4X

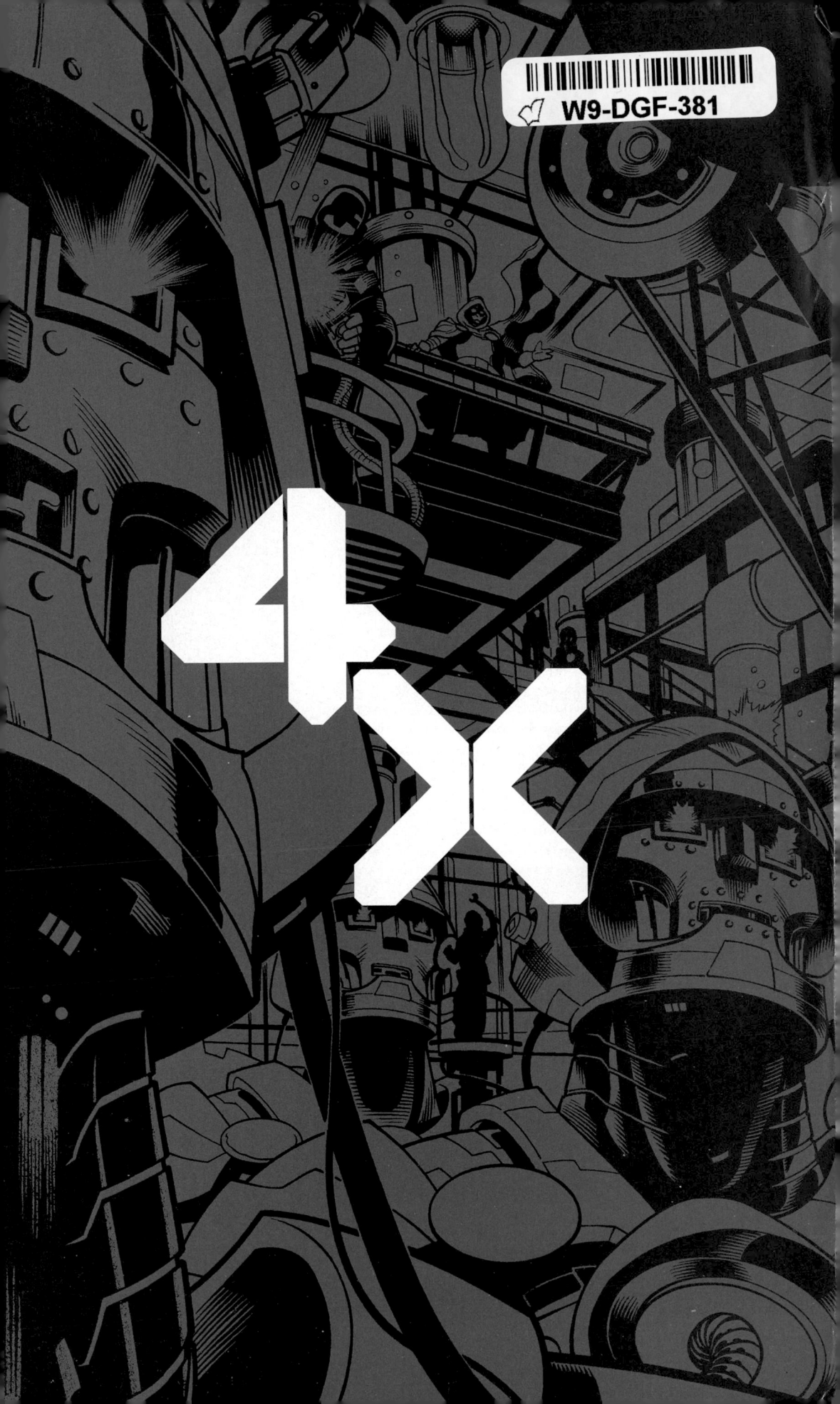

X-MEN / FANTASTIC FOUR

CHIP ZDARSKY	WRITER
TERRY DODSON	PENCILER
RACHEL DODSON	INKER
DEXTER VINES + KARL STORY	INK ASSISTS
LAURA MARTIN	COLOR ART
VC'S JOE CARAMAGNA	LETTERER
TERRY DODSON + RACHEL DODSON	COVER ARTISTS

SHANNON ANDREWS BALLESTEROS	ASSISTANT EDITOR
ALANNA SMITH	ASSOCIATE EDITOR
TOM BREVOORT	EDITOR
C.B. CEBULSKI	EDITOR IN CHIEF

X-MEN + FANTASTIC FOUR CREATED BY STAN LEE + JACK KIRBY

4X

THE WORLD HAS CHANGED

Krakoa has become a safe haven for all mutants, accessible only to those who carry the X-gene. But there is one mutant who has not yet graced this sacred land…

JENNIFER GRÜNWALD — COLLECTION EDITOR
MAIA LOY — ASSISTANT MANAGING EDITOR
LISA MONTALBANO — ASSISTANT MANAGING EDITOR
MARK D. BEAZLEY — EDITOR, SPECIAL PROJECTS
JEFF YOUNGQUIST — VP PRODUCTION & SPECIAL PROJECTS
DAVID GABRIEL — SVP PRINT, SALES & MARKETING
C.B. CEBULSKI — EDITOR IN CHIEF

X-MEN/FANTASTIC FOUR: 4X. Contains material originally published in magazine form as X-MEN/FANTASTIC FOUR (2020) #1-4. First printing 2020. ISBN 978-1-302-92003-6. Published by MARVEL WORLDWIDE, INC., a subsidiary of MARVEL ENTERTAINMENT, LLC. OFFICE OF PUBLICATION: 1290 Avenue of the Americas, New York, NY 10104. **Printed in Canada.** KEVIN FEIGE, Chief Creative Officer; DAN BUCKLEY, President, Marvel Entertainment; JOHN NEE, Publisher; JOE QUESADA, EVP & Creative Director; TOM BREVOORT, SVP of Publishing; DAVID BOGART, Associate Publisher & SVP of Talent Affairs; Publishing & Partnership; DAVID GABRIEL, VP of Print & Digital Publishing; JEFF YOUNGQUIST, VP of Production & Special Projects; DAN CARR, Executive Director of Publishing Technology; ALEX MORALES, Director of Publishing Operations; DAN EDINGTON, Managing Editor; SUSAN CRESPI, Production Manager; STAN LEE, Chairman Emeritus. For information regarding advertising in Marvel Comics or on Marvel.com, please contact Vit DeBellis, Custom Solutions & Integrated Advertising Manager, at vdebellis@marvel.com. For Marvel subscription inquiries, please call 888-511-5480. **Manufactured between 7/24/2020 and 8/25/2020 by SOLISCO PRINTERS, SCOTT, QC, CANADA.**

10 9 8 7 6 5 4 3 2 1

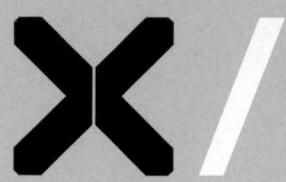

FEARED AND HATED

Mutants around the world are flocking to the island-nation of Krakoa to be a part of the first mutant society. Standing between that sacred land and the human world are the heroes of mutantdom, the X-MEN.

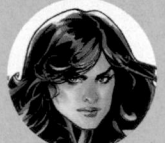
KATE PRYDE

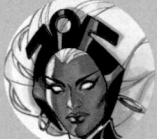
STORM

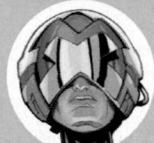
CHARLES XAVIER

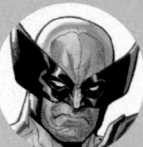
WOLVERINE

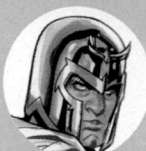
MAGNETO

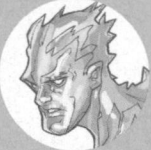
ICEMAN

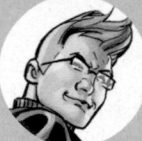
KID OMEGA

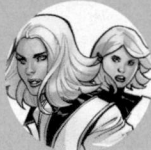
CUCKOOS

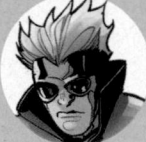
PYRO

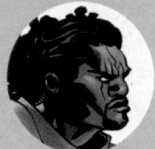
BISHOP

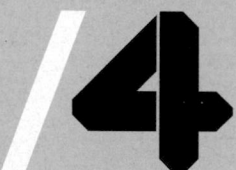

FOUR FEARLESS FRIENDS

A brilliant scientist — his best friend — the woman he loves — and her fiery-tempered kid brother. Together, they braved the unknown terrors of outer space and were changed by cosmic rays into something more than merely human: THE FANTASTIC FOUR.

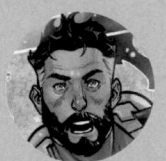
MR. FANTASTIC

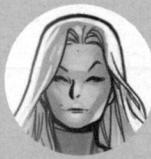
THE INVISIBLE WOMAN

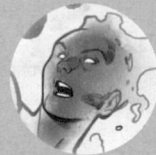
THE HUMAN TORCH

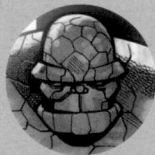
THE THING

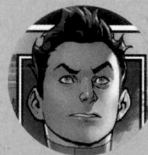
FRANKLIN RICHARDS

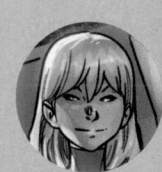
VALERIA RICHARDS

TERRY
DODSON
RACHEL

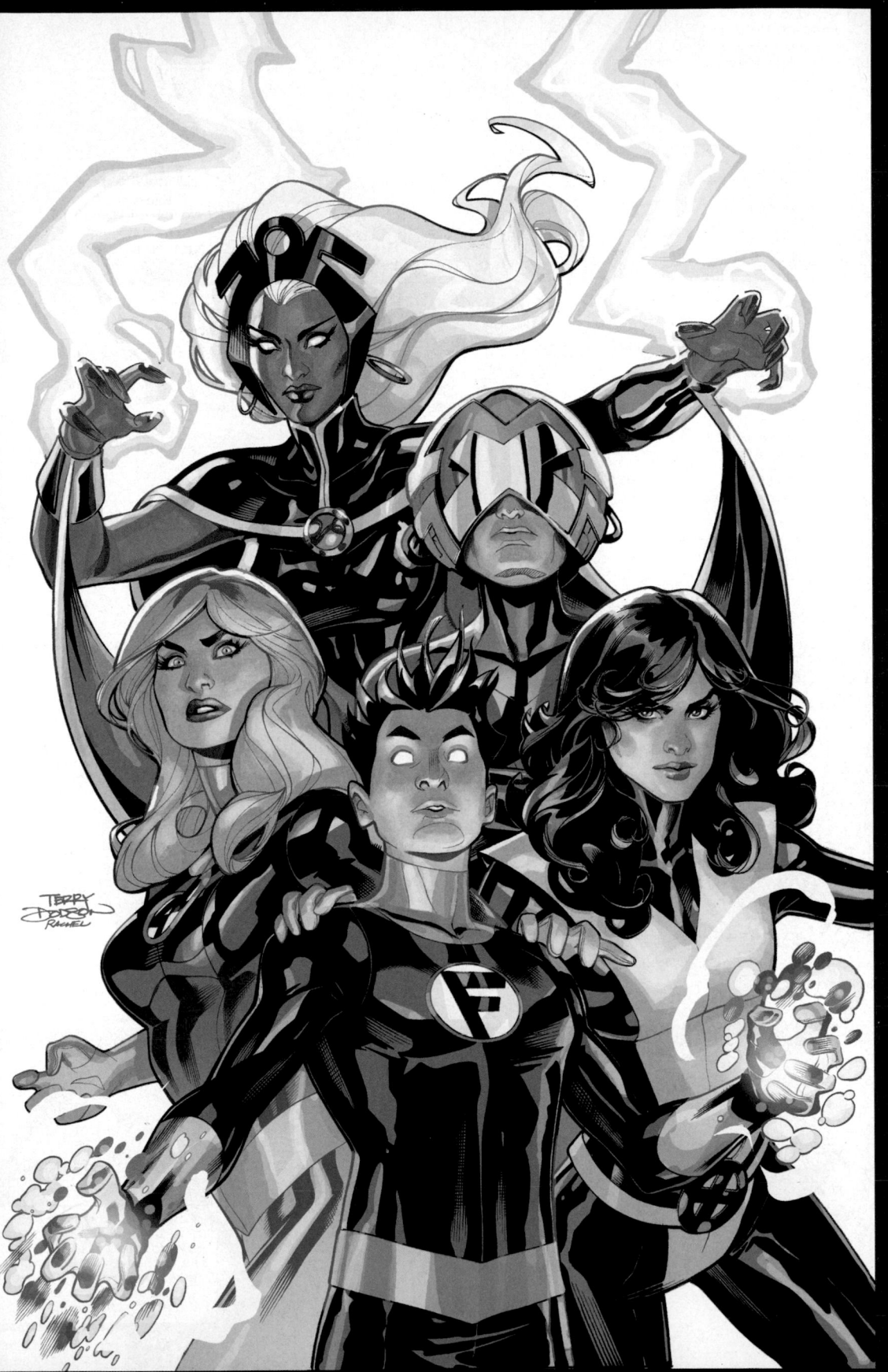

I'm the *Impossible Boy.*
The son of *super heroes*, and not just *any* super heroes...
...the great *Reed Richards* and the powerful *Sue Storm*. Everyone watched me, even as a kid.
Everyone wondered, "What will *he* become?"
It's stupid. That pressure on a *kid*. My parents *gained* powers; I *revealed* them. So what did I reveal?
Well, I became the boy who could *dream* the *future*.
But it wasn't just dreams.
Eventually I could make the impossible *possible*. I could create universes.
A kid who could create universes.
And I did.
Now my powers drain every time I use them. I'm headed toward being someone you'll see in the street and wonder, "Was that Franklin Richards? The guy who was once in the *Fantastic Four?*"
I used to have dreams of the futu I don't anymore

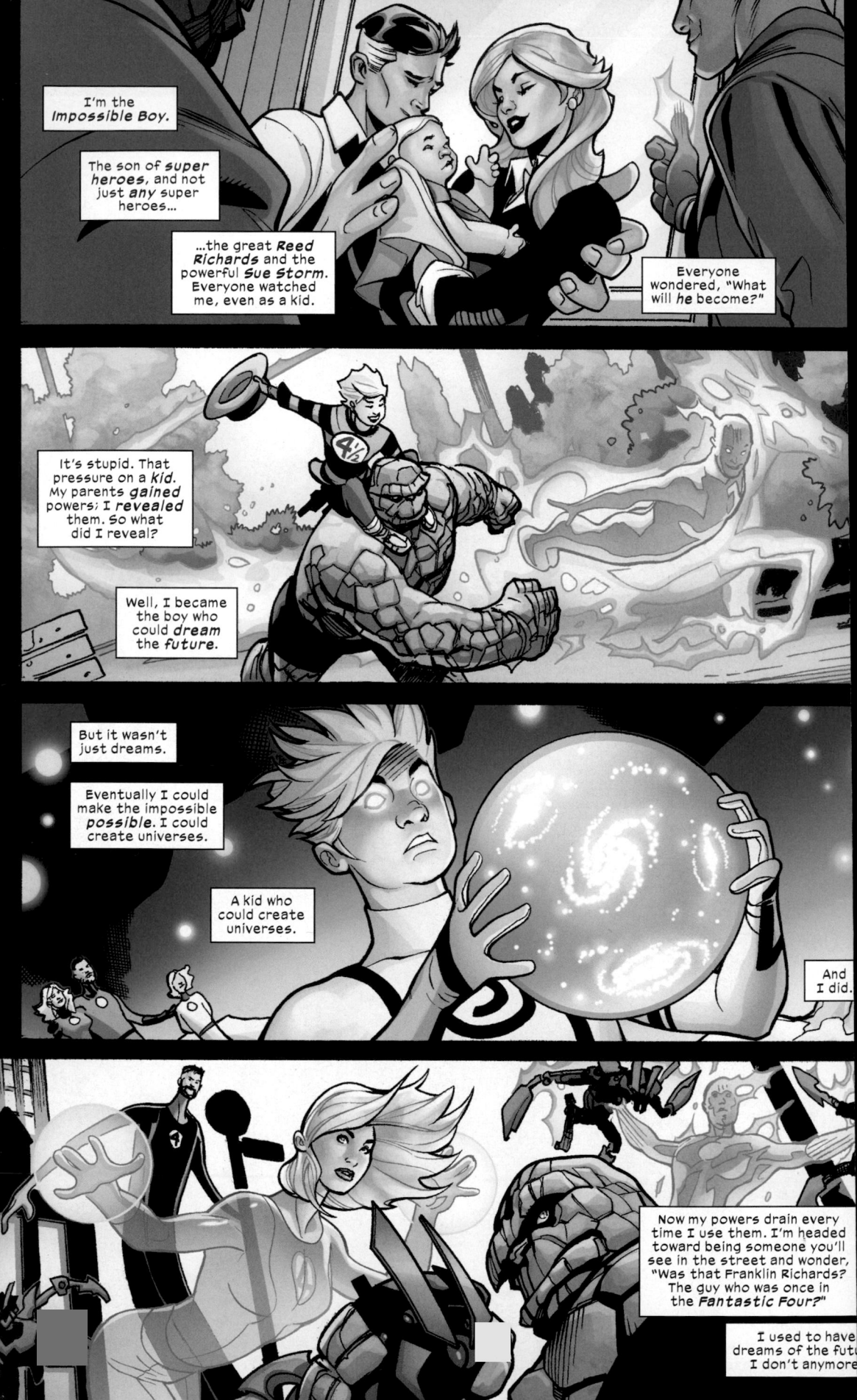

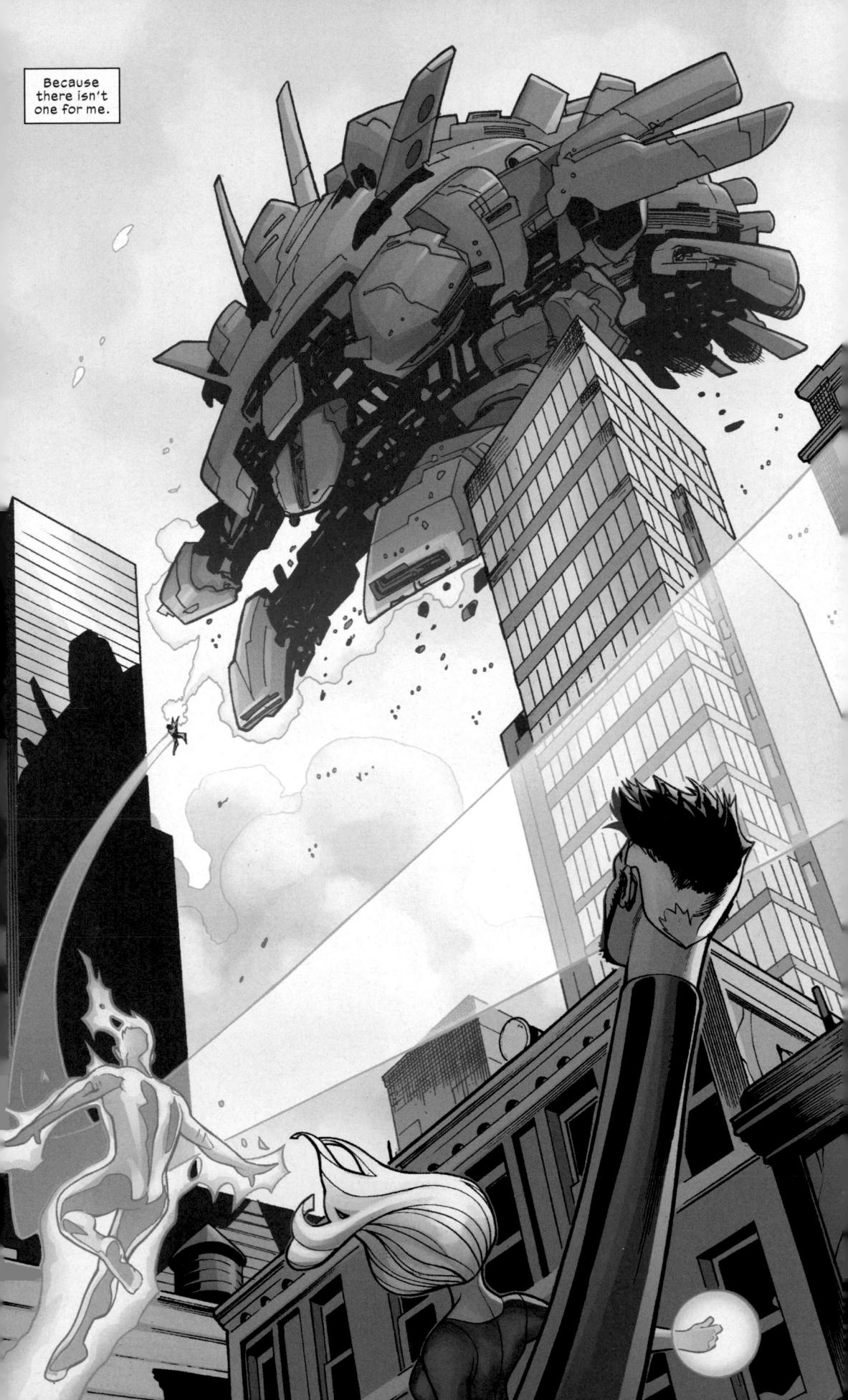
Because there isn't one for me.

X-MEN /
FANTASTIC
FOUR

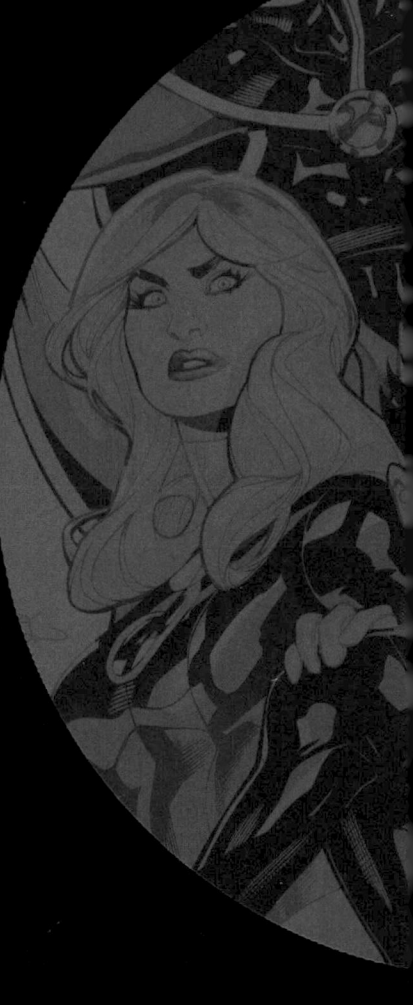

1 THE IMPOSSIBLE BOY

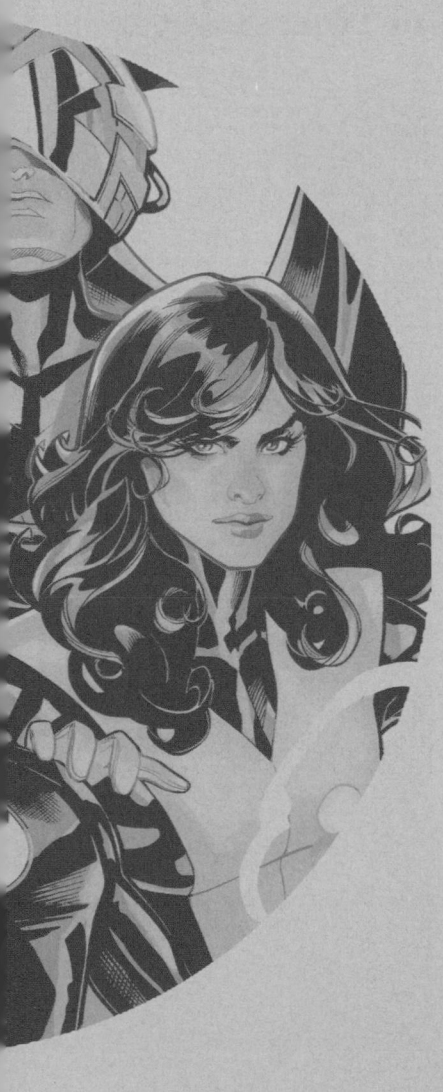

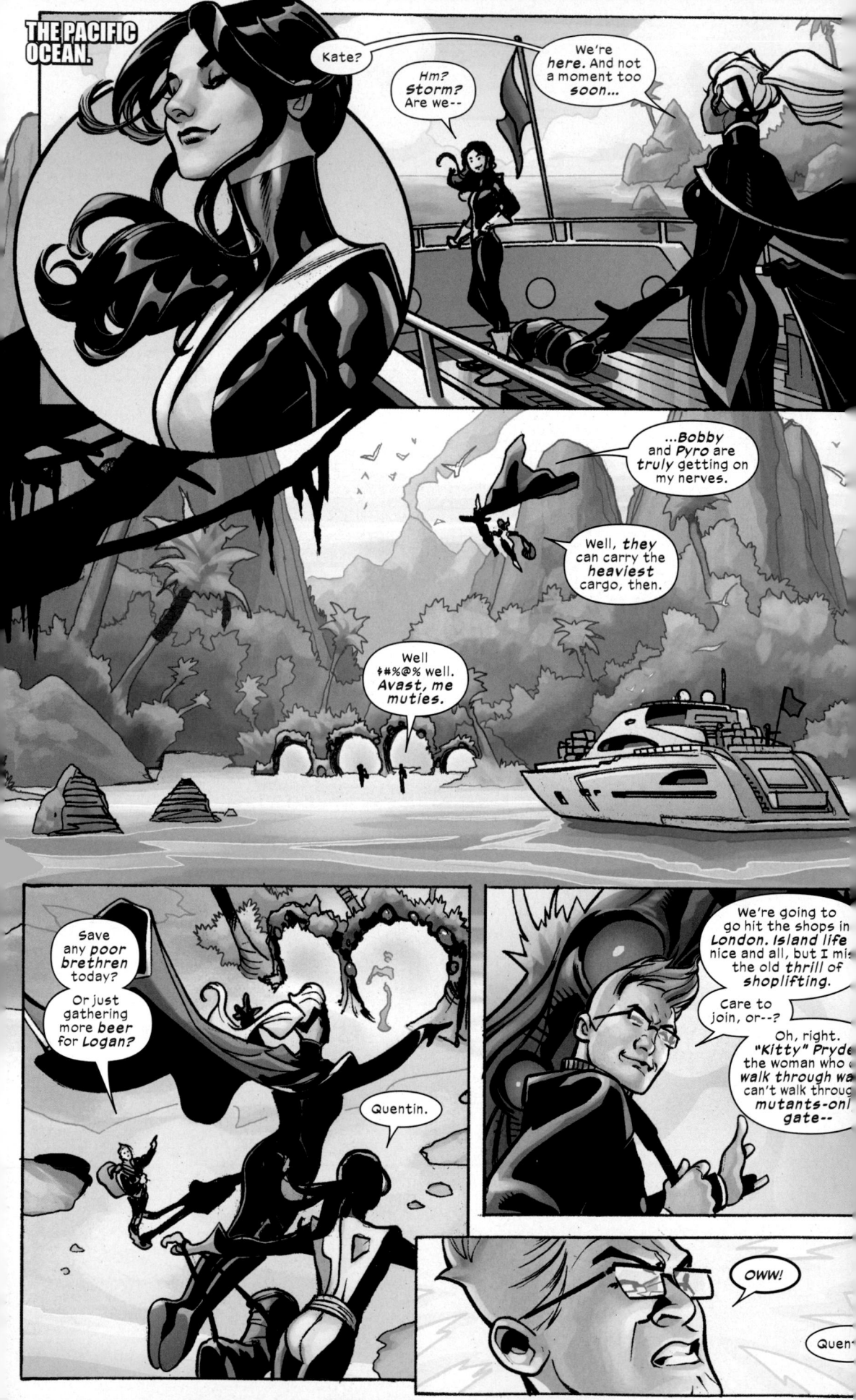

THE PACIFIC OCEAN.

Kate?

Hm? *Storm?* Are we--

We're *here.* And not a moment too *soon...*

...*Bobby* and *Pyro* are *truly* getting on my nerves.

Well, *they* can carry the *heaviest* cargo, then.

Well ǂ#%@% well. *Avast,* me *muties.*

Save any *poor brethren* today?

Or just gathering more *beer* for *Logan?*

Quentin.

We're going to go hit the shops in *London. Island life* nice and all, but I mis the old *thrill* of *shoplifting.*

Care to join, or--?

Oh, right. *"Kitty" Pryde* the woman who walk through wa can't walk throug *mutants-on* gate--

OWW!

Quen

...don't be rude.
Yes, don't be *Quentin.*
Whatever. Creeps.
Thanks, but I didn't need your pity psychic attack--
We don't care what you need.
We're here to let you know...
"...the *Professor* needs to see you."
THE MUTANT NATION OF KRAKOA.
God, not a moment's rest.
I'm going to go tend to my *garden.* If it's another *Marauders mission,* send word.
Will do. Though if Charles sent the *Cuckoos* to greet me instead of just reaching out psychically, *that* means he's *busy.* And if he's *busy...*

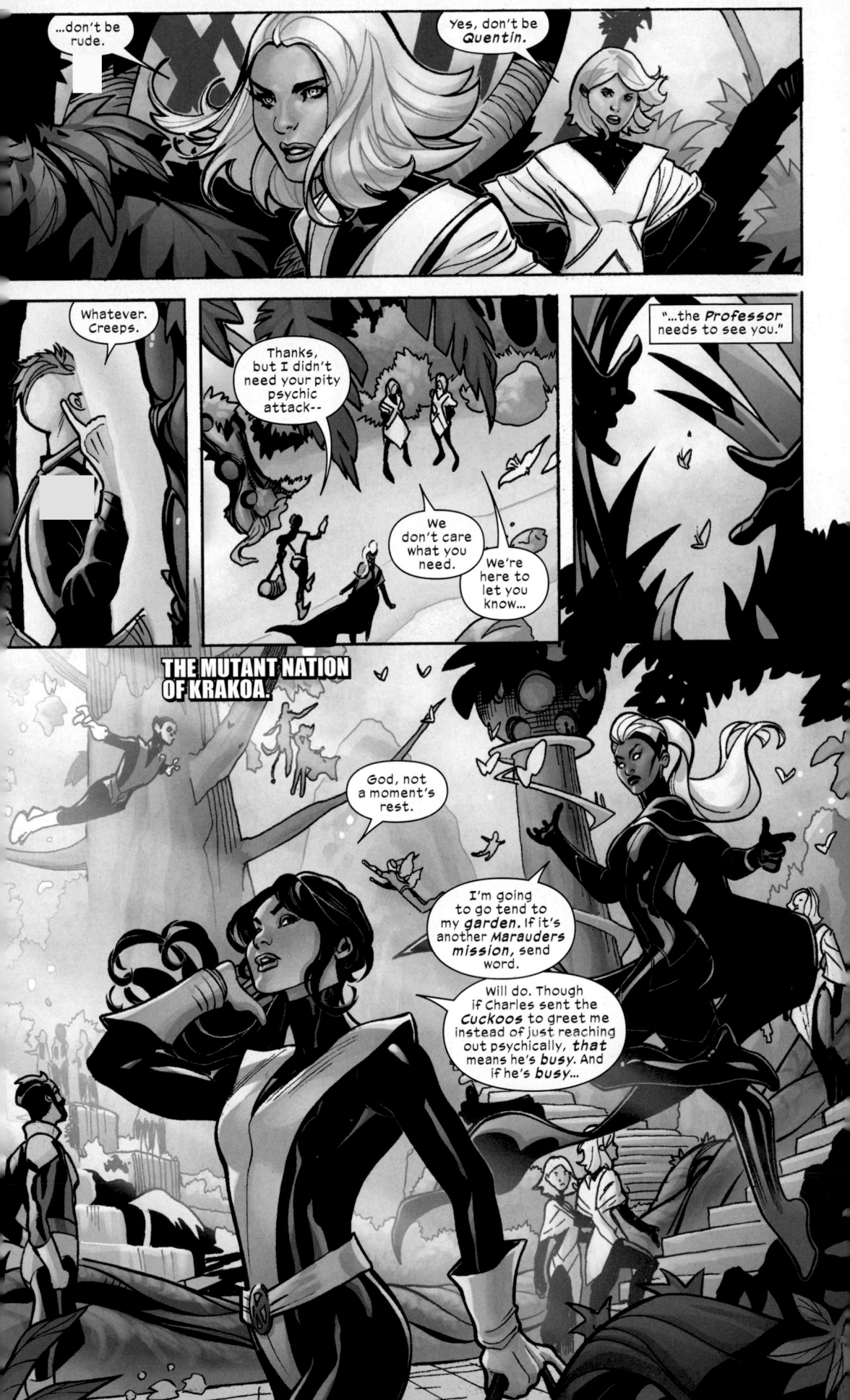

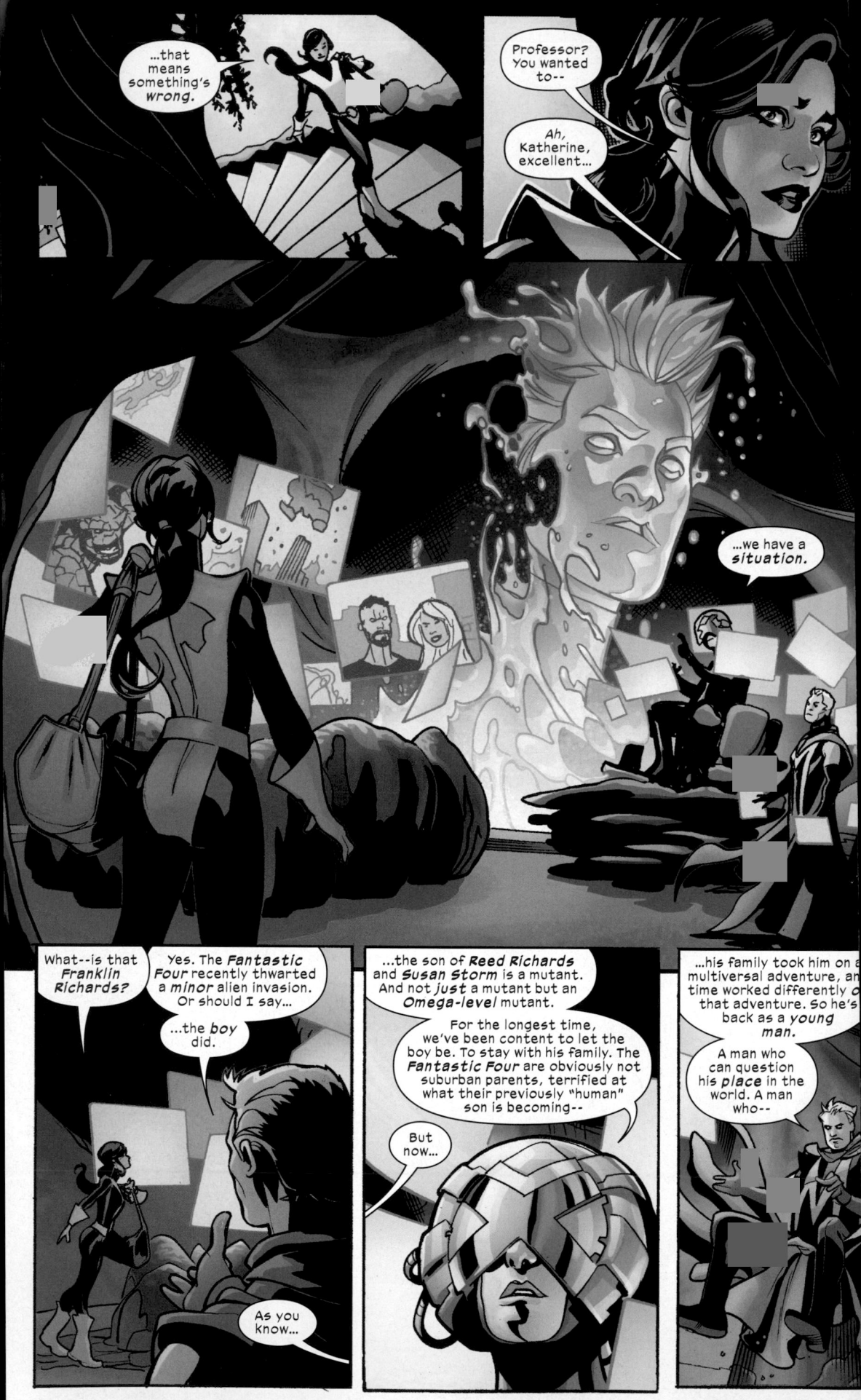

...that means something's *wrong.*

Professor? You wanted to--

Ah, Katherine, excellent...

...we have a *situation.*

What--is that *Franklin Richards?*

Yes. The *Fantastic Four* recently thwarted a *minor* alien invasion. Or should I say...

...the *boy* did.

...the son of *Reed Richards* and *Susan Storm* is a mutant. And not *just* a mutant but an *Omega-level* mutant.

For the longest time, we've been content to let the boy be. To stay with his family. The *Fantastic Four* are obviously not suburban parents, terrified at what their previously "human" son is becoming--

But now...

As you know...

...his family took him on a multiversal adventure, and time worked differently on that adventure. So he's back as a *young man.*

A man who can question his *place* in the world. A man who--

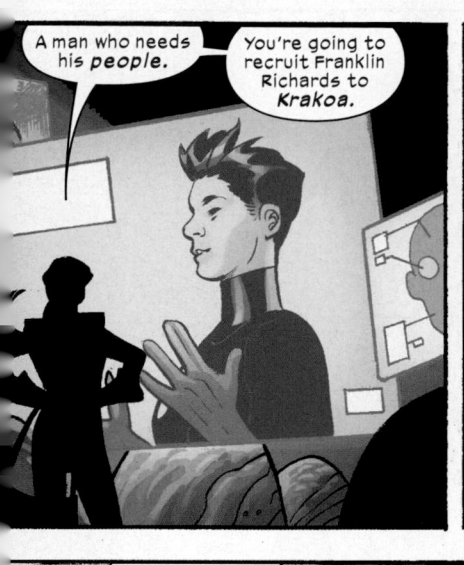

A man who needs his *people.*

You're going to recruit Franklin Richards to *Krakoa.*

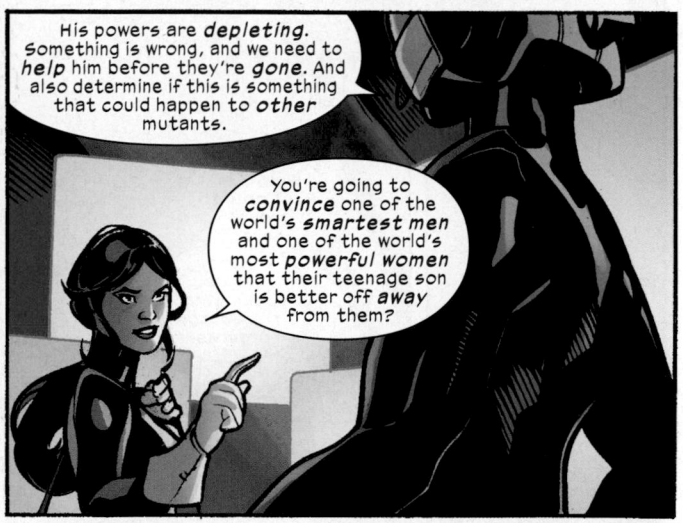

His powers are *depleting.* Something is wrong, and we need to *help* him before they're *gone.* And also determine if this is something that could happen to *other* mutants.

You're going to *convince* one of the world's *smartest men* and one of the world's most *powerful women* that their teenage son is better off *away* from them?

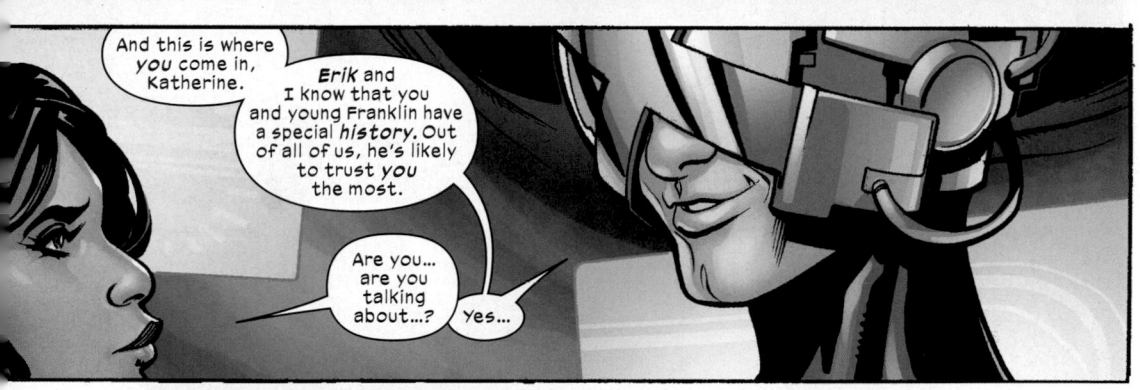

And this is where *you* come in, Katherine. *Erik* and I know that you and young Franklin have a special *history.* Out of all of us, he's likely to trust *you* the most.

Are you... are you talking about...?

Yes...

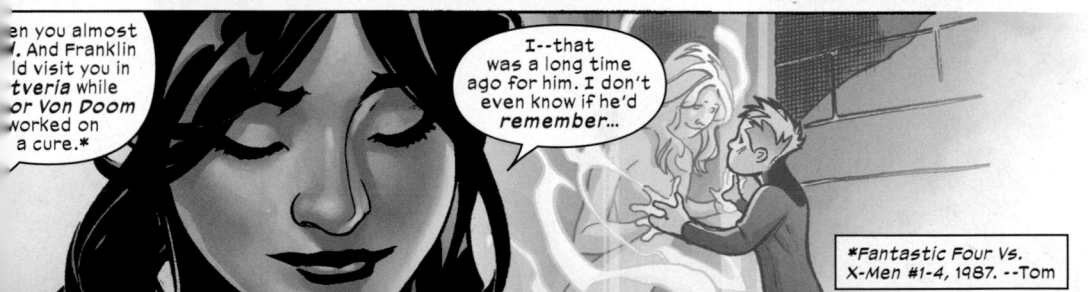

en you almost . And Franklin ld visit you in tveria while or Von Doom worked on a cure.*

I--that was a long time ago for him. I don't even know if he'd *remember...*

*Fantastic Four Vs. X-Men #1-4, 1987. --Tom

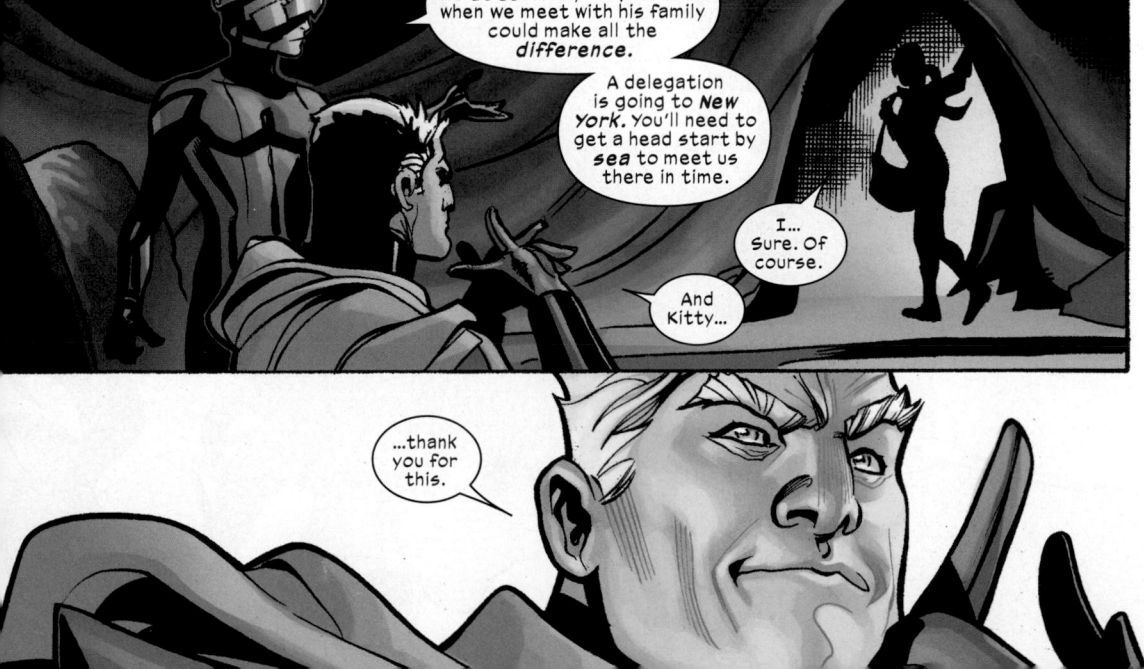

He *does.* And your presence when we meet with his family could make all the *difference.*

A delegation is going to *New York.* You'll need to get a head start by *sea* to meet us there in time.

I... Sure. Of course.

And Kitty...

...thank you for this.

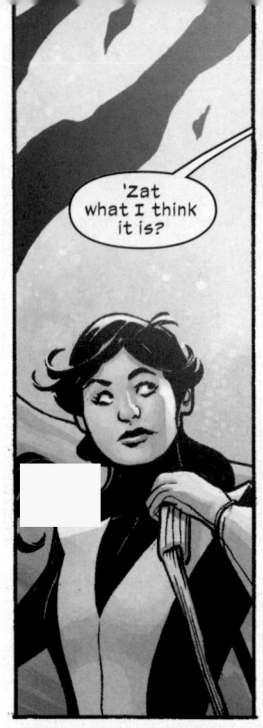

'Zat what I think it is?

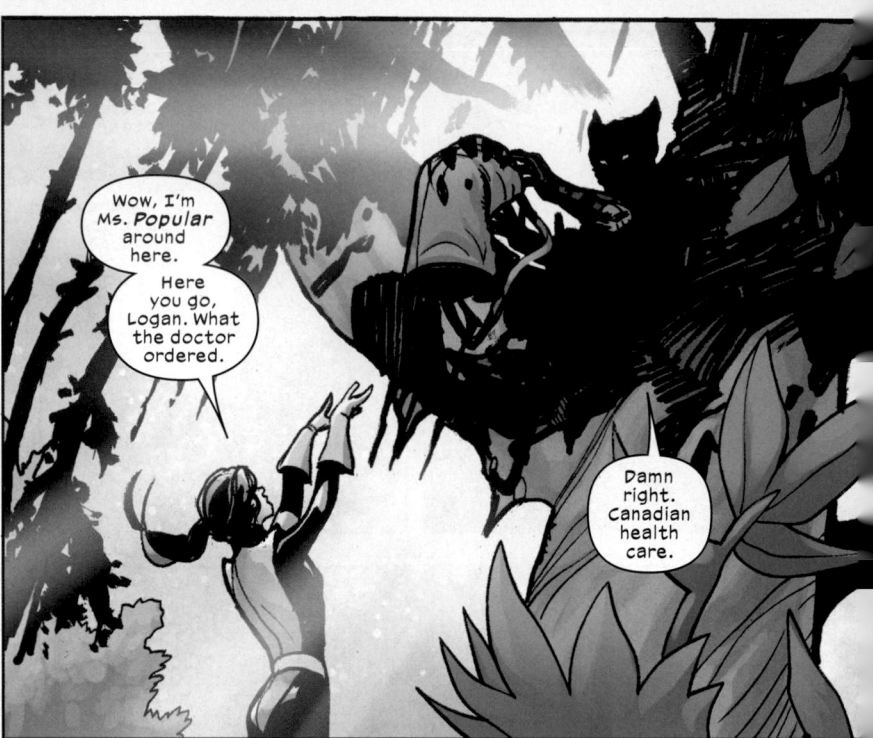

Wow, I'm *Ms. Popular* around here.

Here you go, Logan. What the doctor ordered.

Damn right. Canadian health care.

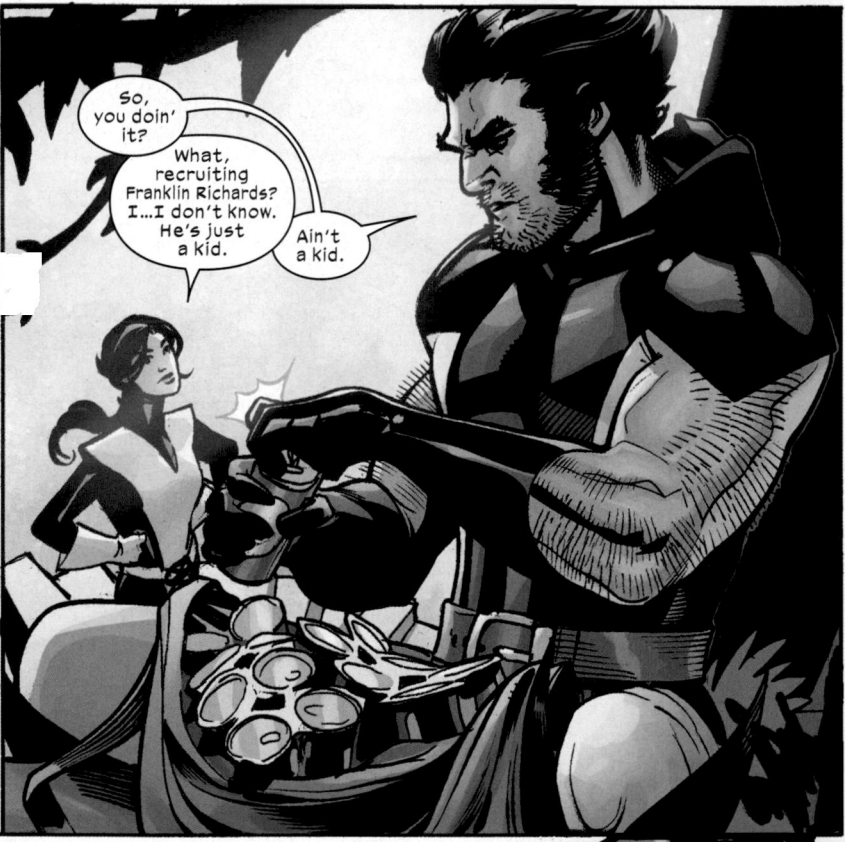

So, you doin' it?

What, recruiting Franklin Richards? I...I don't know. He's just a kid.

Ain't a kid.

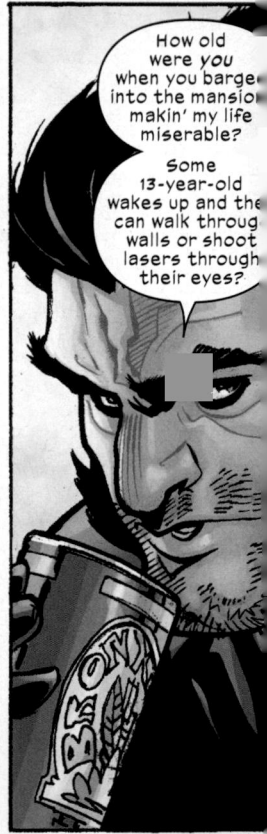

How old were *you* when you barged into the mansion makin' my life miserable?

Some 13-year-old wakes up and then can walk through walls or shoot lasers through their eyes?

You know as well as I do...

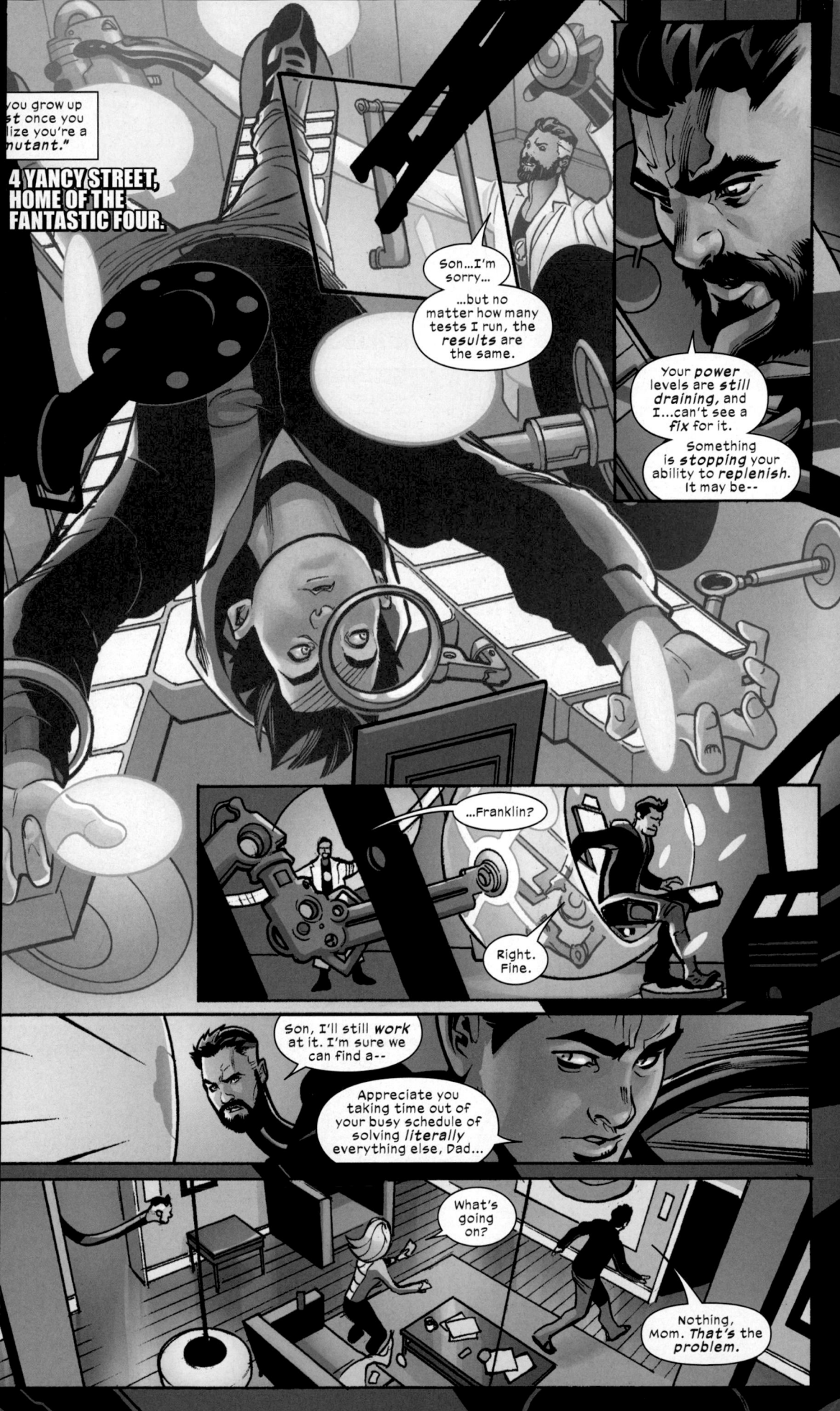

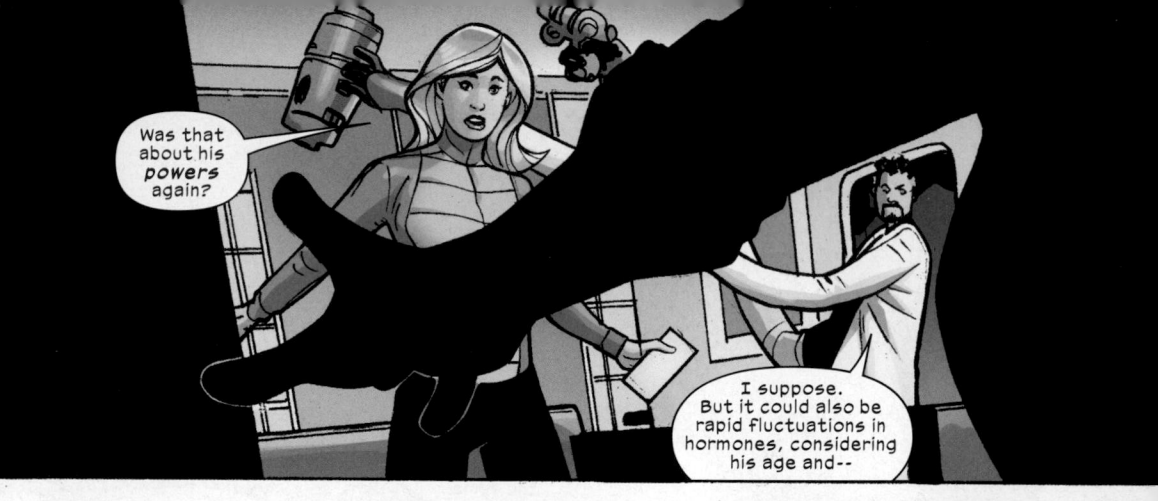

Was that about his **powers** again?

I suppose. But it could also be rapid fluctuations in hormones, considering his age and--

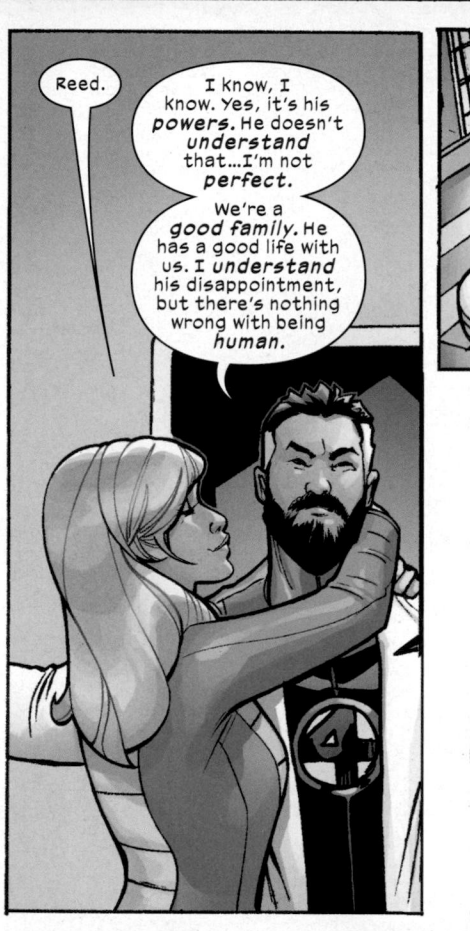

Reed.

I know, I know. Yes, it's his **powers**. He doesn't **understand** that...I'm not **perfect**.

We're a **good family**. He has a good life with us. I **understand** his disappointment, but there's nothing wrong with being **human**.

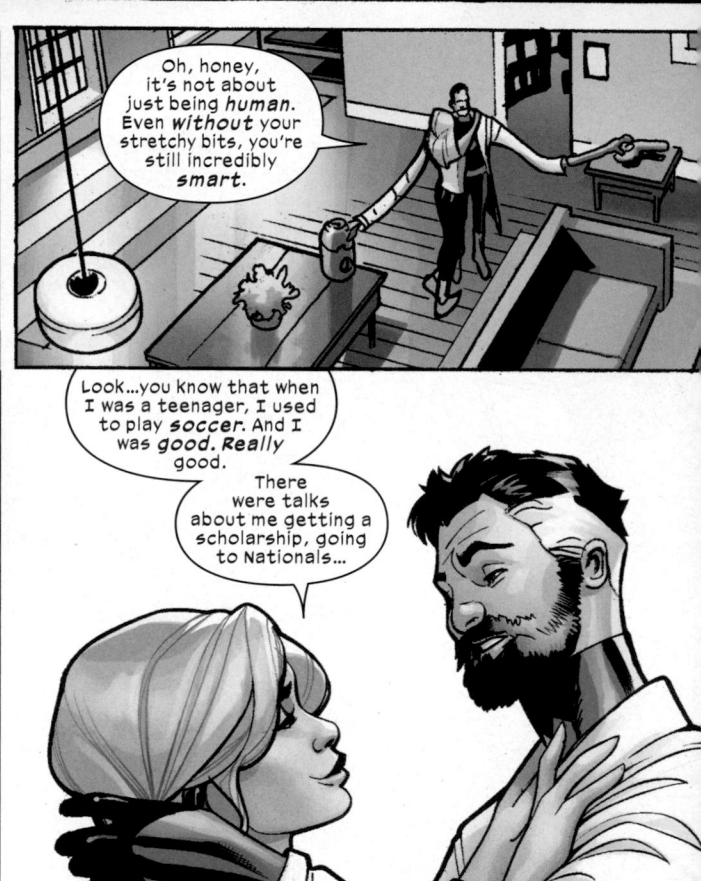

Oh, honey, it's not about just being **human**. Even **without** your stretchy bits, you're still incredibly **smart**.

Look...you know that when I was a teenager, I used to play **soccer**. And I was **good**. **Really** good.

There were talks about me getting a scholarship, going to Nationals...

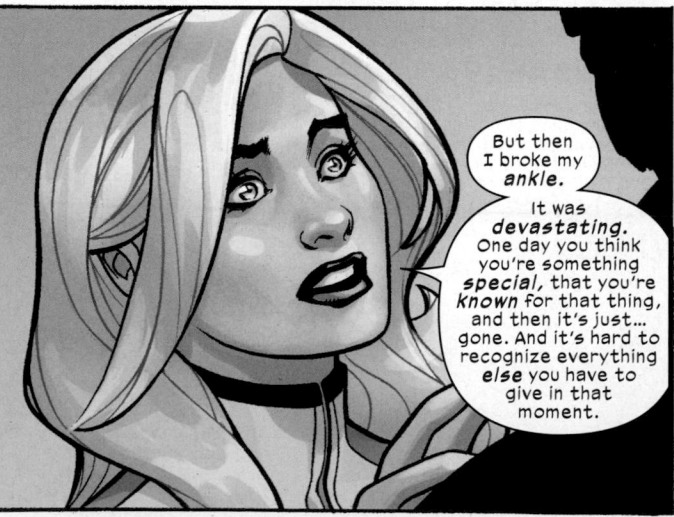

But then I broke my **ankle**.

It was **devastating**. One day you think you're something **special**, that you're **known** for that thing, and then it's just... gone. And it's hard to recognize everything **else** you have to give in that moment.

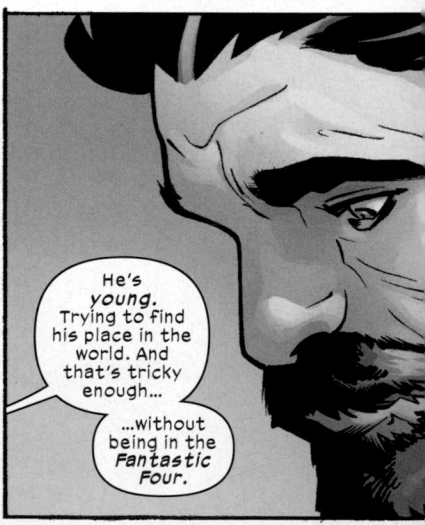

He's **young**. Trying to find his place in the world. And that's tricky enough...

...without being in the **Fantastic Four**.

REED RICHARDS

Entry 66109

Ever since the accident that gave us our extra abilities, I've been trying to reconcile the high energy expenditure of each of our power sets with our seemingly unchanged individual energy intake. The most basic laws of physics make this seem impossible. At first I suspected we were absorbing energy from the air, possibly low-level radiation, but the numbers never added up.

Then I came across the work of Dr. Rachna Koul, who specialized in imperiumology, the science of super-powers. She posited that superhumans are each connected to one or more intradimensional sources of energy, which she dubbed "Godpower." A solid theory, though I'm still unable to find that conduit in my studies of the Fantastic Four's power sets.

Franklin's diminishing powers would appear to lend credence to the Godpower theory, as he seems to be running out of the energy needed to use his powers. If we were to believe there is a Godpower source, then it's possible that Franklin's connection to that source is broken.

Whether or not it can be repaired depends on first proving its existence.

Somehow.

RR
SR
JS
G
BG
FR

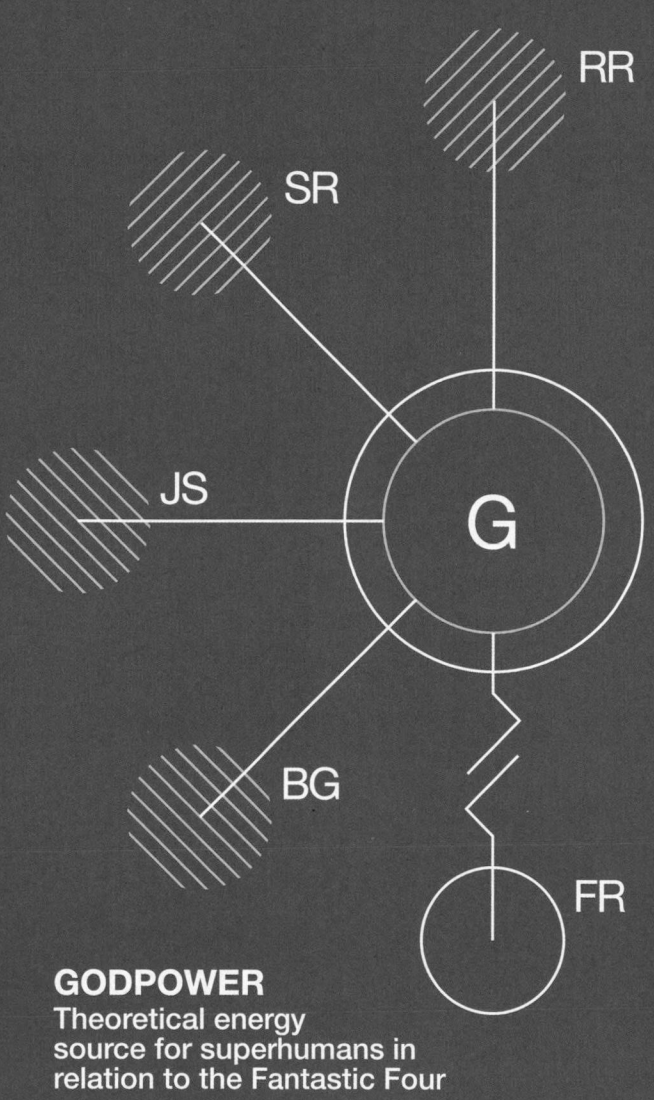

GODPOWER
Theoretical energy source for superhumans in relation to the Fantastic Four

diagram 20031-X

I get it, kid. I *do*. But *trust* me, this super-power garbage ain't *everything*.

I'd *gladly* live a normal life with *Alicia,* bein' *regular* handsome instead 'a, you know...

...*chiseled* handsome.

Come on, *Uncle Ben*...

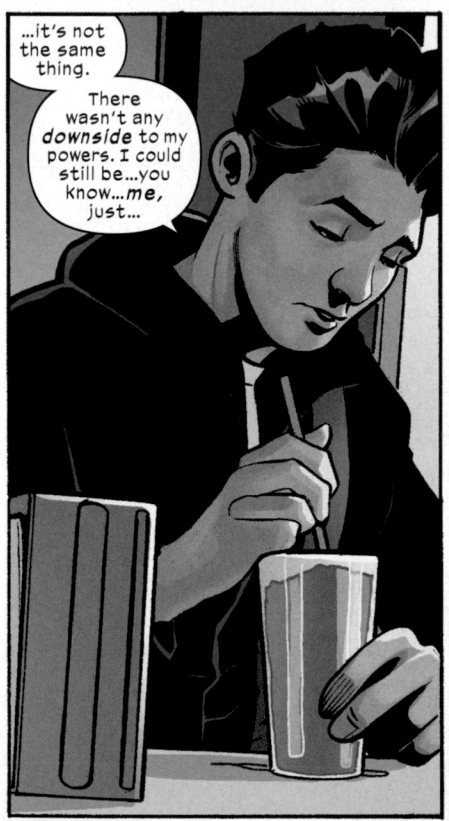

...it's not the same thing.

There wasn't any *downside* to my powers. I could still be...you know...*me*, just...

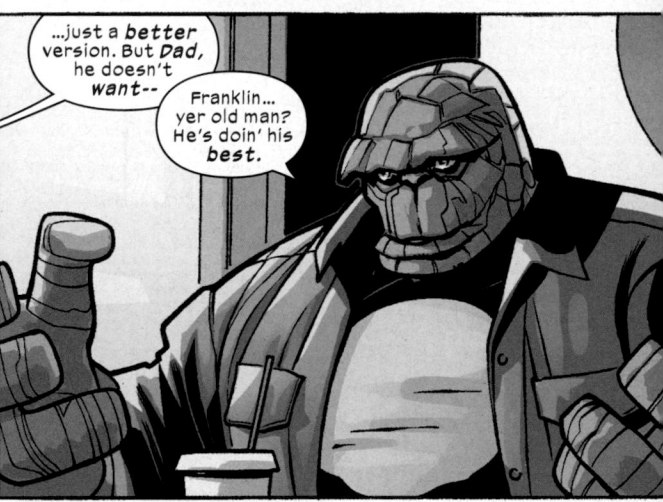

...just a *better* version. But *Dad*, he doesn't *want*--

Franklin... yer old man? He's doin' his *best*.

Is he?

Dad's the *smartest man alive*. He solves the universe's problems *daily*.

So why *is* it exactly that the *two* problems he can't solve...

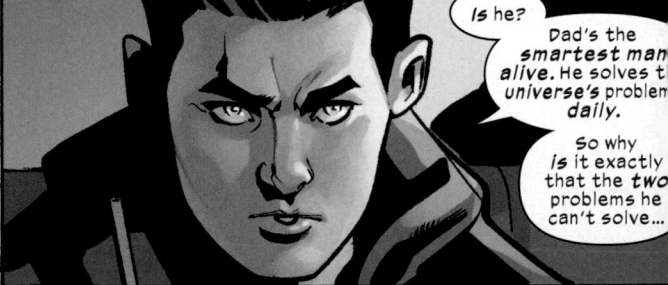

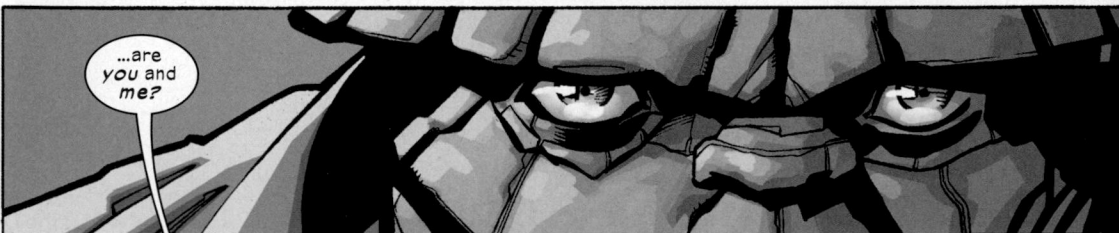

...are *you* and *me*?

Happy's
I don't think it's on purpose.
But he's always acted weird about me having so much power.
And the Fantastic Four have needed your strength since the beginning.
I'm just saying, maybe, you know, unconsciously--
Don't.
Reed's a good man. He cares about you, about us. If he didn't want to "fix" either of us, he'd tell us. 'Cause if he didn't...
...he knows we'd never forgive him...
There you are!
We've got ourselves some visitors!
And honestly...
Happy's

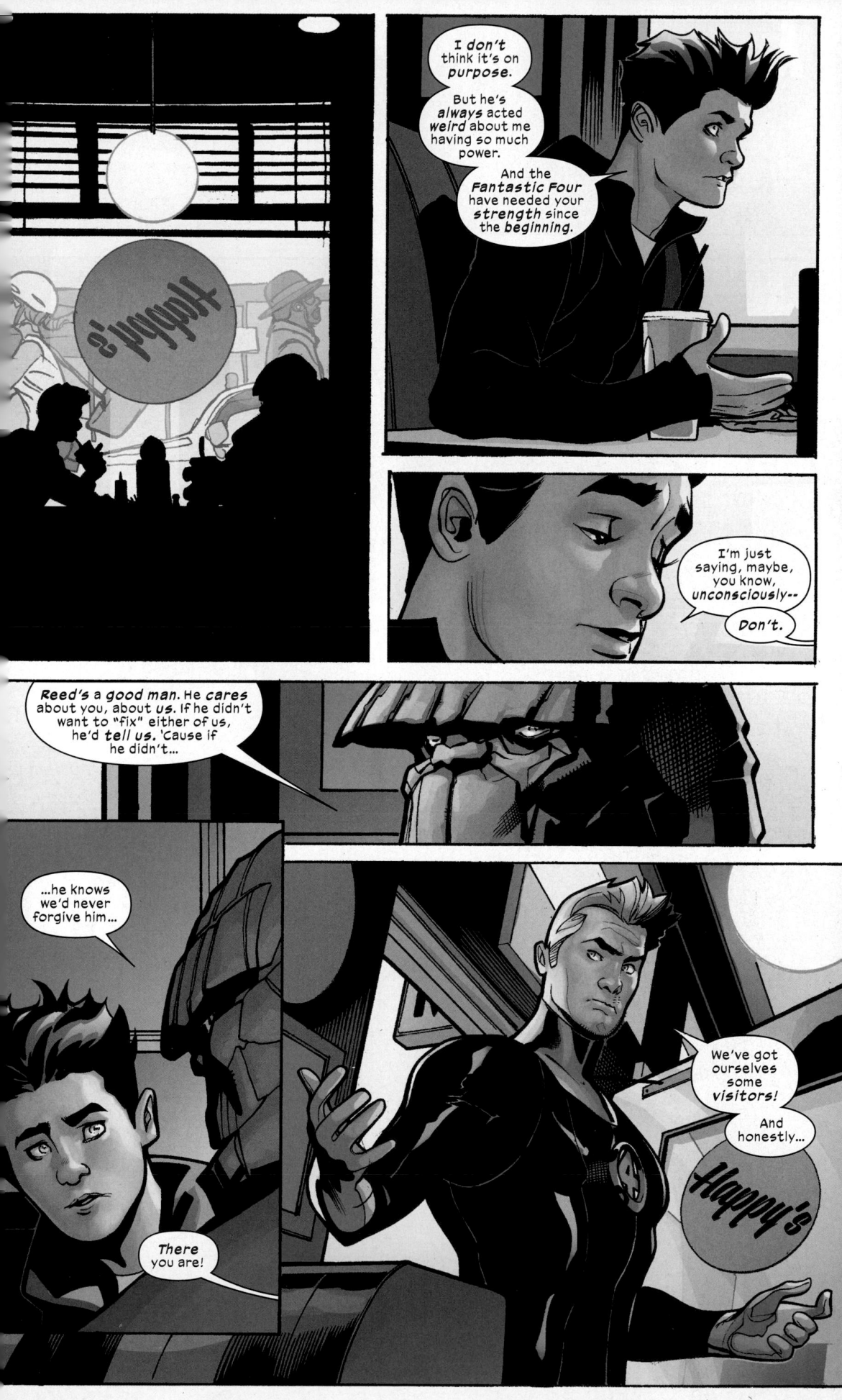

"...not the *good* kind."
Ya know, if I was the *suspicious* type...
...I'd suspect we weren't *welcome* here.
I'll ask you one more time, *Wolverine:* Why are you here?
You know why we're here, Susan.
We're h about t futur

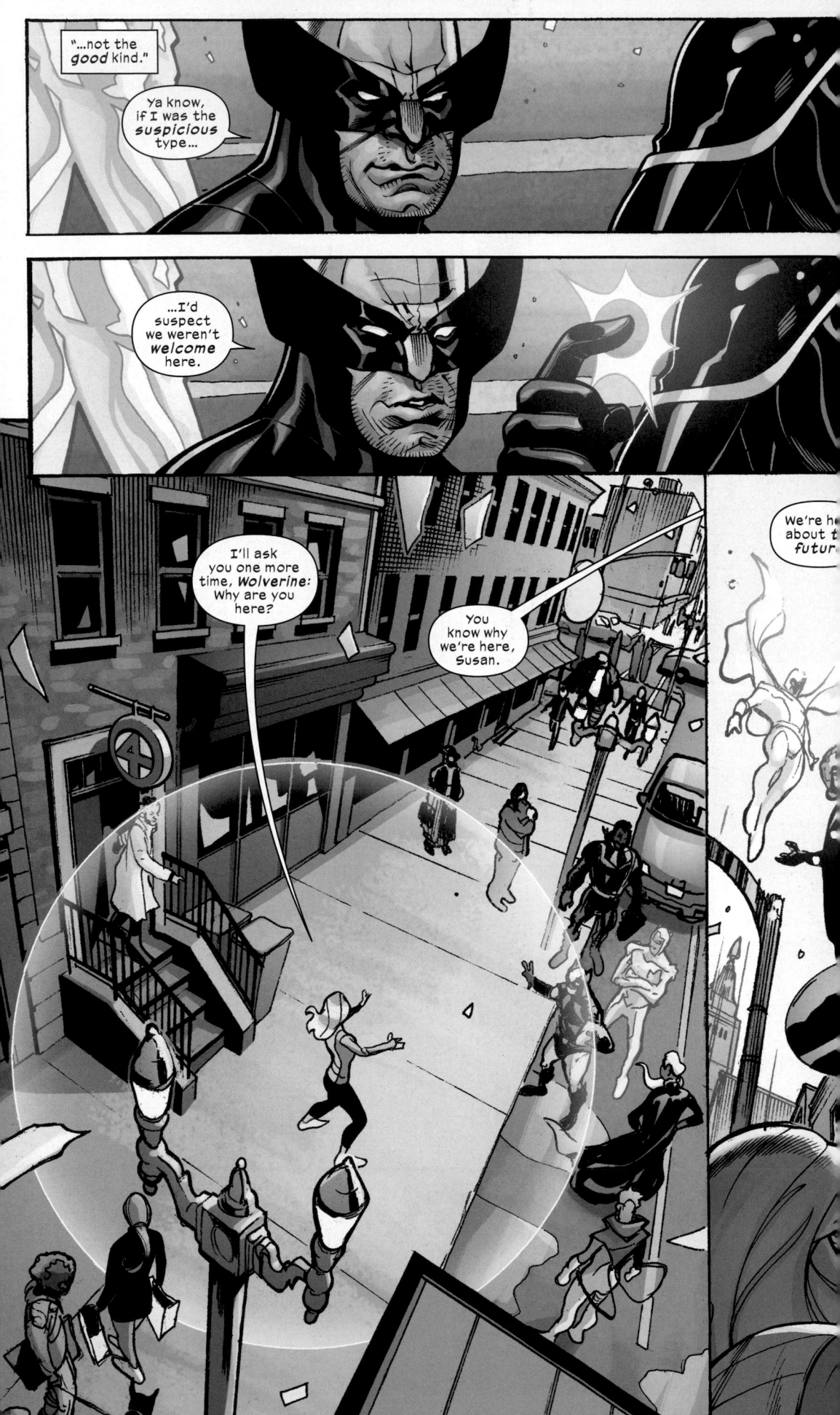

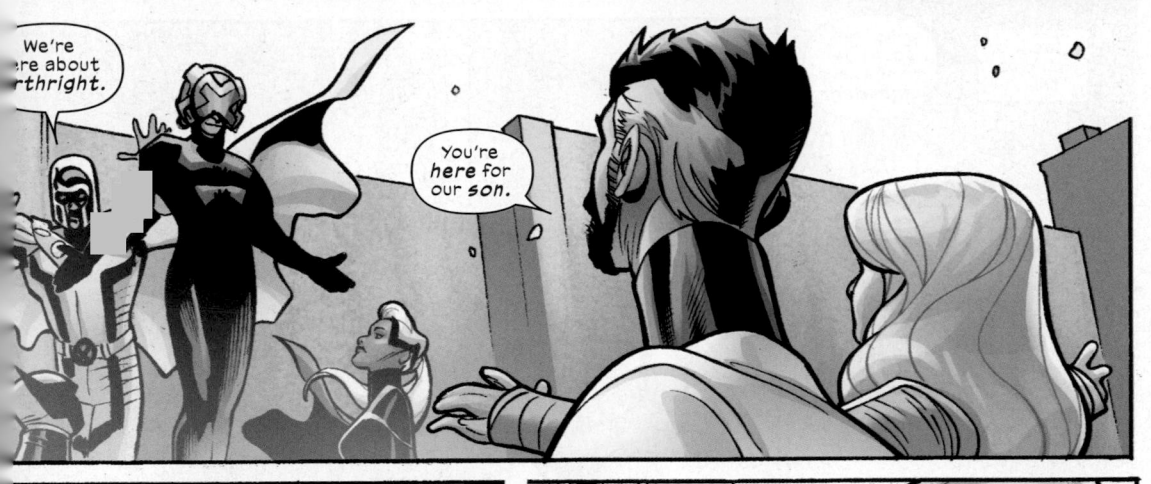

We're here about birthright.

You're *here* for our *son*.

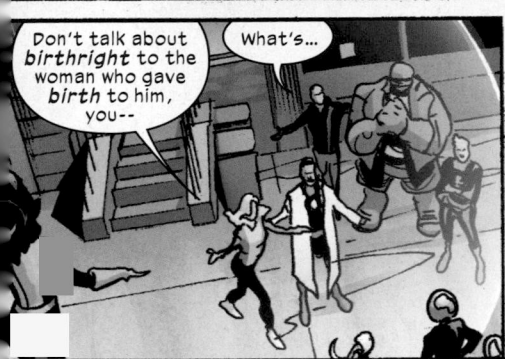

Don't talk about *birthright* to the woman who gave *birth* to him, you--

What's...

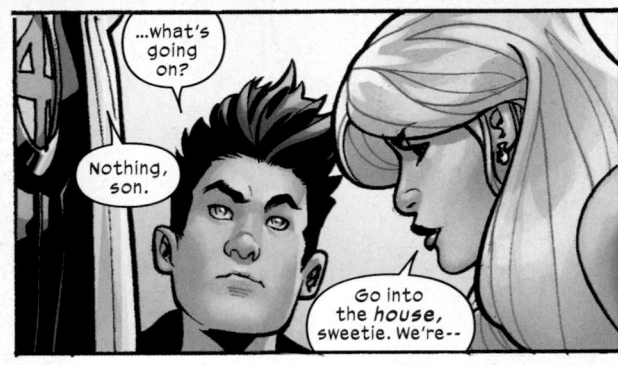

...what's going on?

Nothing, son.

Go into the *house*, sweetie. We're--

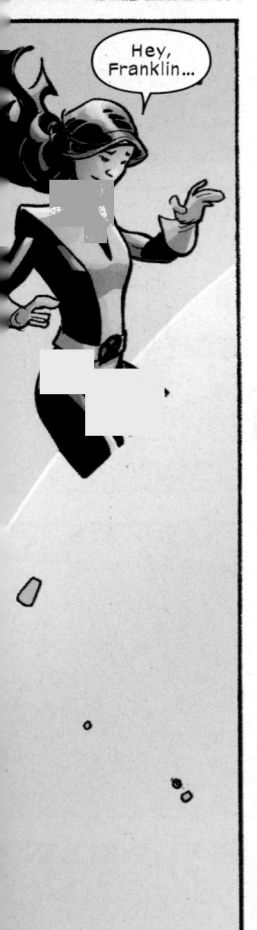

Hey, Franklin...

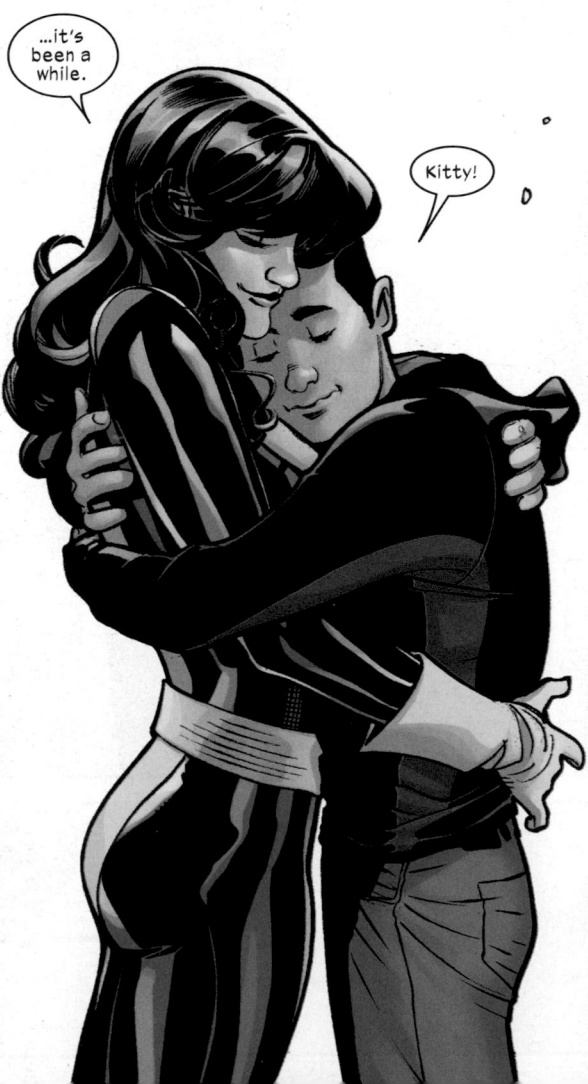

...it's been a while.

Kitty!

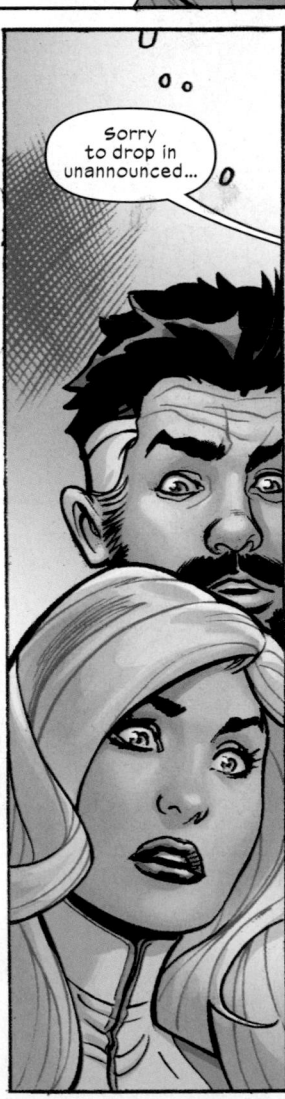

Sorry to drop in unannounced...

"...we just want to talk."
So, as you know, things have changed.
Yes. You changed things, Charles.
I just took the next logical step after years of persecution, Reed. Krakoa is home to all mutants now.
We're recognized by the United Nations. We have diplomatic immunity in more than 100 countries.
You're acting like you're above humanity, buying us off with "gifts" of medicine.
We are above them...
...and above you.
Erik is being blunt, but we are the next step in evolution, and we're finally embracing it.
We can't control h others feel. We ne to do what's right us and the worl which we still protect.
But our m priority protecti
...is all of mutantkind. Including your gifted son.
Nearly every mutant on the planet is in Krakoa now. As it should be. It's a paradise where we can be free.
Franklin Richards is one of us and belongs there. We can help him with--
Absolutely not.

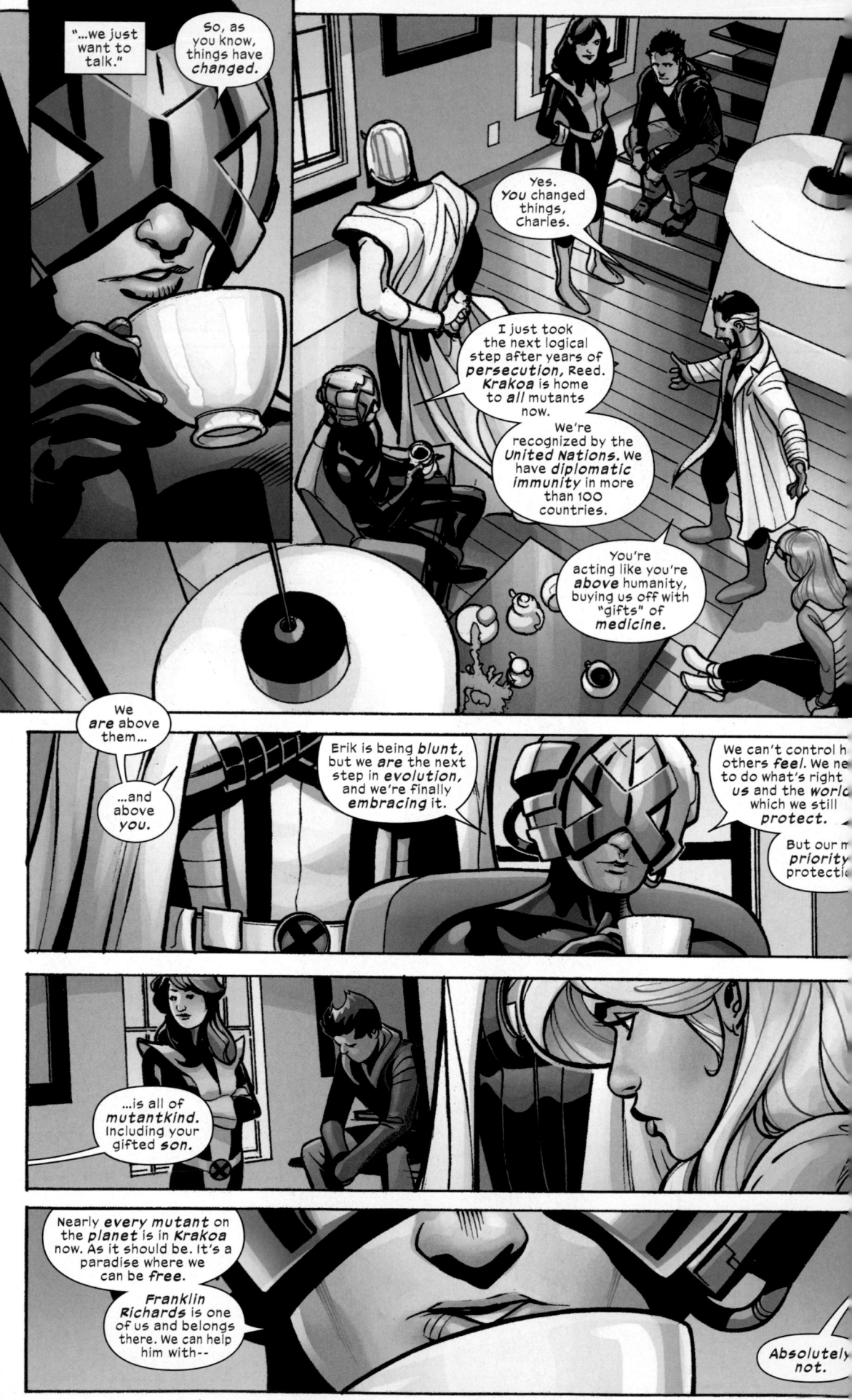

s family isn't segregation. t our children to modern society ney can learn and with people who ve different xperiences!
It's why we chose to live here on Yancy Street! So we can be around people!
Don't you mean...
...so you can endanger people?
How long until this city block is destroyed because enemies of the Fantastic Four attack, or enemies of...
...mutants?
Son, you've done well among the humans, but your people are waiting for you to truly discover home.
Come with us. Claim that home.
I... maybe I could just...
Stay away from my son!
Sue! It's okay! Let's just--
You do not want to do this, Susan.
elease Erik...
...or I will make you release him.
Don't you dare, Charles. We'll handle this with discussion, not your mental violations.

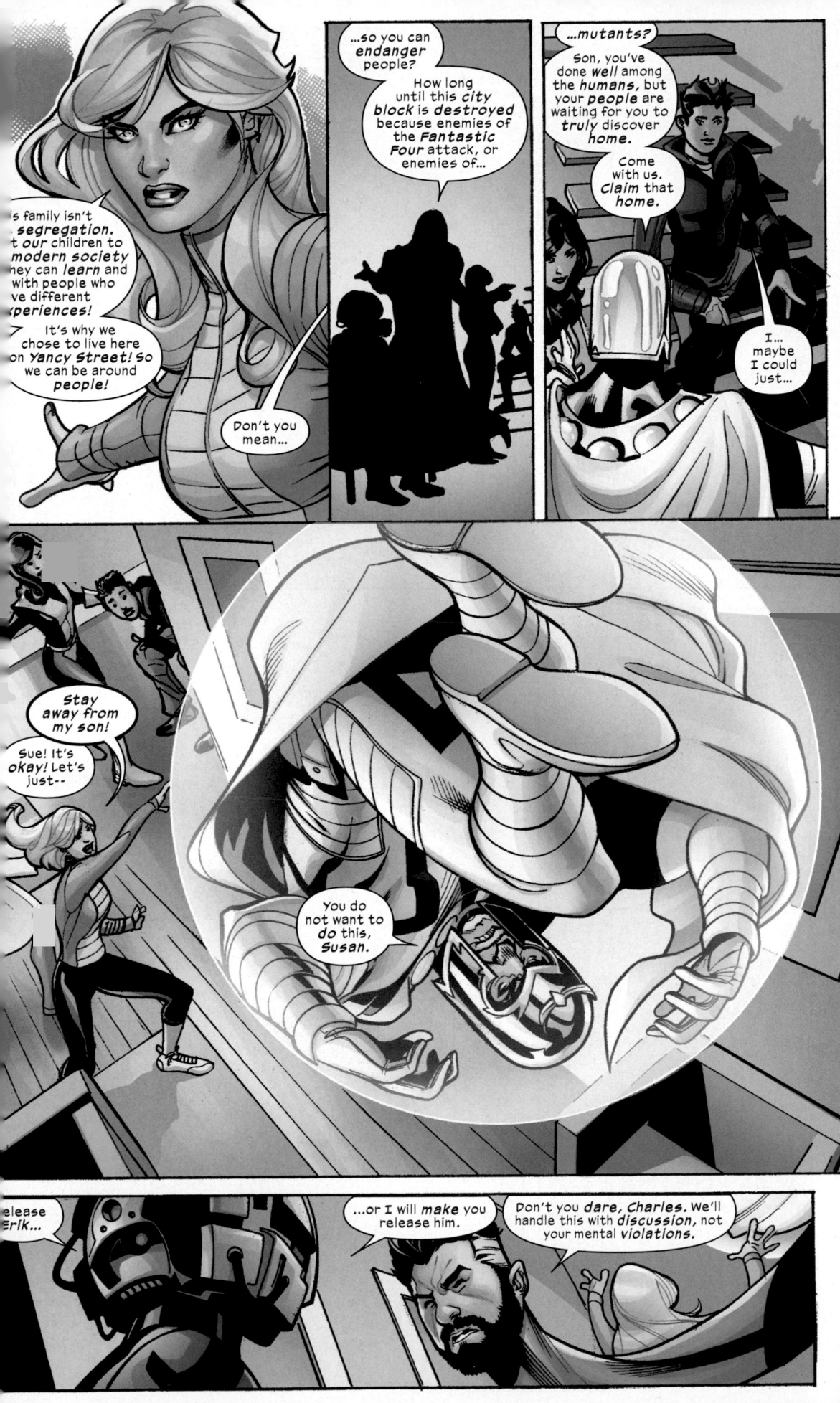

Your *wife* is the one committing *violence.* We're only responding to--
Excuse me?!
Oh, man... this isn't good...
Wanna get out of here?
Yeah...
You come in *here* and threaten to take my *child* and--
Cool.
So, *Stormie,* you think this is a *good* idea?
I do.
Mutants are hated and feared. *Millions* of us died at Genosha as a result of that hatred.

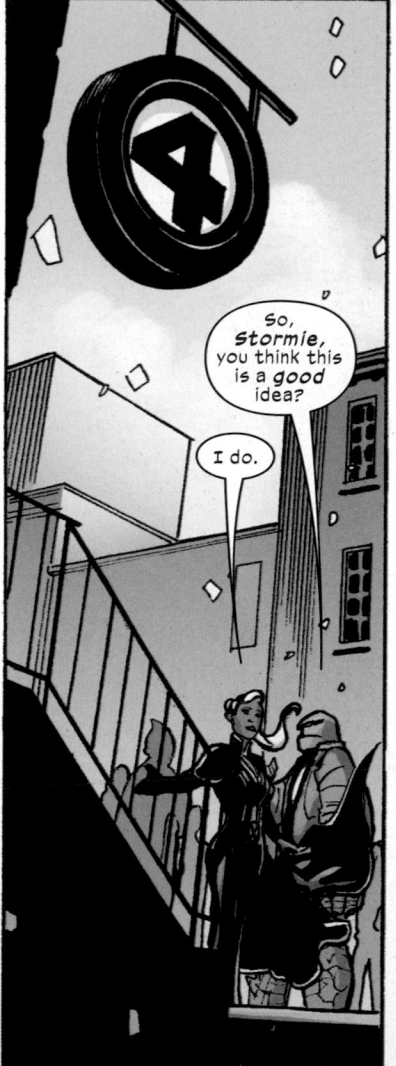

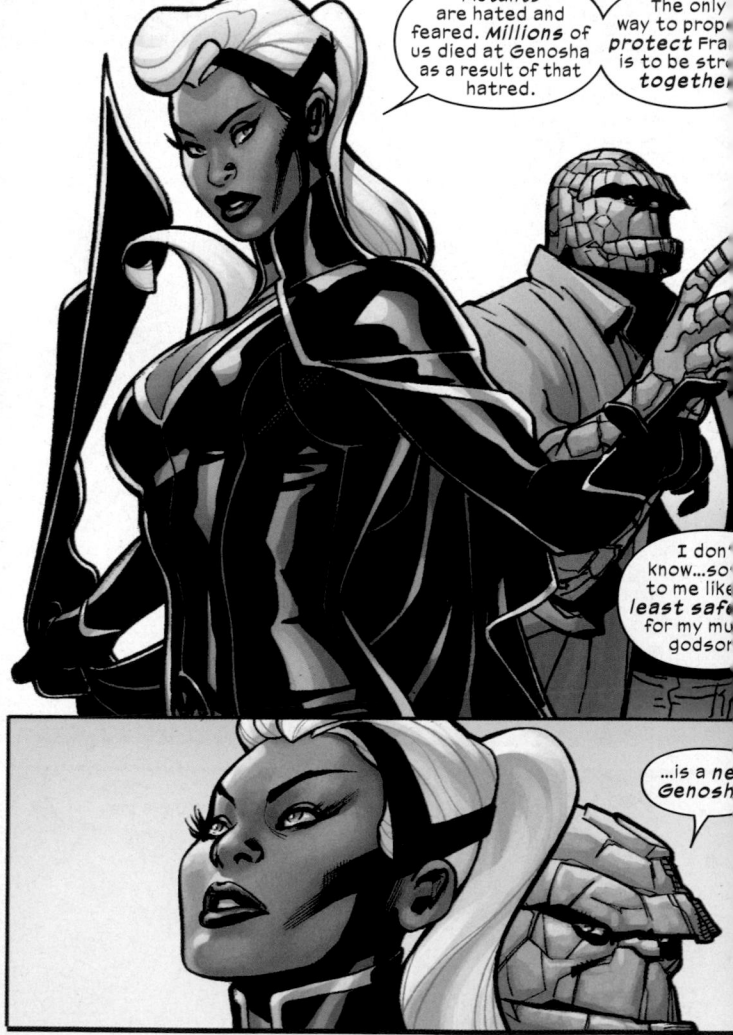

I'm orry this is appening...
...I know it's a *lot* to take in.
I just hate that nobody even *cares* what I think.
Like, this is *my life!*
So, in that case...
...what do you want to do?
don't...I don't know. I nk I want to go? Maybe you can *help* me with my *powers*...
But I know my parents will lose their *minds*.
Yeah, at first. But they'll *get it*. Eventually.
I just want you to know...
...no matter what you *decide*, I'll *back* you. I won't let Charles push you to do anything you don't *want* to do. *Or* your parents.
Thanks...
I've missed you, *Kitty*.

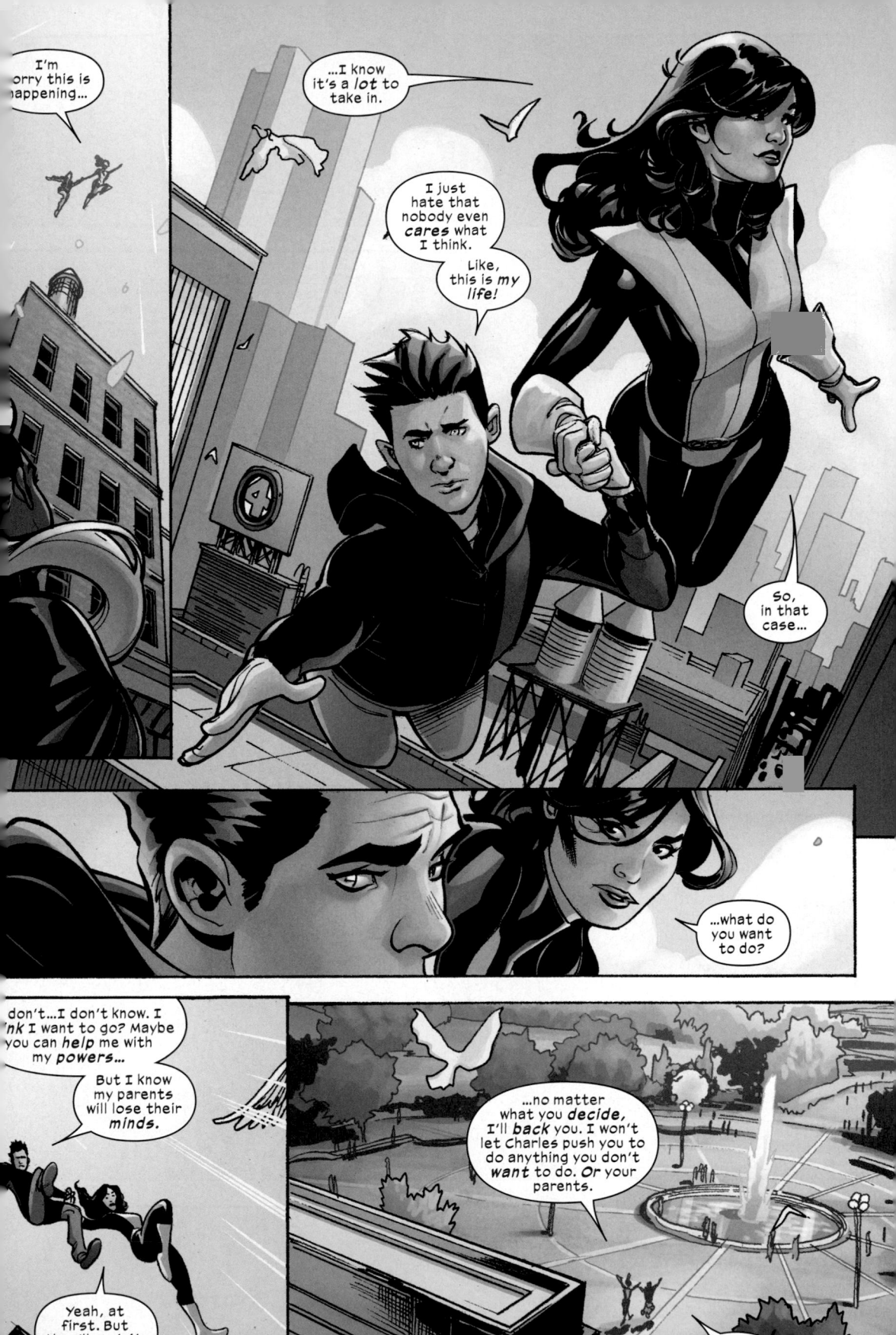

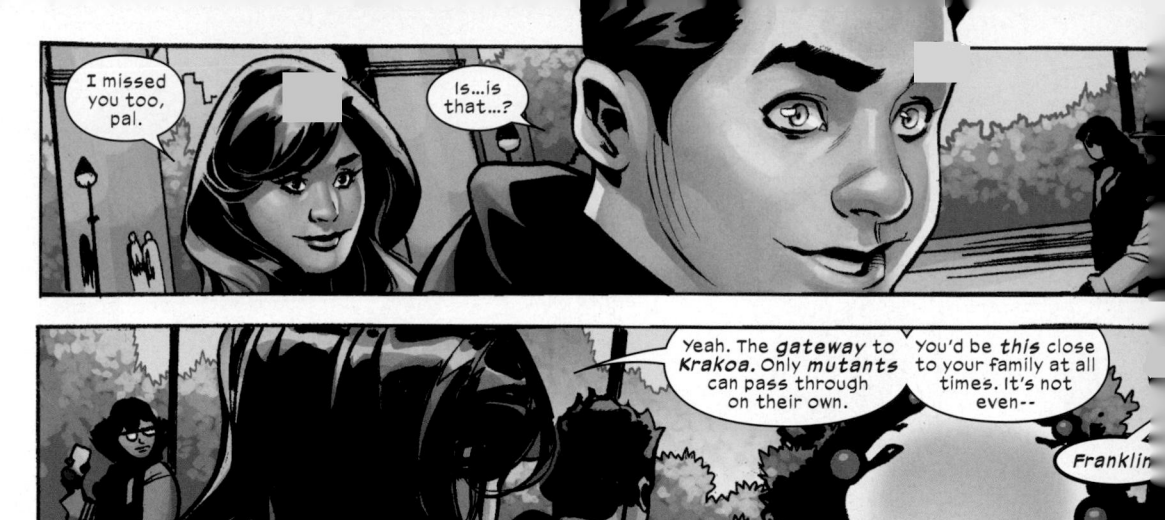

I missed you too, pal.

Is...is that...?

Yeah. The *gateway* to *Krakoa.* Only *mutants* can pass through on their own.

You'd be *this* close to your family at all times. It's not even--

Franklin

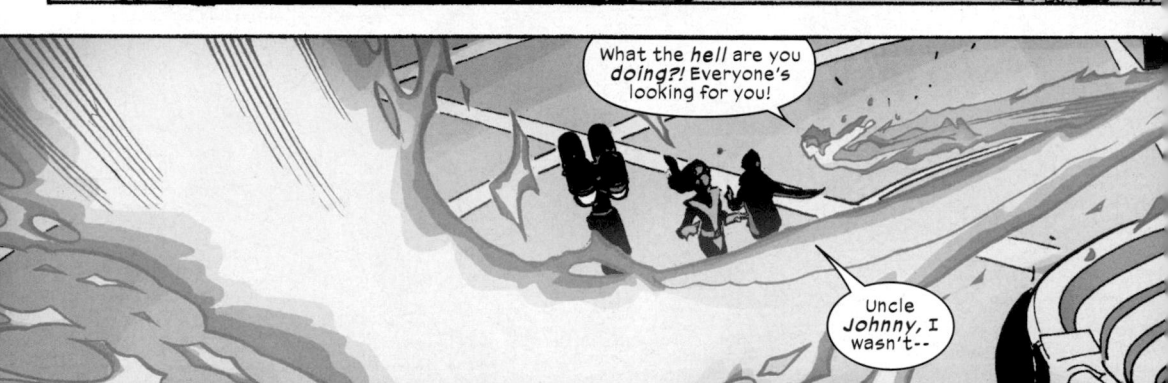

What the *hell* are you *doing?!* Everyone's looking for you!

Uncle *Johnny,* I wasn't--

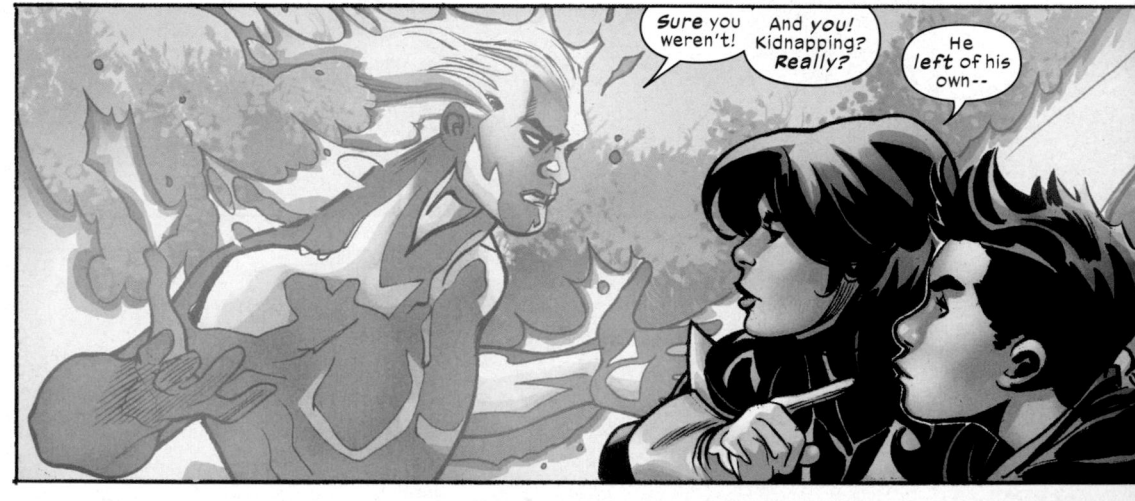

Sure you weren't!

And *you!* Kidnapping? *Really?*

He *left* of his own--

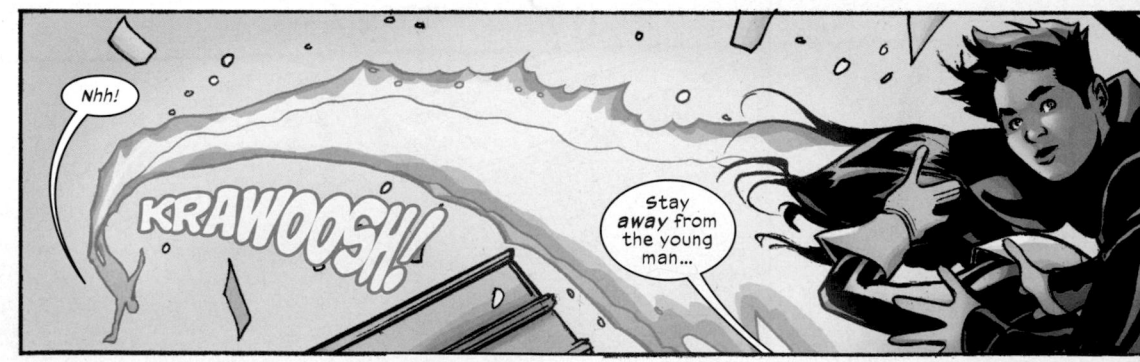

Nhh!

KRAWOOSH!

Stay *away* from the young man...

...he has diplomatic immunity.
Yeah, bub. And so do I, so get ready for some--

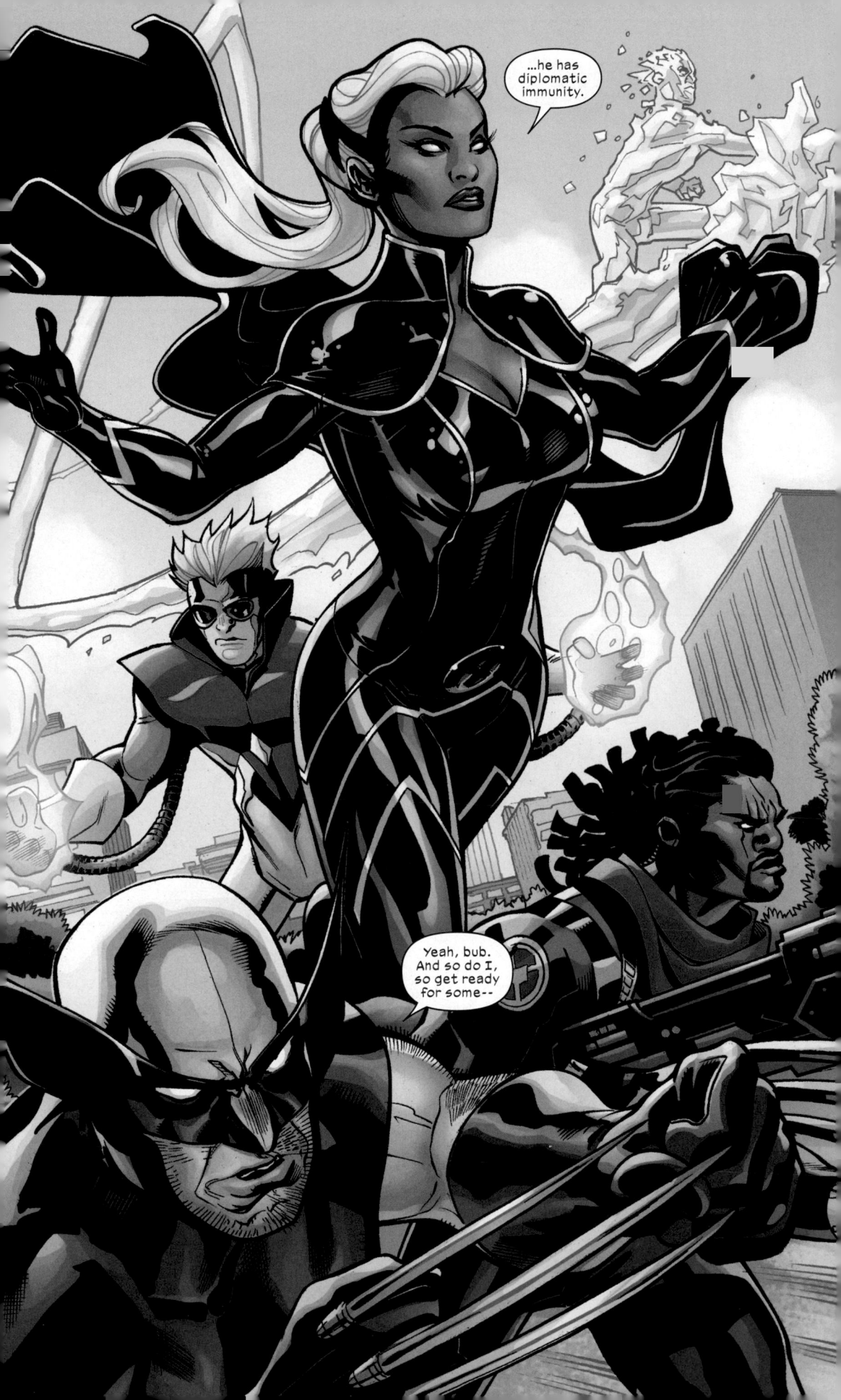

--@#$%!
'S funny how the only folks who need "diplomatic immunity"...
KRSSZH!
...are the ones doin' things *wrong.*
Ah!
Oh, *Bishop,* this is going to be *fun...*
Remember, *no* human casualties, *Pyro!* Just-- what?!
FWOOSH
FZAM!
I'll only say this *once...*

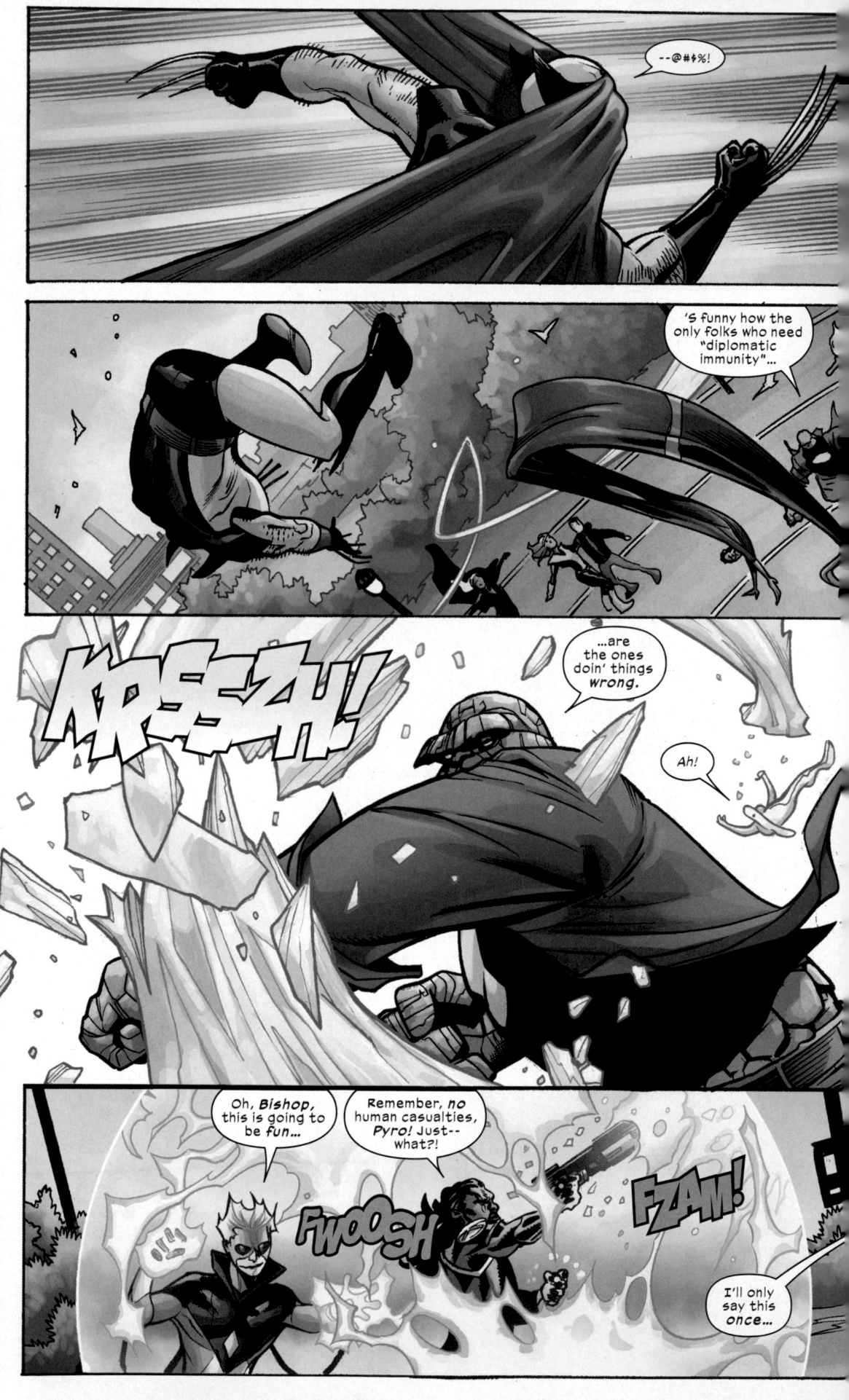

TOOM!
...you're done here. This is over.
You fools!
Your child does not belong to you like some precious bauble! He is a mutant! He is power!
Erik... let's not escalate.
No. Let's.
So you learn your lesson and stay away from my family.

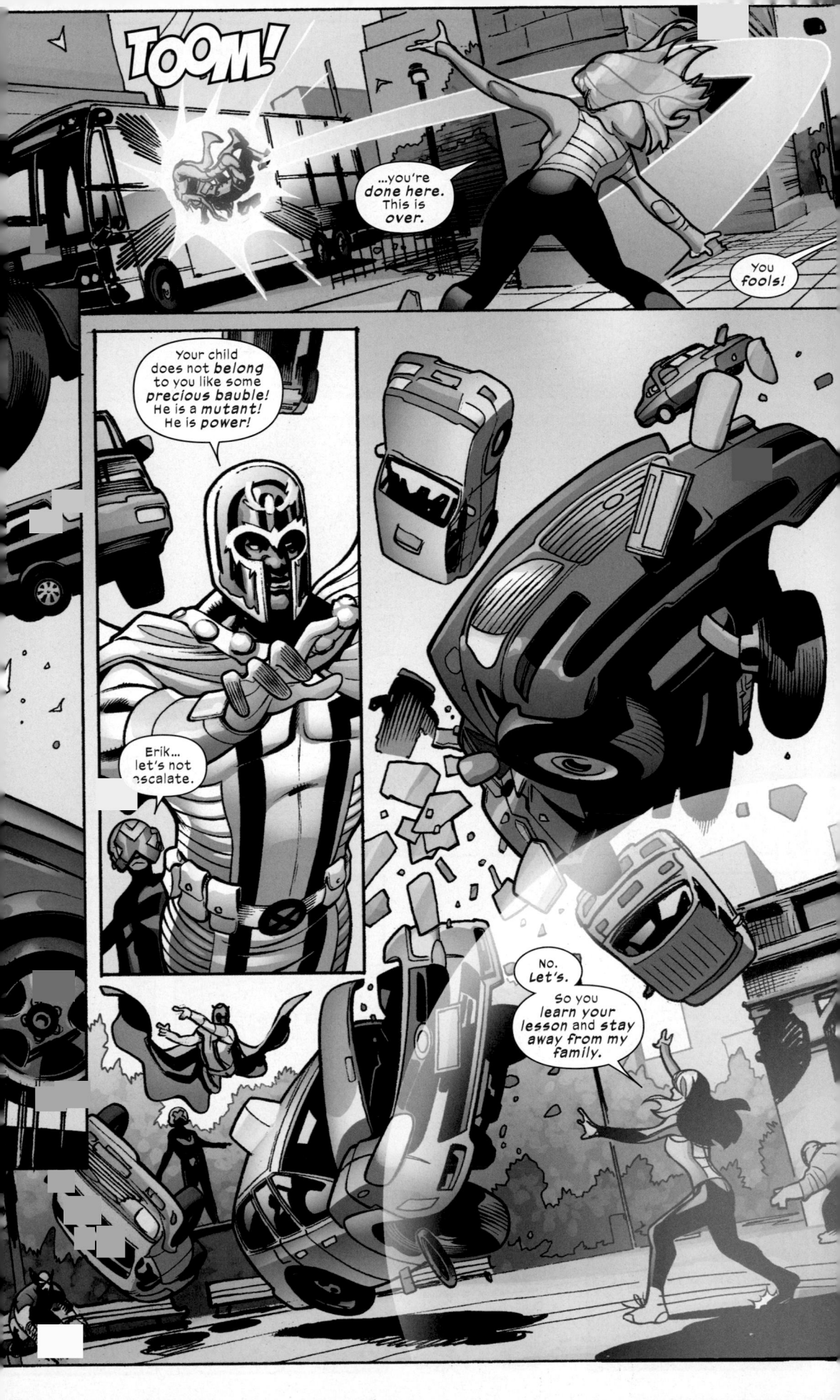

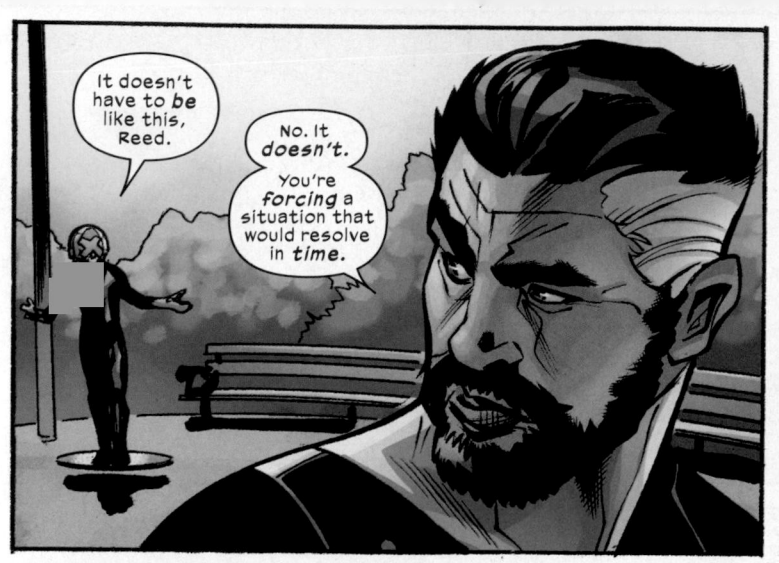

It doesn't have to be like this, Reed.

No. It doesn't. You're forcing a situation that would resolve in time.

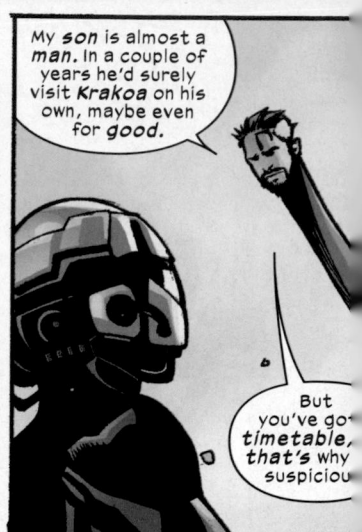

My son is almost a man. In a couple of years he'd surely visit Krakoa on his own, maybe even for good.

But you've go timetable, that's why suspiciou

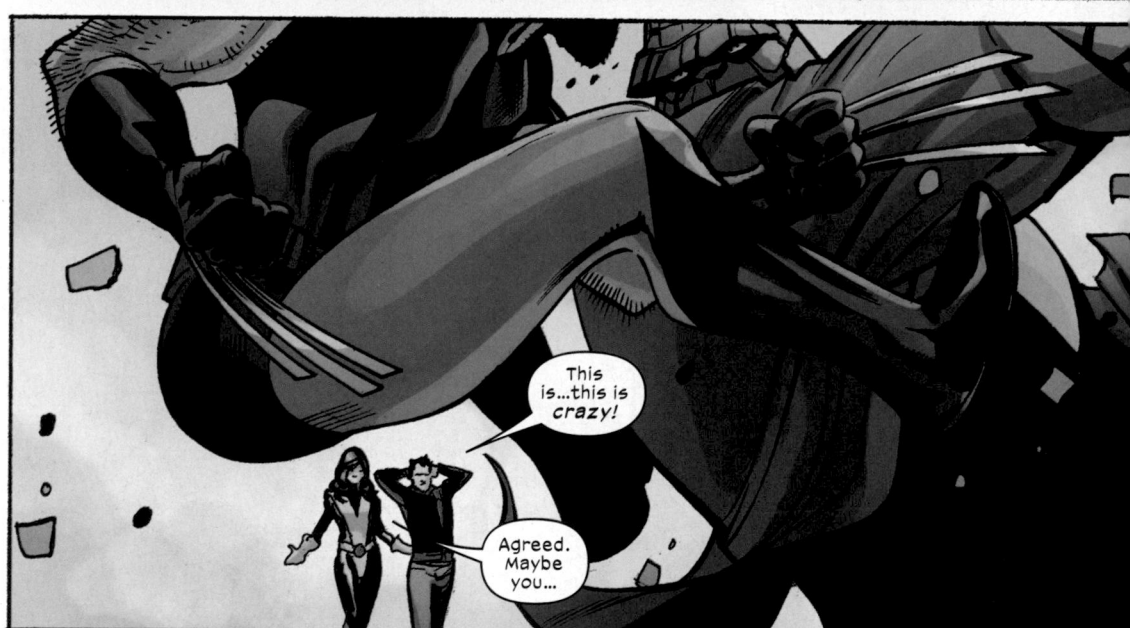

This is...this is crazy!

Agreed. Maybe you...

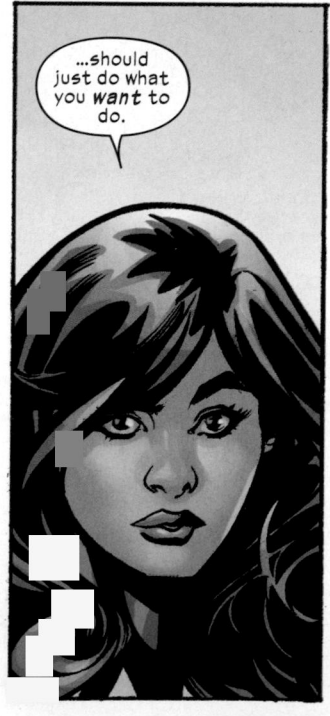

...should just do what you want to do.

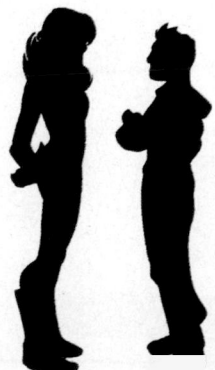

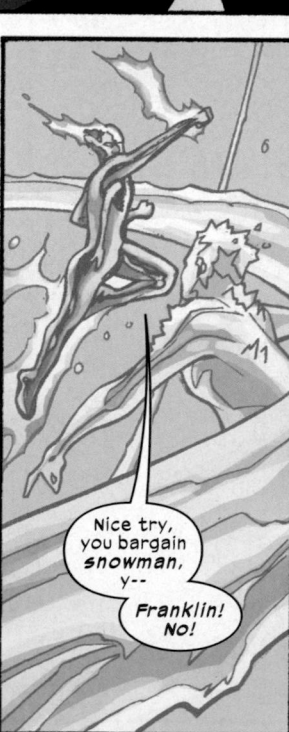

Nice try, you bargain snowman, y--

Franklin! NO!

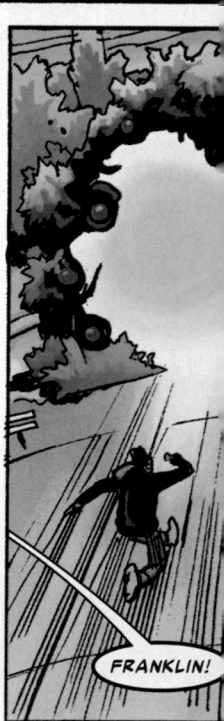

FRANKLIN!

What...
F-Franklin? How--
I'm...I'm sorry, son.
I knew this might happen. So I...I created a device that masks your mutant gene. Which prevents you from accessing the gates. I--
You what?!
You--you were supposed to be fixing me!
I'm just trying to protect you...
You're too young to just go. I'm your father. Your place is--

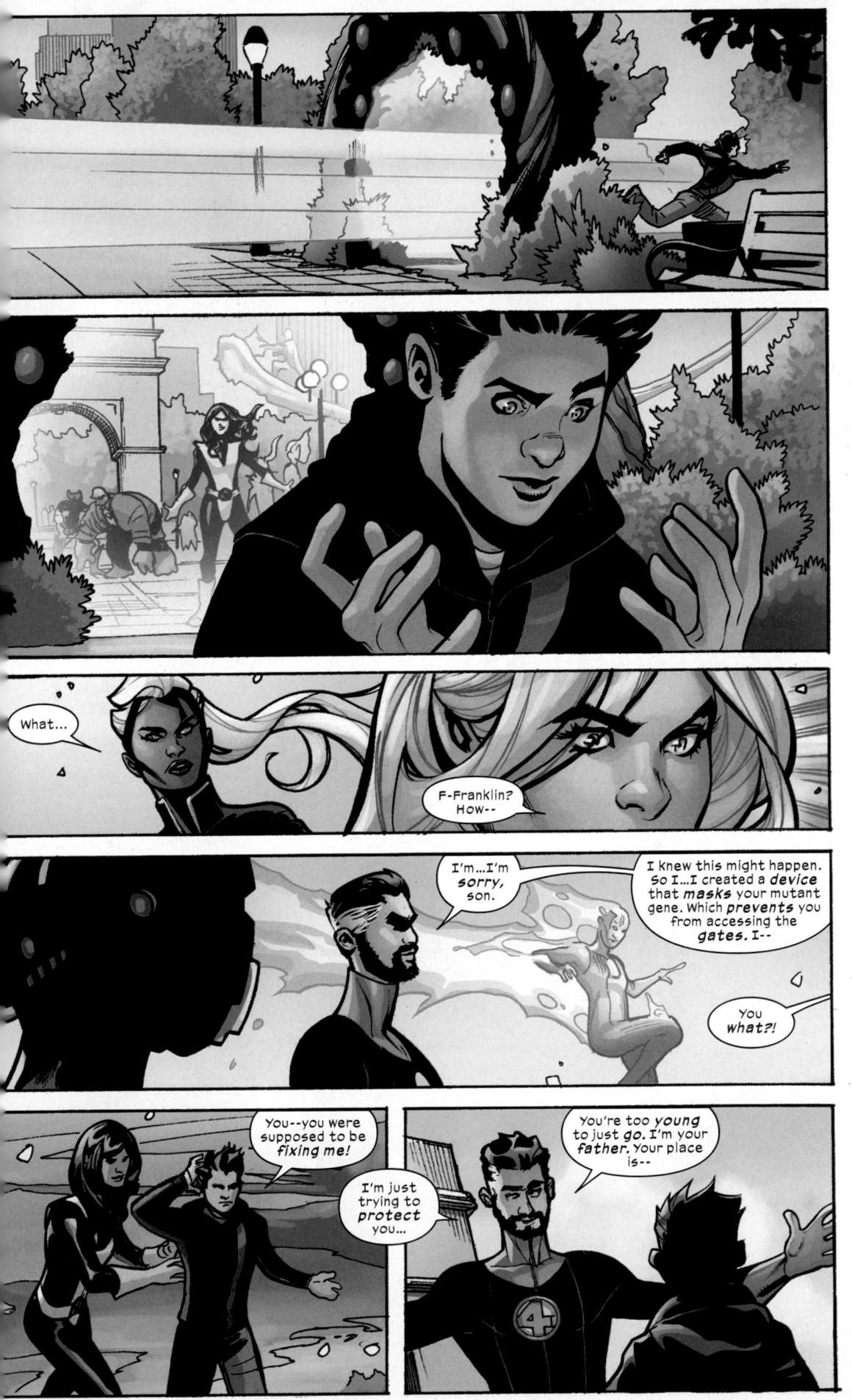

It would appear that you're right, *Reed*.

I suspect this *will* resolve itself in time.

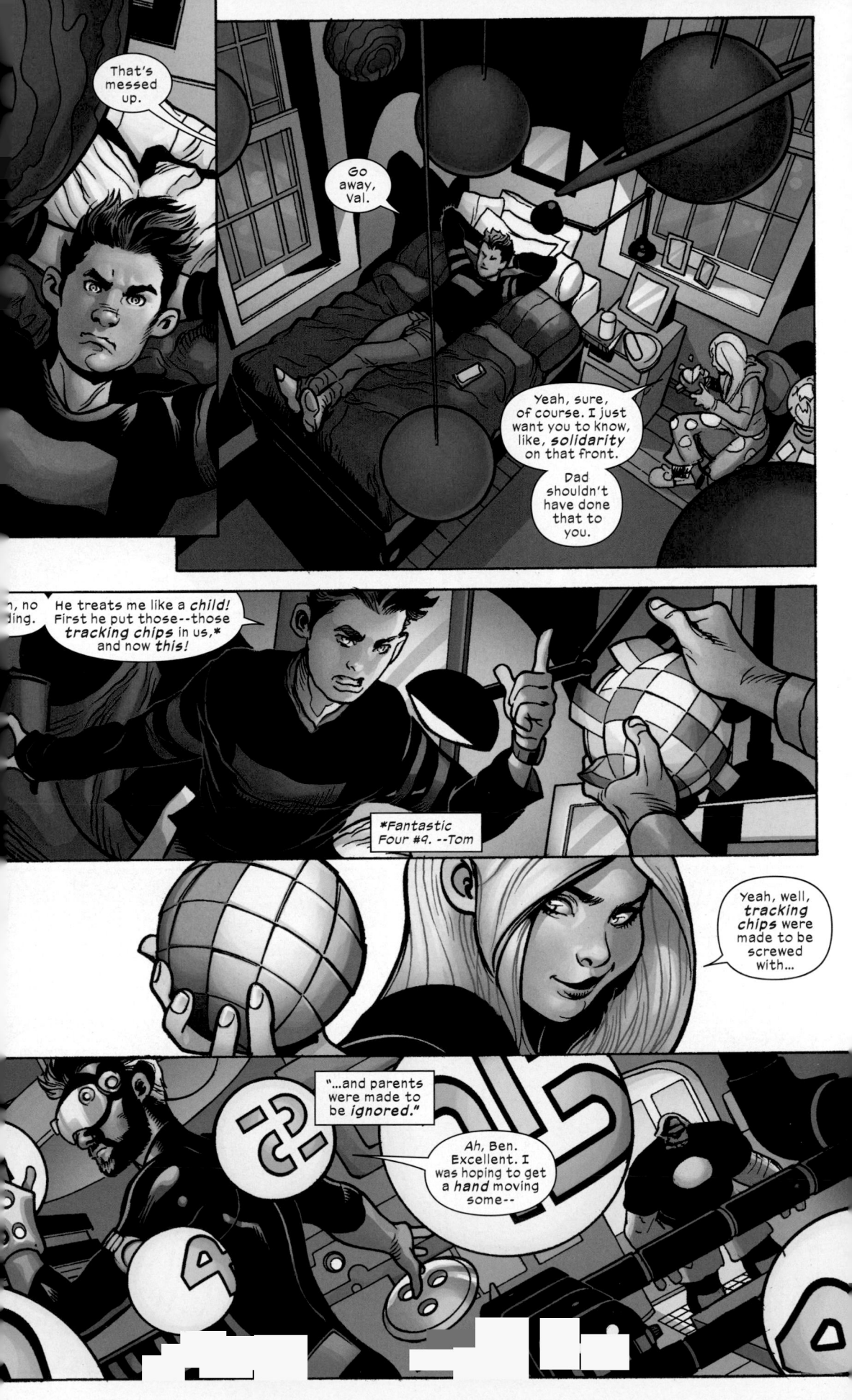

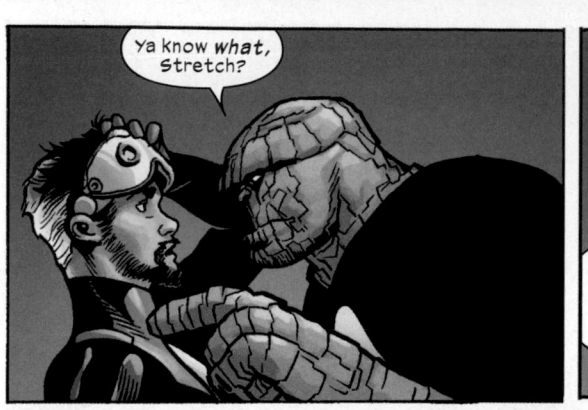

Ya know *what*, Stretch?

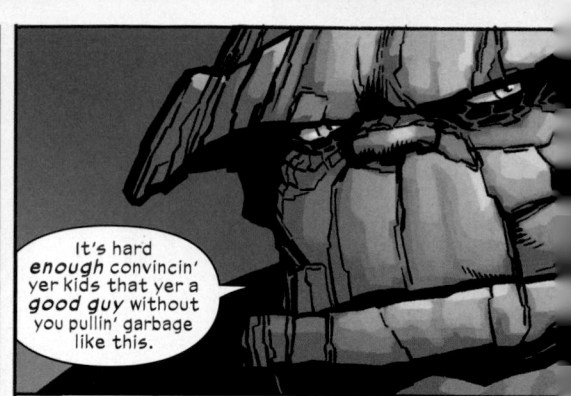

It's hard *enough* convincin' yer kids that yer a *good guy* without you pullin' garbage like this.

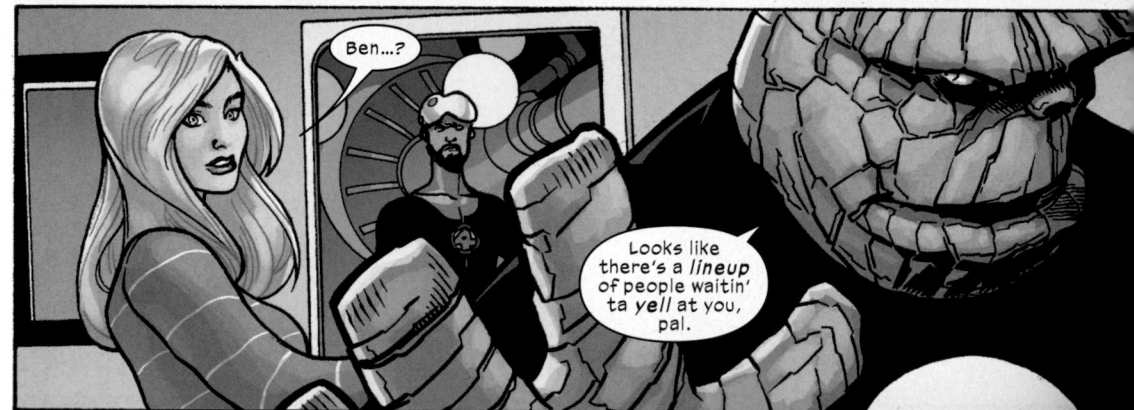

Ben...?

Looks like there's a *lineup* of people waitin' ta *yell* at you, pal.

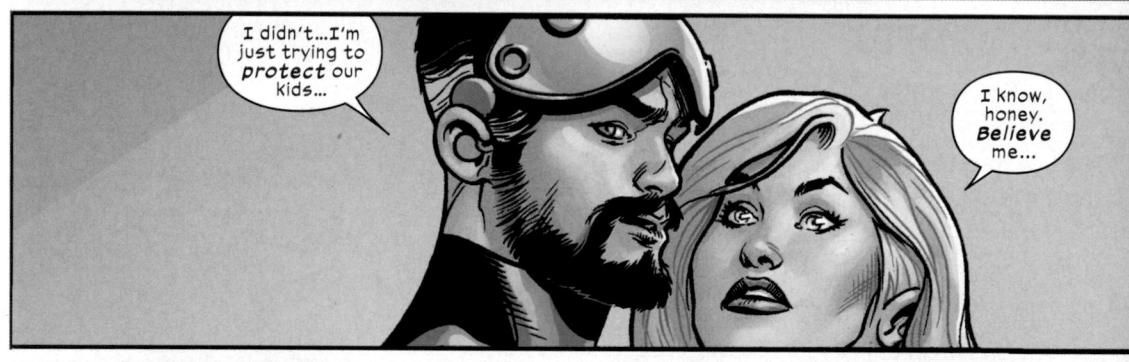

I didn't...I'm just trying to *protect* our kids...

I know, honey. *Believe* me...

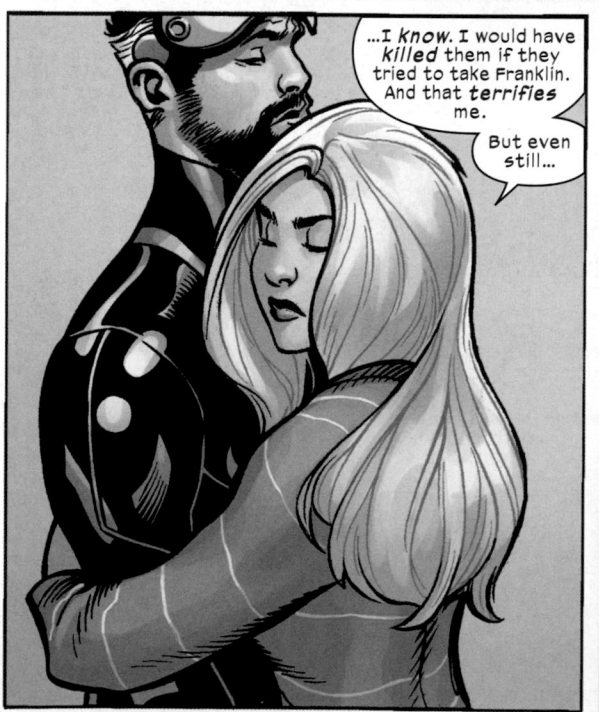

...I *know*. I would have *killed* them if they tried to take Franklin. And that *terrifies* me.

But even still...

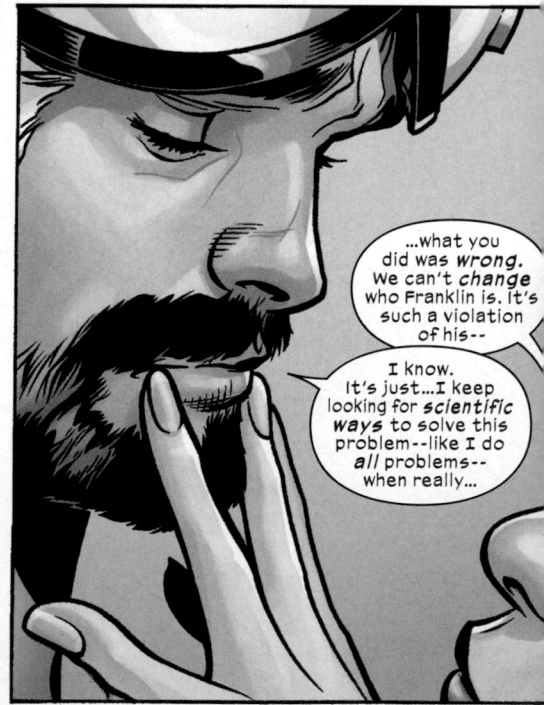

...what you did was *wrong*. We can't *change* who Franklin is. It's such a violation of his--

I know. It's just...I keep looking for *scientific ways* to solve this problem--like I do *all* problems-- when really...

...I just need to be a better father."
Professor? I'm assuming they didn't welcome you with open arms.
No, Scott, they did not.
But based on the way Reed Richards treated his son and, frankly, mutants in general...
...I suspect we no longer have to approach young Franklin. Rather...
"...he will approach us."
Dammit, weather's getting a little rough.
Pyro, go wake Storm so we can get her to clear things up a bit.
Aye aye, Captain.
And don't be a creep about it or wake her with fire.
Nay nay, Captain...
I'm gonna grab some flares in case we can't see the...

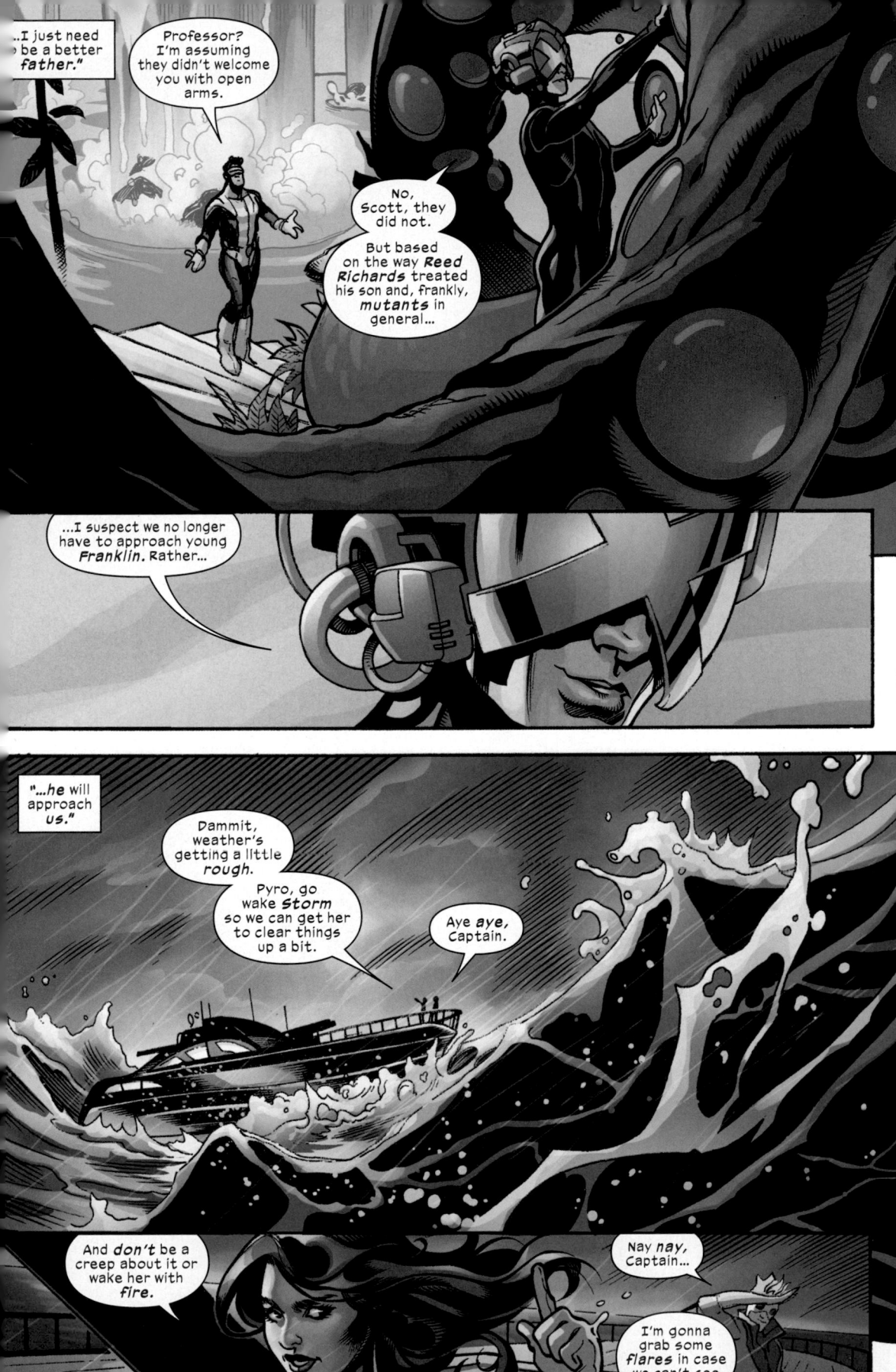

...mutants...
Uh, hey, Kitty...
...been a while. Have you met my sister, Val?
Hey.
What on Earth are you--
Look, you said it yourself. You'd back me on whatever I wanted to do. Well, I want to come back to Krakoa with you.
I...and you?
I want to go too! For a bit at least.
But you're... you're human!
Barely! I just want
make sure my brother
to where he wants
so I can, you kno
have his room.
But we're not going to Krakoa!
What do you m--
We left New York for a mutant rescue mission! There's a boat stranded in the ocean of refugee--

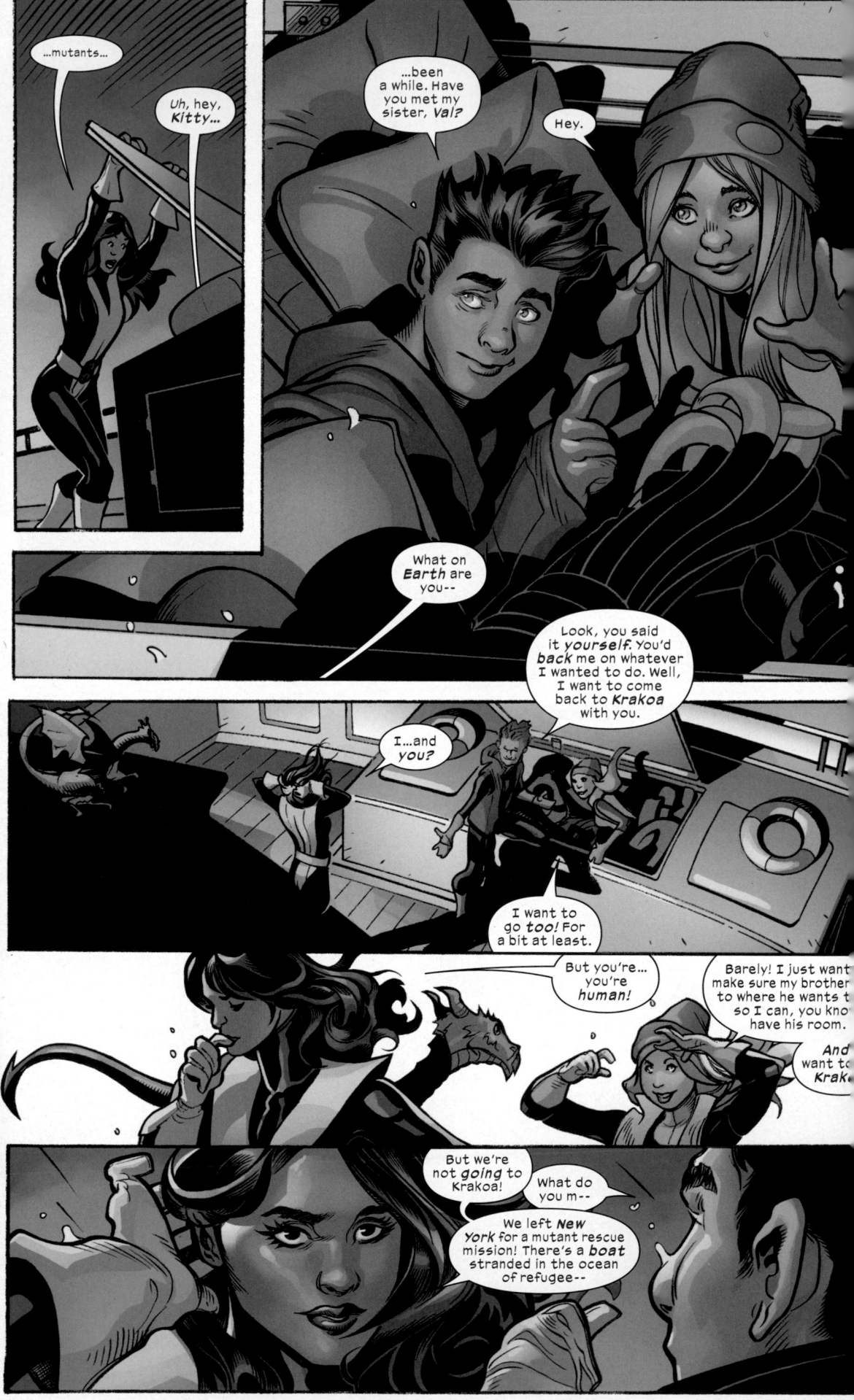

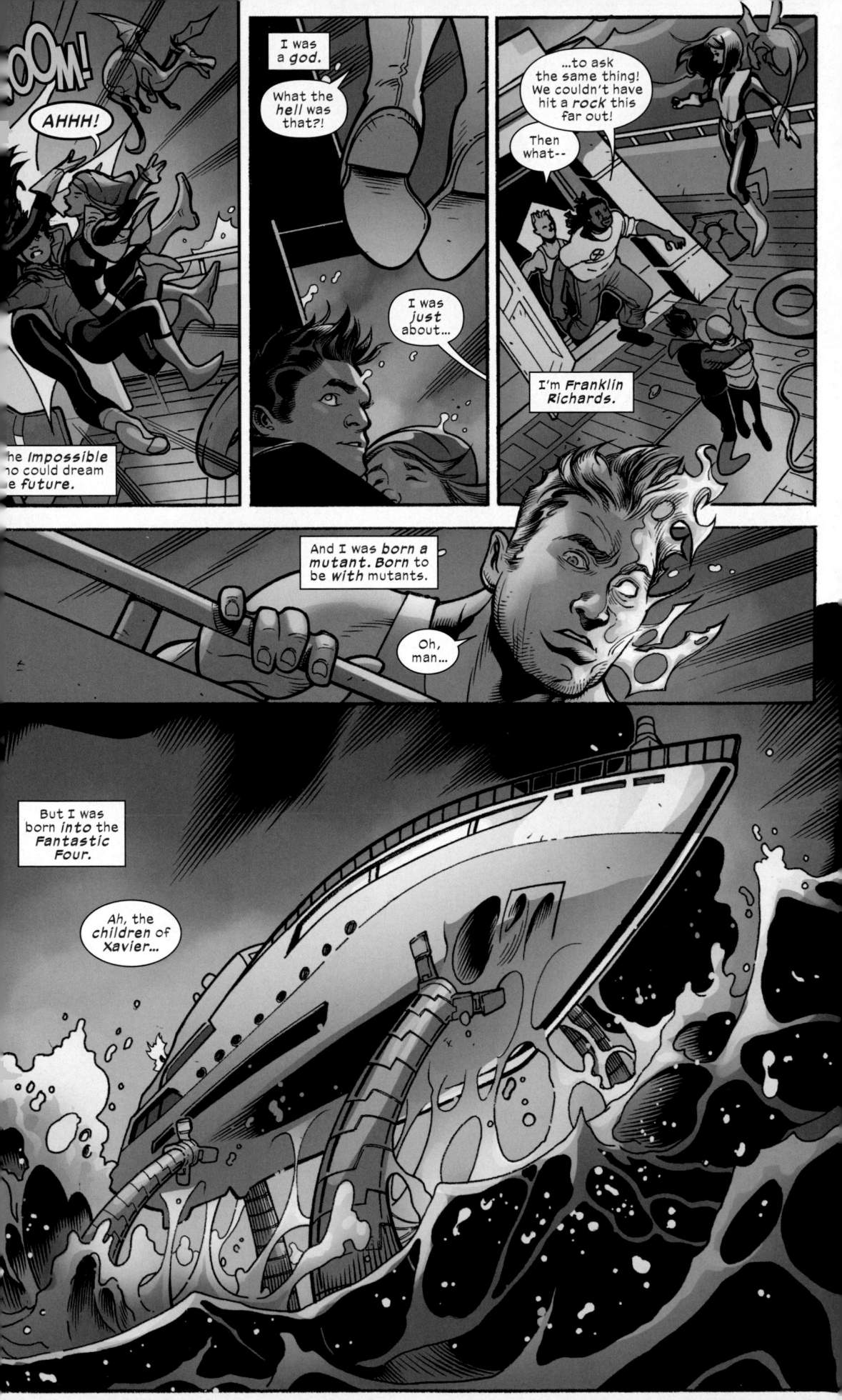

...and where is your *father?*
Which means I have *twice* as many enemies...

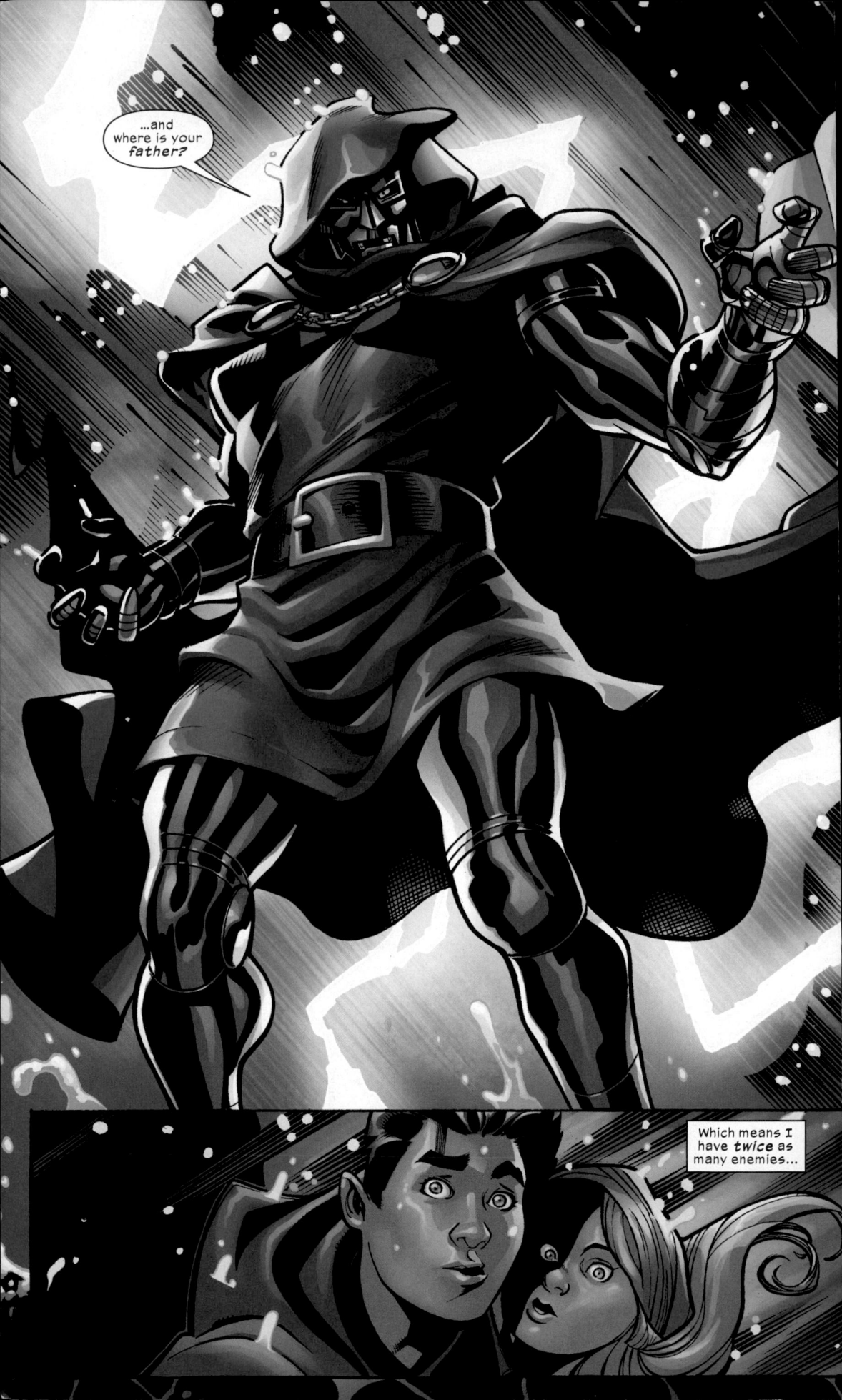

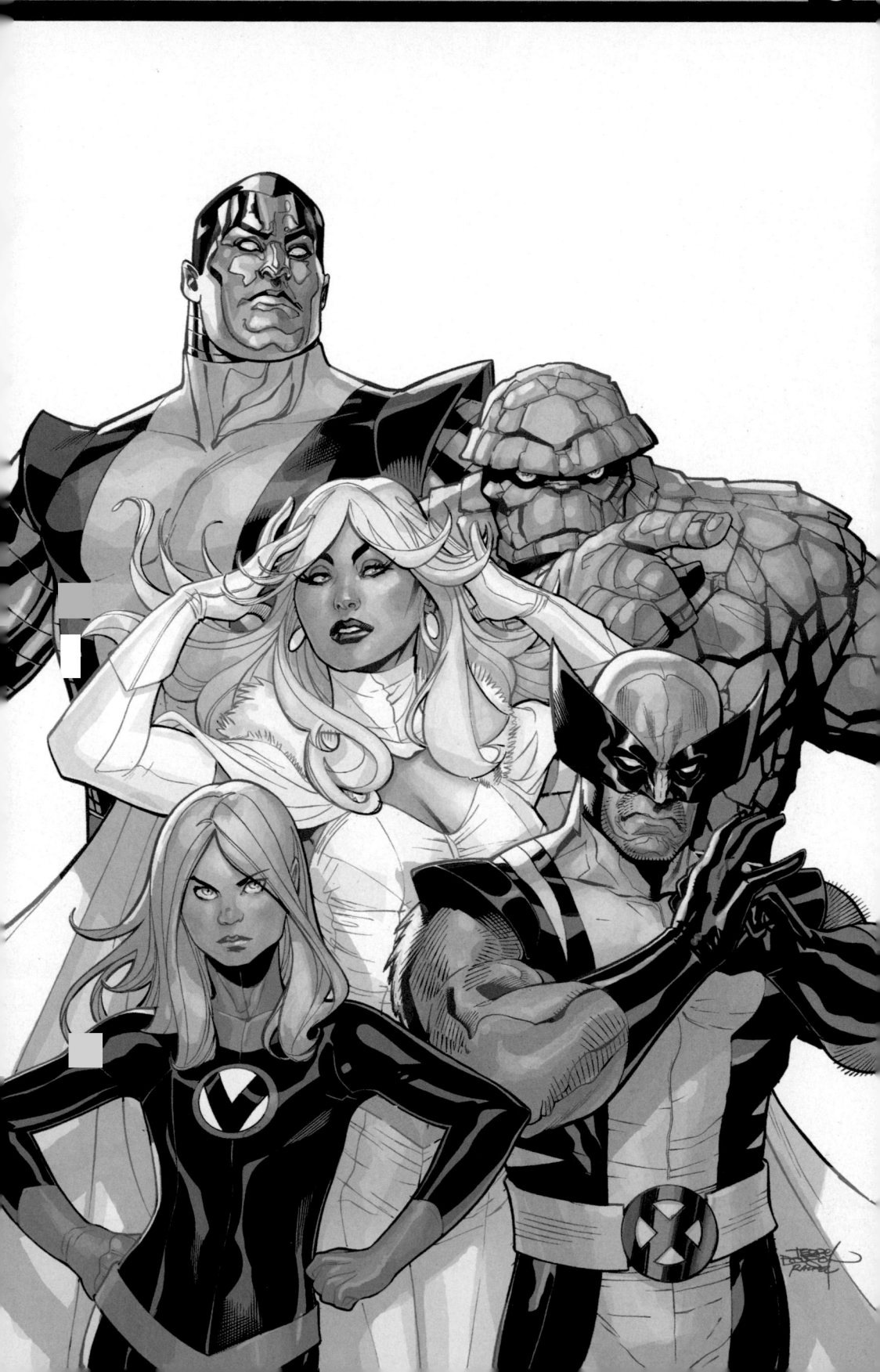

I assure you, we don't know where your children are.
I know your meeting went...poorly...and I understand Charles and Erik can be a little intense...
...but they're not kidnappers.
I know they're not, Cyclops.
But their agenda is clear--your agenda is clear. Krakoa is for all mutants, and you want them all to join you.
Franklin wanted to go, and I have no doubt you'd let him, despite our wishes as parents...
...because we're human.
Reed, we respect you and everything your tea has done for the world c humans and mutants, s believe me when I say your children are not here.
And to be perfectly clear...
...Krakoa is Franklin's birthright, but not Valeria's.

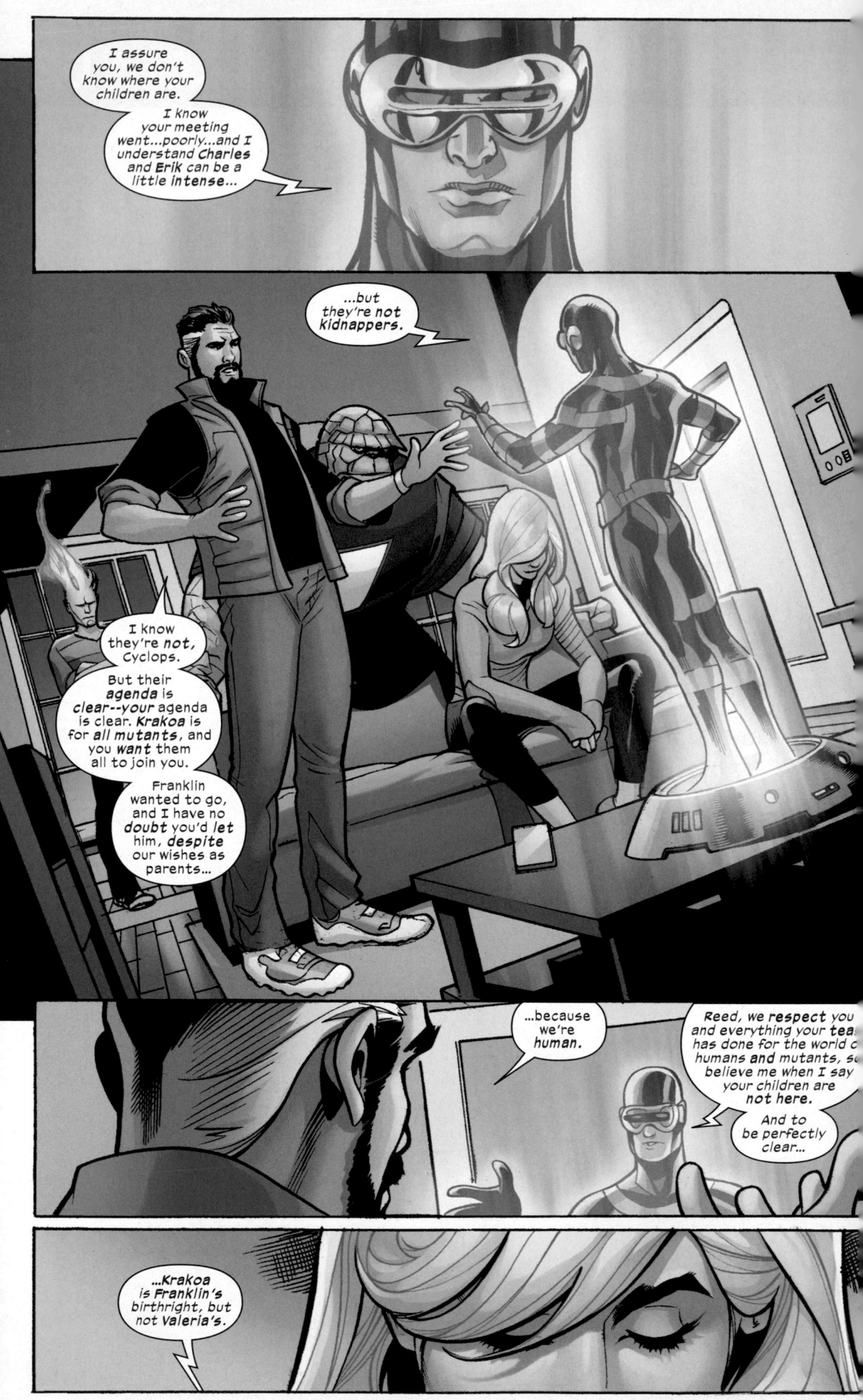

We're not an island of runaway humans. Of course we'd let you know if--

One's better than the other, is that it?

Um-- Sue?

...why should we believe you?

Of my children. You value the life of Franklin over Valeria.

My genius daughter wouldn't be allowed in your paradise compound because she's not pure enough for you. Not mutant.

You value her life less. All your actions make that perfectly clear. So, tell me, Scott...

I'm not--Sue, you do not want to--

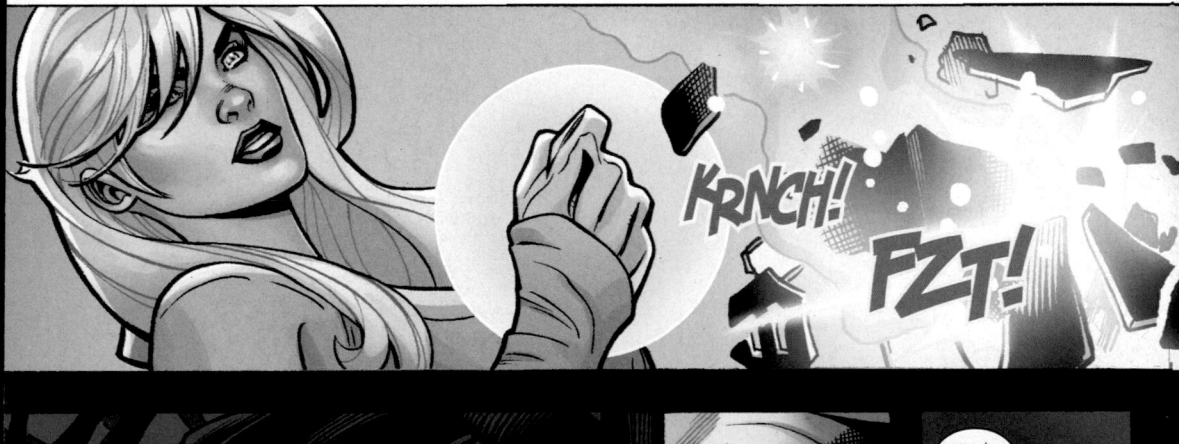

KRNCH!

FZT!

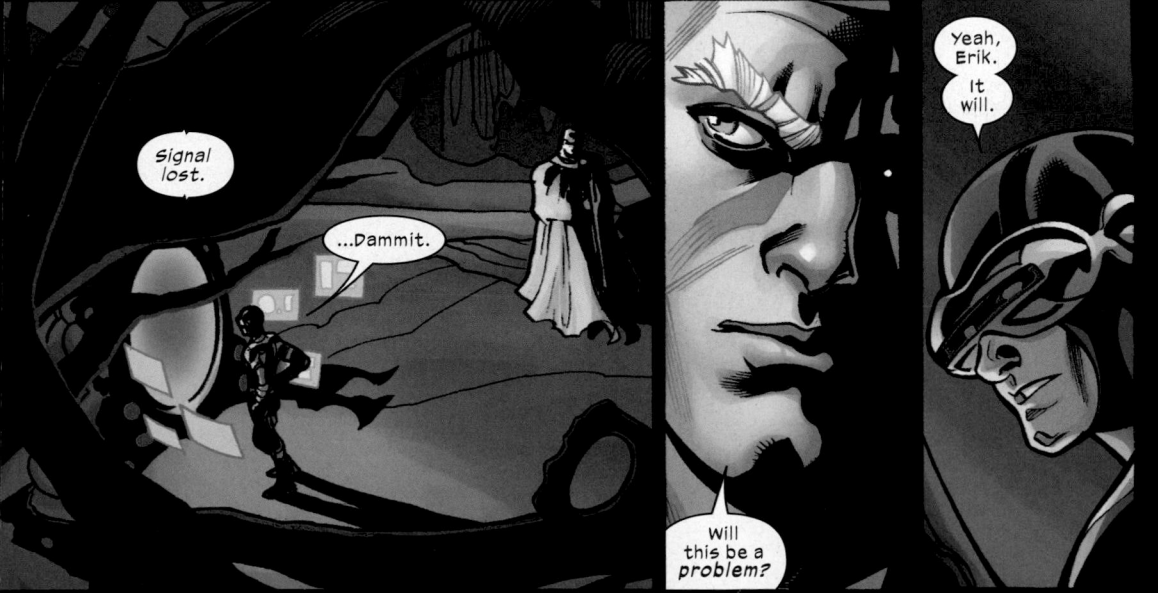

Signal lost.

...Dammit.

Yeah, Erik. It will.

Will this be a problem?

X-MEN /
FANTASTIC
FOUR

2 BROKEN BORDERS

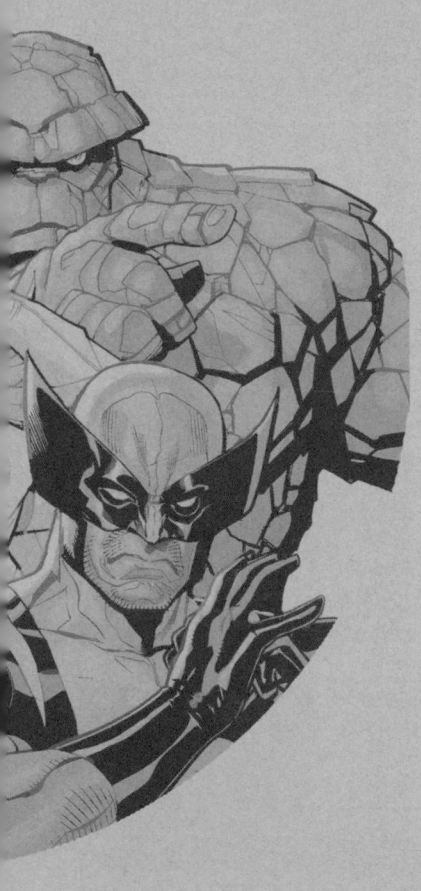

Sue! This isn't a time for escalation!
Reed, you've heard them. You've witnessed their actions.
They're a nation that thinks they're better than everyone. They're helping people, for a price!
Sabretooth has diplomatic immunity! Apocalypse is with them, for--
They're not the people we once knew. They're not heroes.
You're right. They're a nation now. And we can't just attack a nation. There are--
...ya @#$% up. Ya messed with yer kids and they ran and it's your fault.
And I hear what yer sayin', all of us do. But--
We're going. To get the kids.
This team isn't just you, Reed. We're a democracy--
Unlike Krakoa, I'd imagine.
Help us help our kids, Reed.

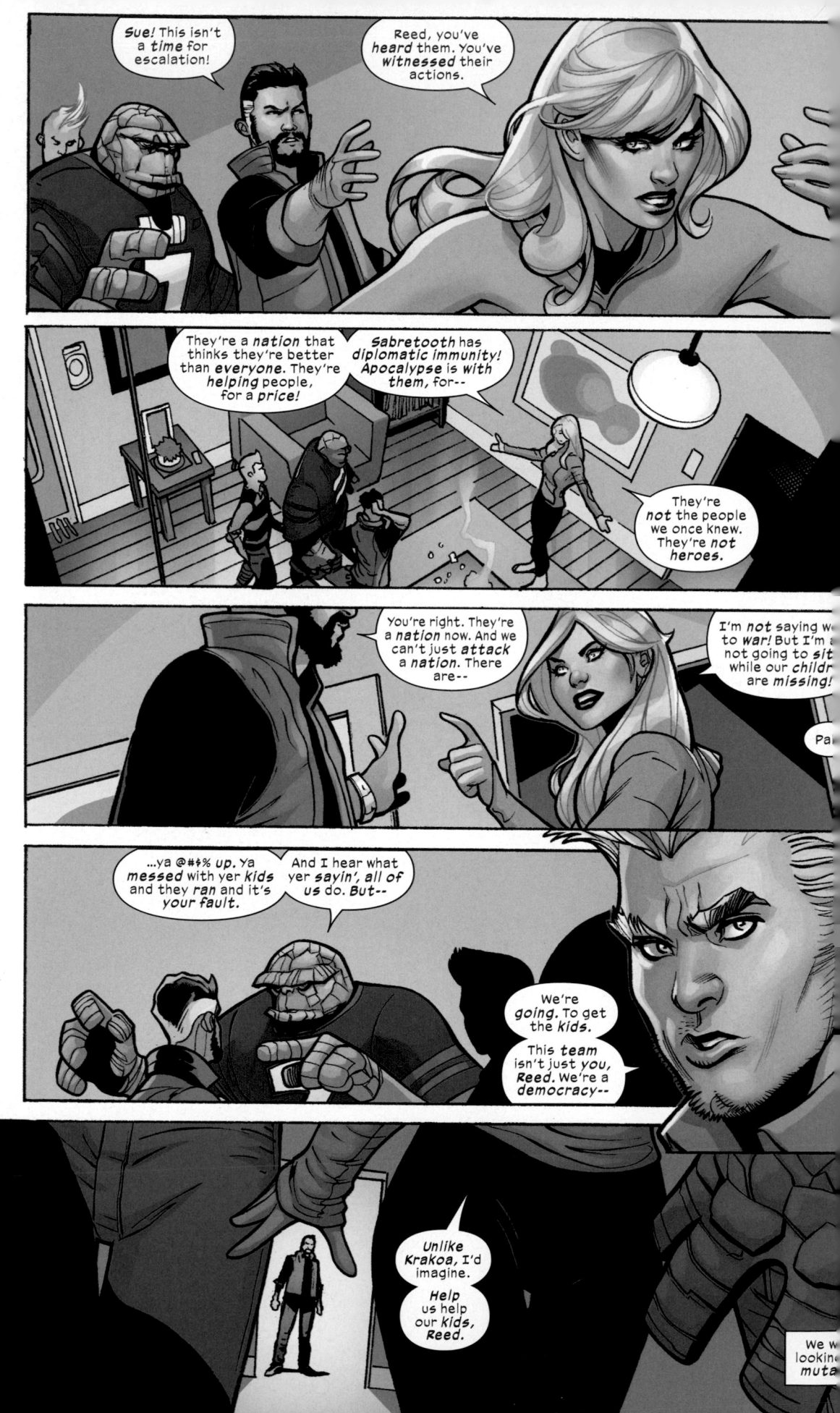

Mutants lost at sea.
Refugees searching for Krakoa...
Their promised land.
A safe place.
ut the auder was tacked.
Because nowhere in this world is truly safe...

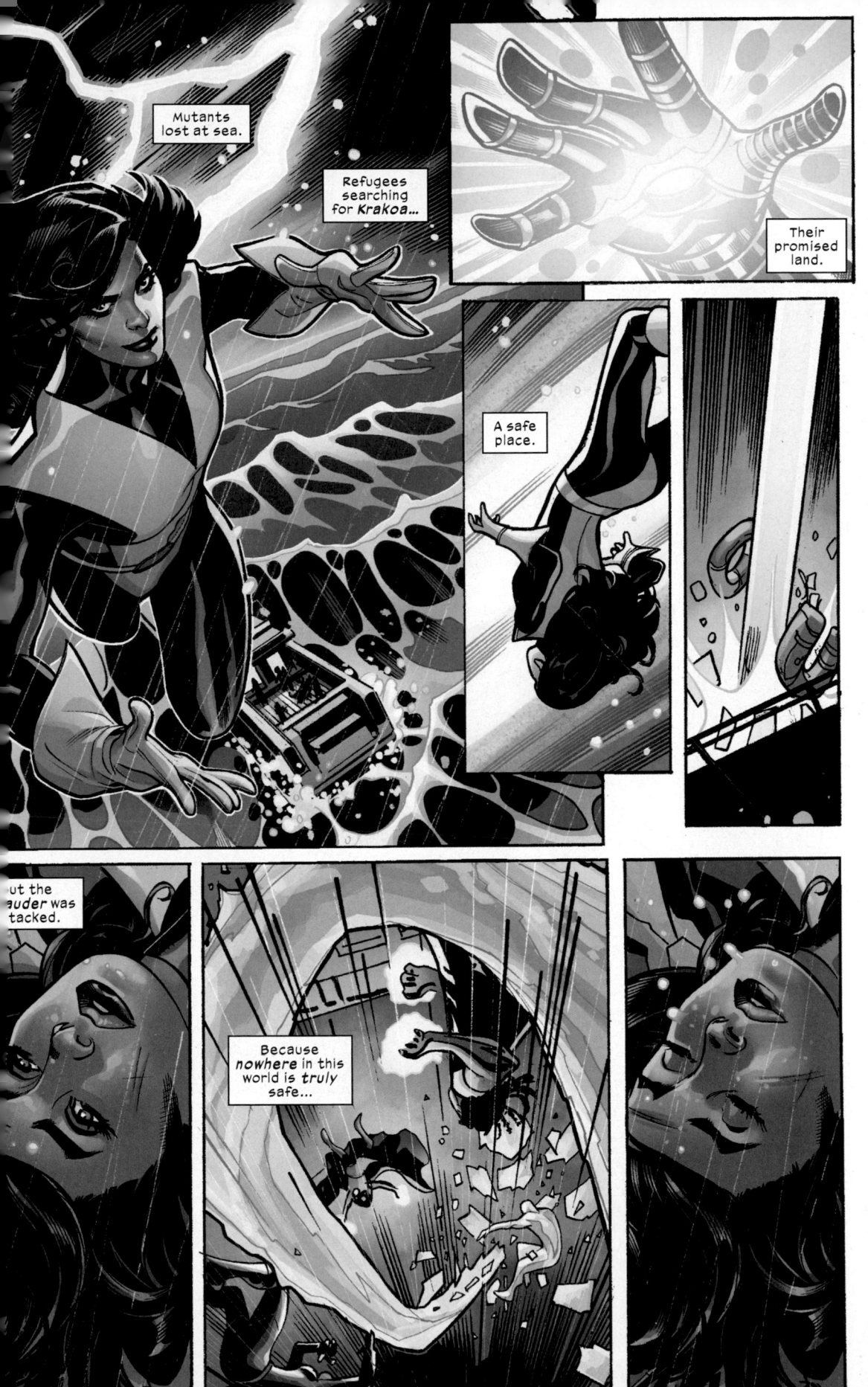

...when you're a *mutant*.

Nhhh... what's...

...going on...

Ah. Aw
Excelle

It's *okay*, Kitty. Don't freak out.

Now we can eat.

Finally.

Doom.

Where-- if you *hurt*--

Your *people?* Katherine, I've only ever been a *benevolent hand* when it comes to *mutantkind*.

They are *safe.* For the *moment.*

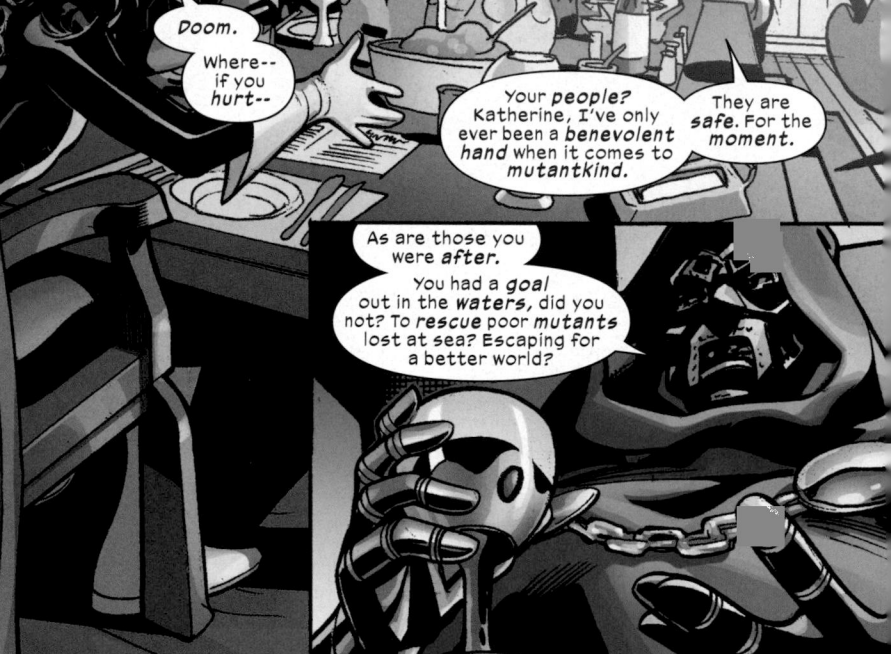

As are those you were *after.*

You had a *goal* out in the *waters*, did you not? To *rescue* poor *mutants* lost at sea? Escaping for a better world?

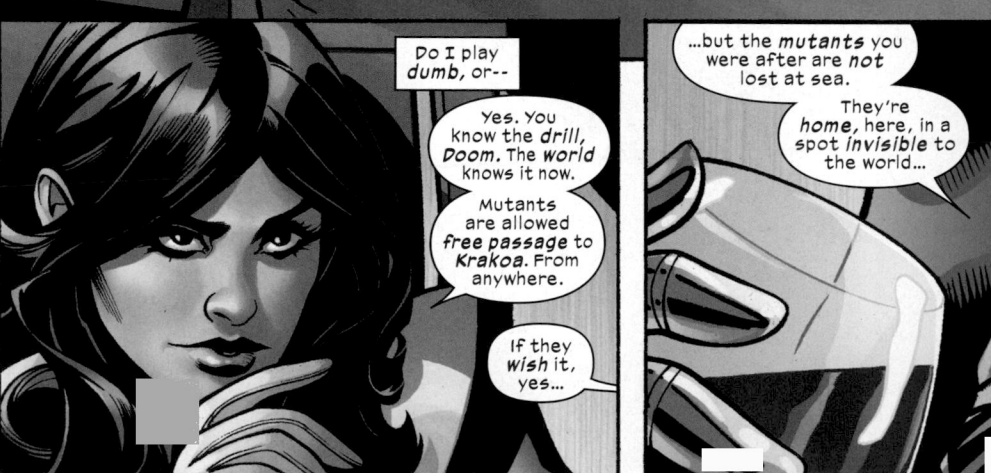

Do I play *dumb*, or--

Yes. You know the *drill*, *Doom.* The *world* knows it now.

Mutants are allowed *free passage* to *Krakoa*. From anywhere.

If they *wish* it, yes...

...but the *mutants* you were after are *not* lost at sea.

They're *home*, here, in a spot *invisible* to the world...

...DOOM ISLAND.
I can understand how you'd make the *mistake.*
Uncle Doom, it is *very* obvious that you're *hiding* something.
Besides the *salt.*
Valeria's right.
Why aren't your country's mutants in *Latveria?* Why aren't *you?*
It is *clear* to me, and anyone with *eyes,* that this new *paradigm shift* will have one outcome: *war.*
The protection of *Latveria* is my *priority,* so to remove the target...I brought my "genetically advanced" citizens *here,* to my *home away from home.*
This *island* is where I go when I do not wish to involve...Latveria *proper* in my plans. Such as my *new* one...
...to *help Franklin Richards...*
...be *all* that he can *be.*

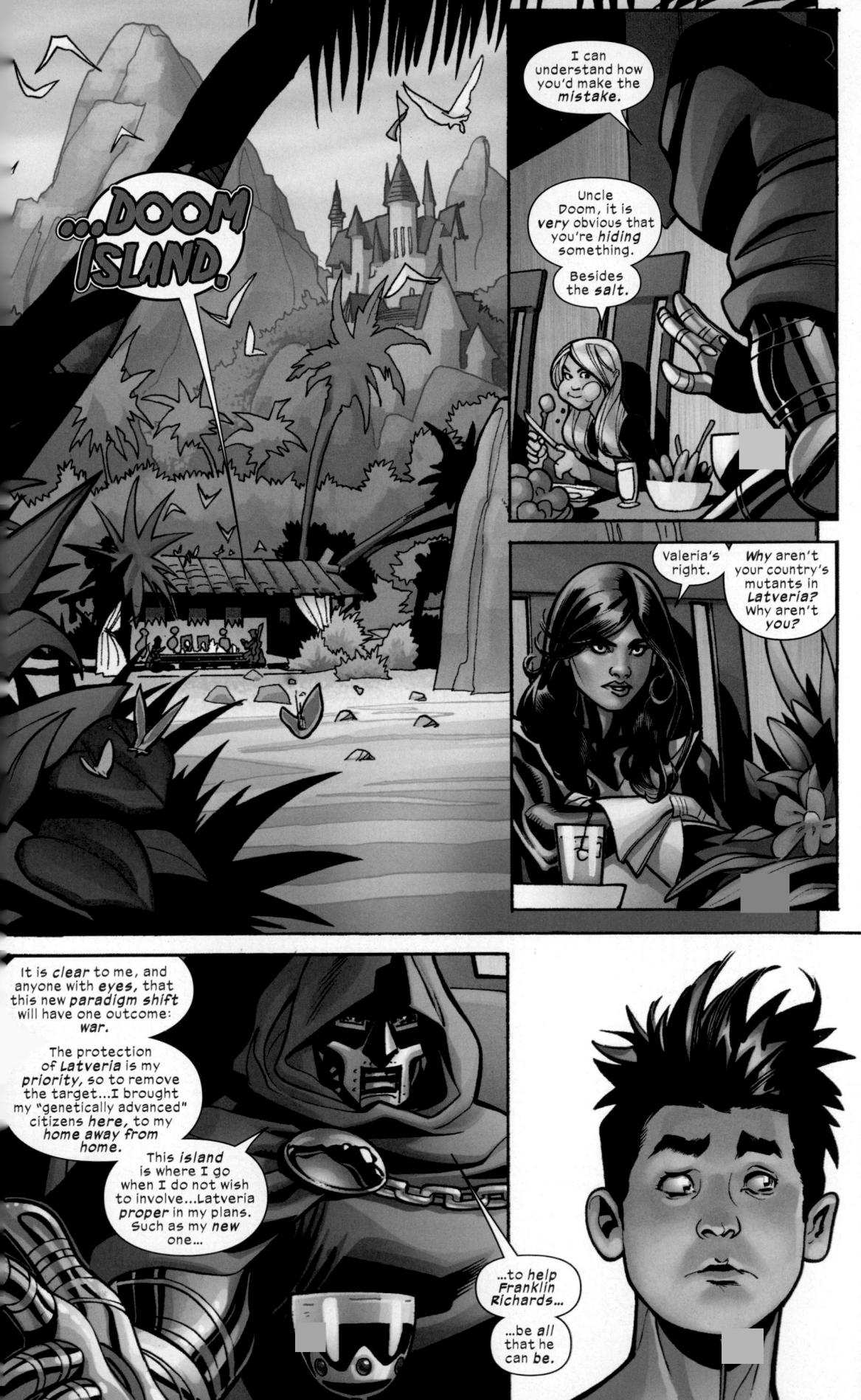

REED RICHARDS

Entry 661026 THE MUTANT POPULATION

Exponential growth and horrific decimation has marked the mutant population in the last decade. Is it any wonder they wish to band together, away from the humans who would harm them?

At this point, the island of Krakoa houses almost every mutant, which makes it the most powerful stronghold on the planet. And also the biggest target. Having our son move there feels wildly irresponsibl especially considering he's an "Omeg level mutant." While I don't know th specifics of the designation, I understar it puts him in rarified air within the muta community as one of their most powerf members.

I have no doubt the X-Men will come f my son, regardless of our wishes.

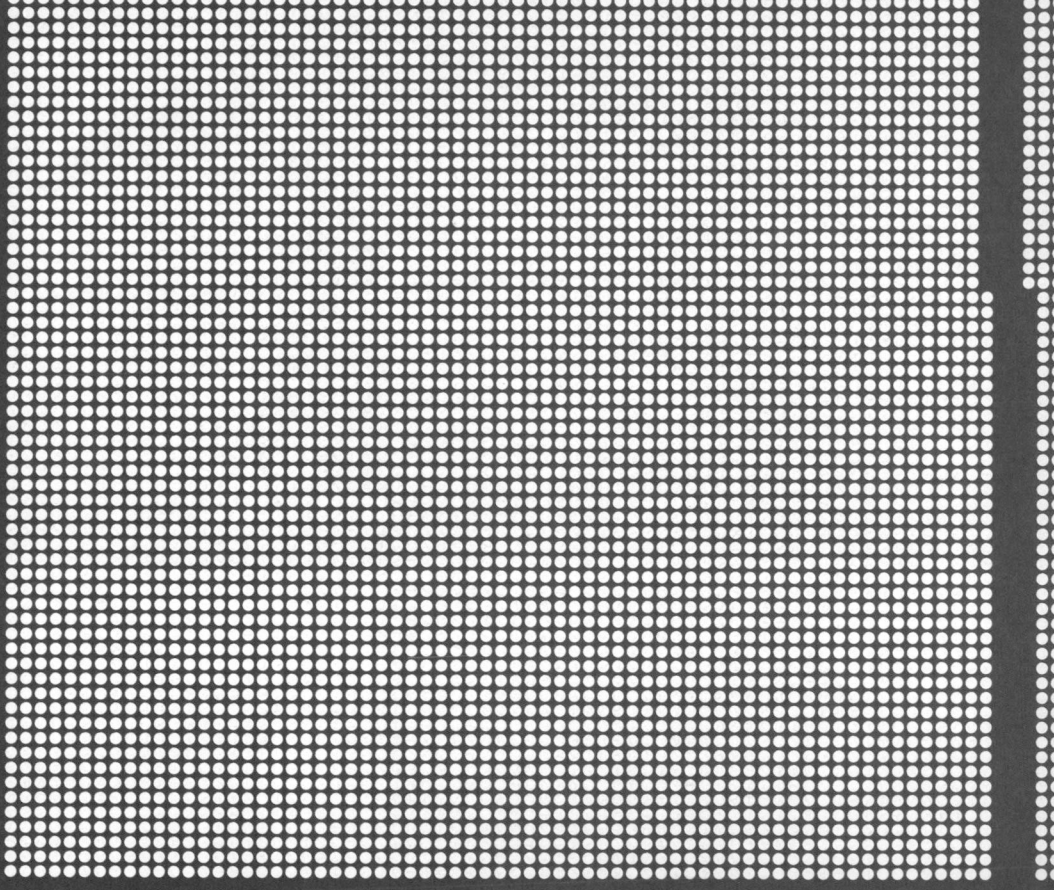

MUTANTS ON KRAKOA
est. 200,000

● =50 mutants

MUTANTS OFF KRAKOA
est. 10,000

OMEGA-LEVEL MUTANTS

Sorry, gang.
The Marauder is fully abandoned and drifting off the coast of Japan, no crew in sight.
Thank you, Jamie. We'll send others to search the area.
So, the boy is missing...
And Katherine and her team, from Cerebro no less. Surely no coincidence.
Where was she headed?
Mein Gott, the level of communication around here...
...So do we know where she was supposed to go?
Supposedly to rescue mutants at sea after our New York debacle.
But I was not led to believe they were off the Japanese coast...
The mutants at sea...
...aren't registering on Cerebro anymore. Give me a moment and I'll search the system for the last time they did...

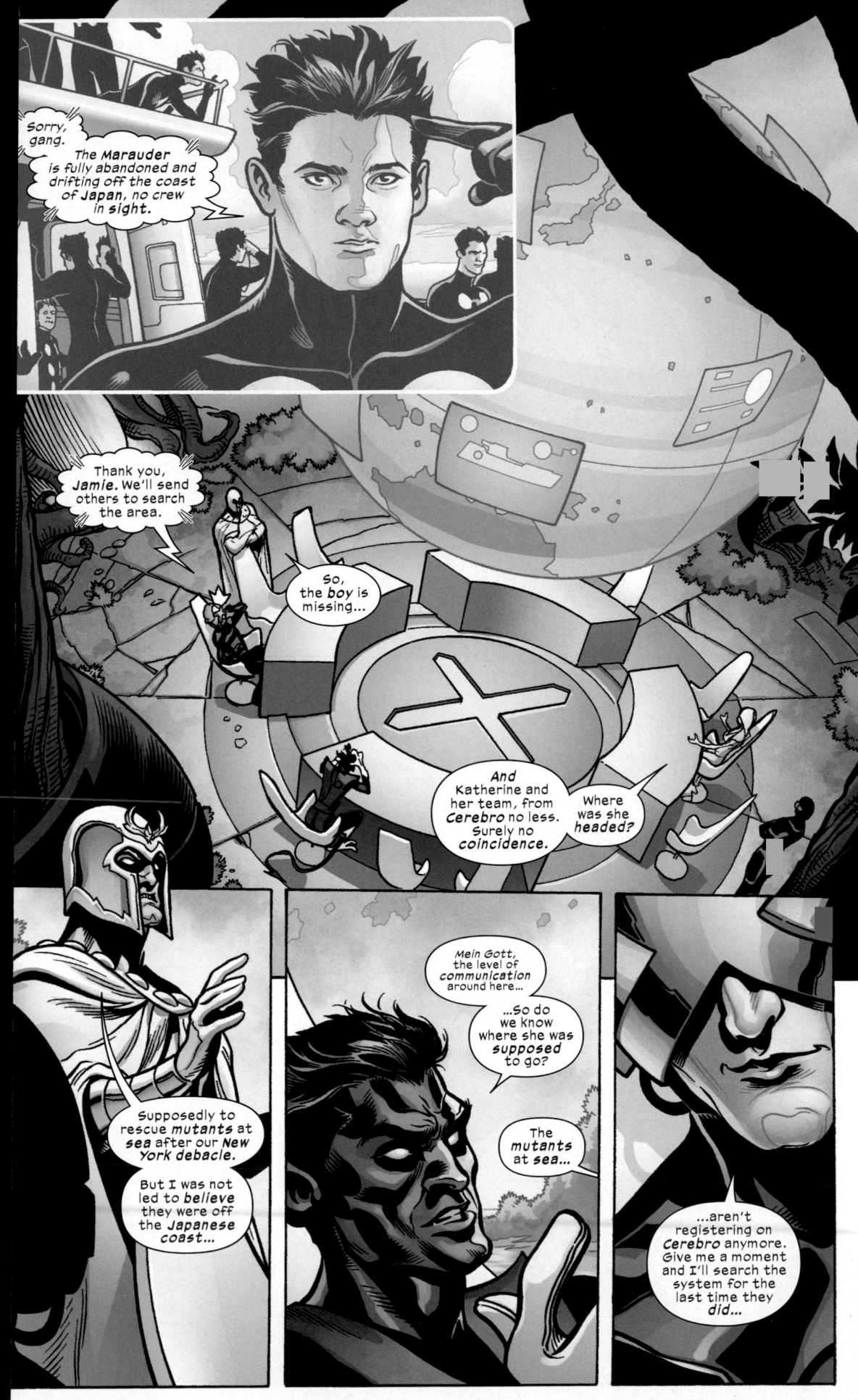

Look at you, Mr. Summers. In the chambers with the upper class.
Does it kindle any desire to be on the Quiet Council?
Absolutely not. You know me, Ms. Frost...
...I live to serve.
Ah, there we go...
...1,000 miles north...2,200 miles west of us.
We should assemble a team...
Cyclops, I'll join you and whoever you think--
Wait.
We still haven't discussed the Fantastic Four.
They think we have their children.
That means Krakoa is in danger.
There is a strong possibility that the Richards children will be where Kitty is.
They'll be here before you find the kids, Professor. You didn't see Sue Storm's eyes.
I'm telling
as a father,
suspected
took my
children...

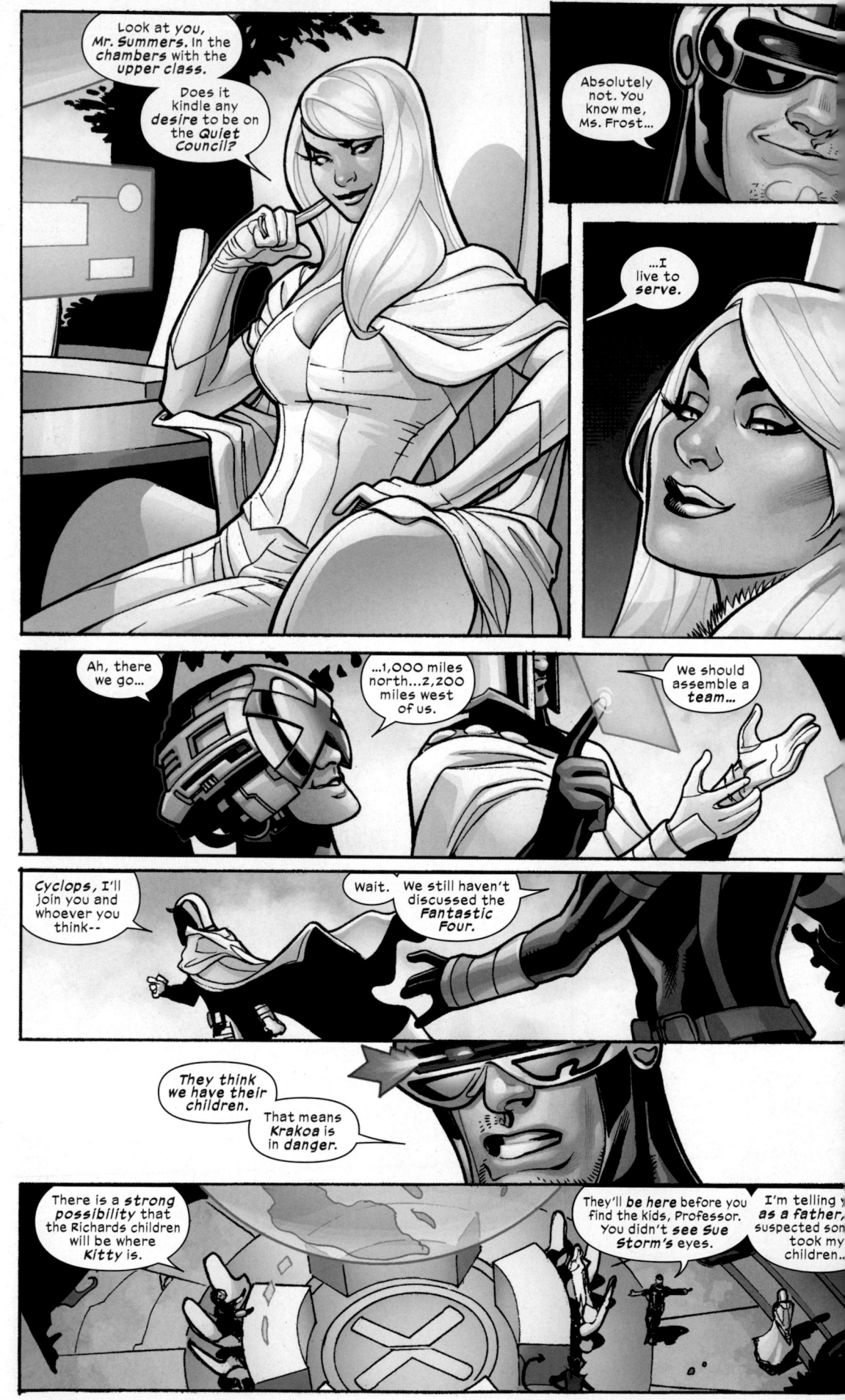

...I'd move heaven and earth to get them back. Honestly, I'm surprised they're not here already.
I do hate to say it, but Scott is correct.
Before you send a team, we need a plan to repel an attack from them and defend Krakoa.
We're a nation of mutants. This island is the most powerful place on the planet!
We do not need a plan for-- for a man who throws fire, or a rock-studded brute--
That may be true, mein freund...
...but you can't plan for the mind of Mr. Fantastic.
He can do most anything he wishes. Or be most anywhere with...
...the Invisible... Woman...

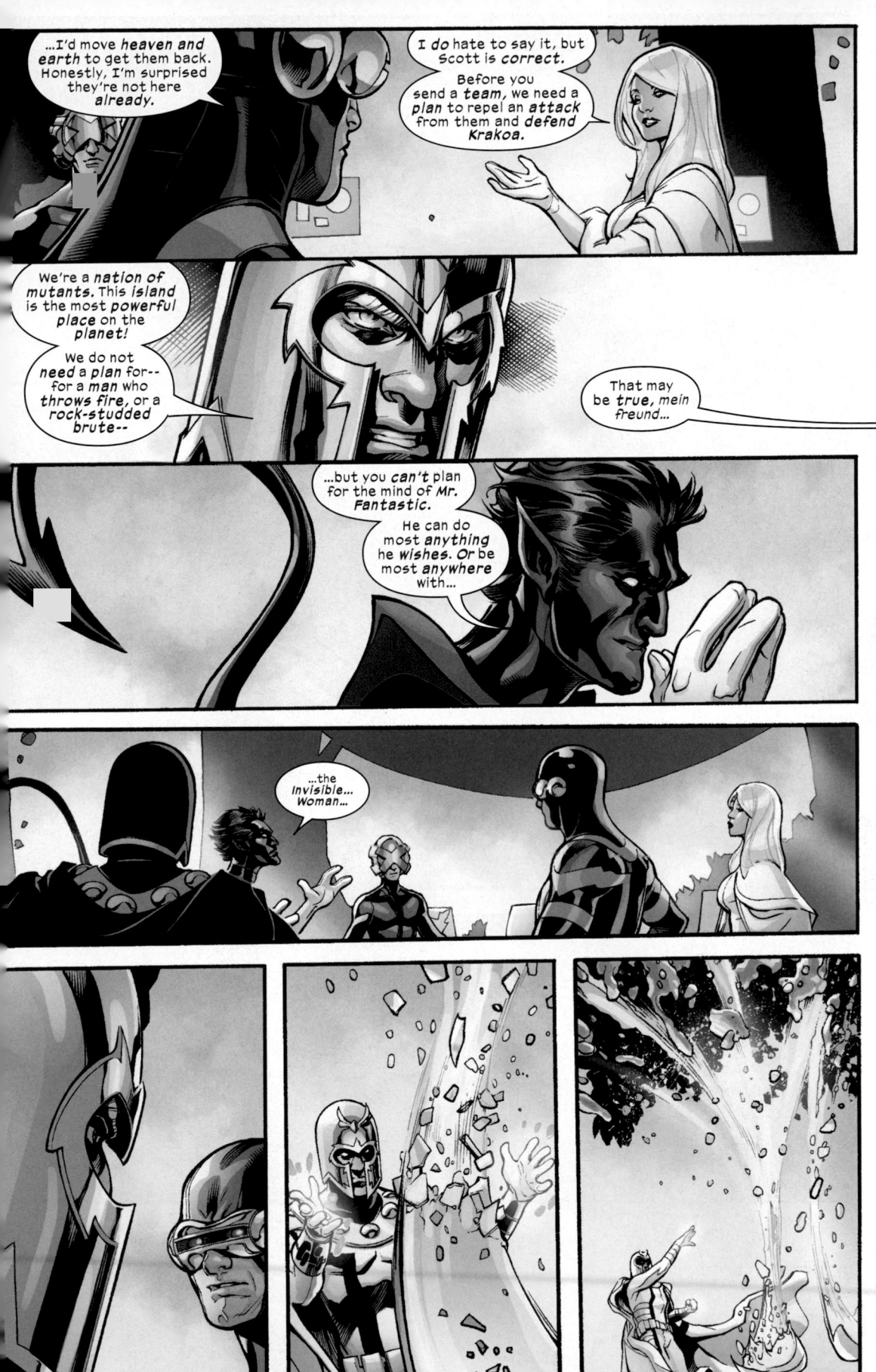

Hey, traditionally evil guy...
...this is fer callin' me "brute."
PAF!
Nh!
They're here!
Push outward--
Hnf!
Well, you're off the hook for kidnapping...
Nh!
...but you all still sound like creeps!
Quick! Sue's down! And without her...
Nhhh...

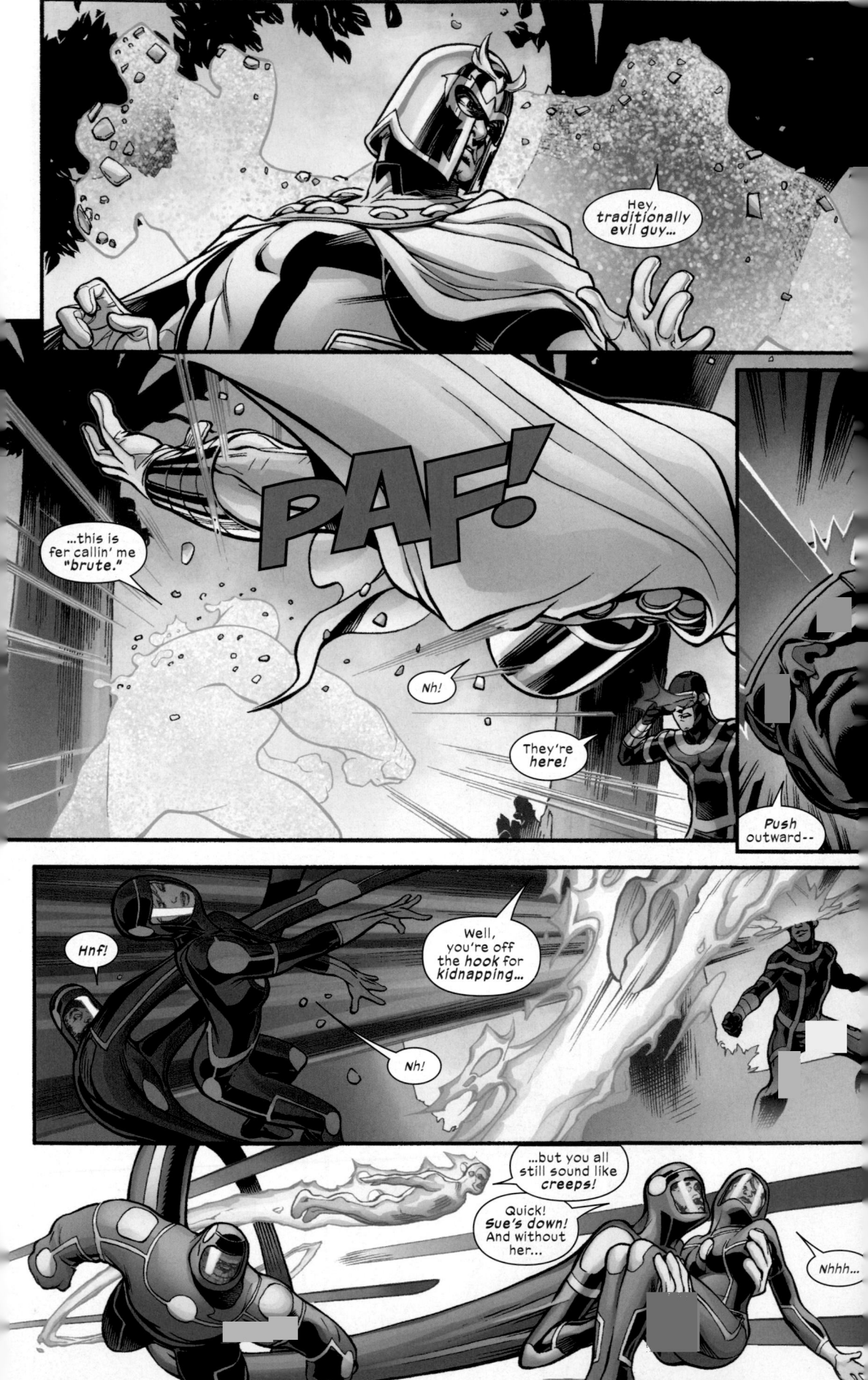

e won't
and a
ance!"

I need
to see my
people,
Doom.

Patience.
They're
safe.

Did you--
did you
depower
them...

...like
you did to
me?

Ah. No,
Ms. Pryde. I
see how you
would be
confused...

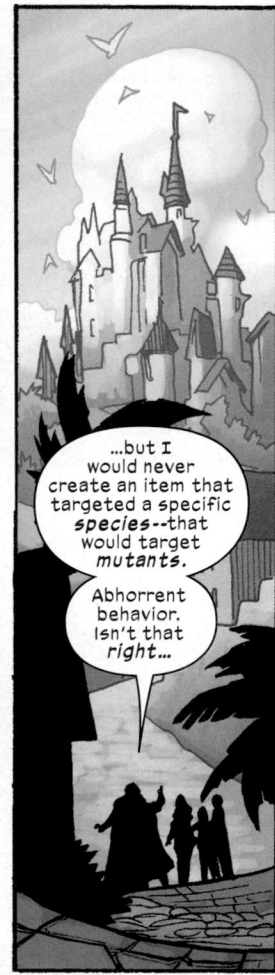

...but I
would never
create an item that
targeted a specific
species--that
would target
mutants.

Abhorrent
behavior.
Isn't that
right...

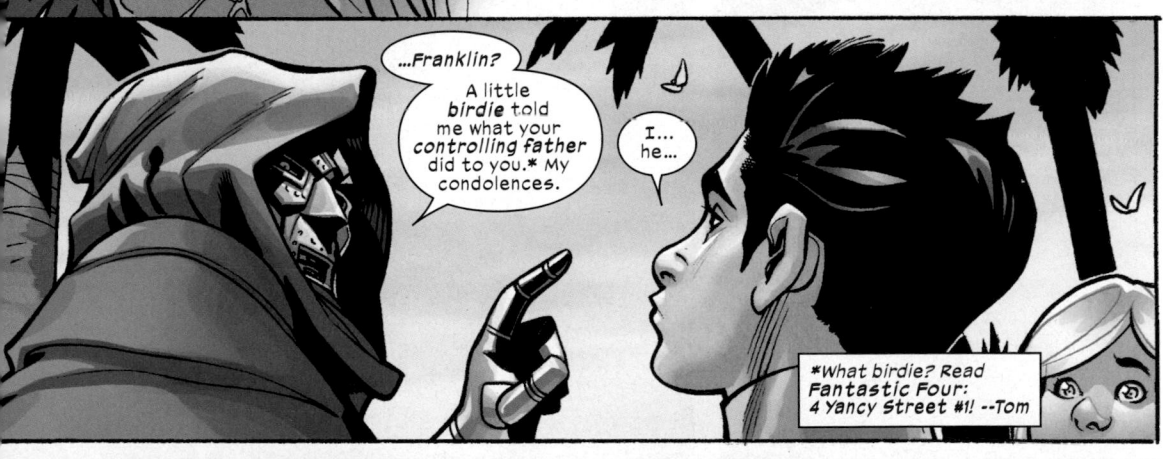

...Franklin?
A little
birdie told
me what your
controlling father
did to you.* My
condolences.

I...
he...

*What birdie? Read
Fantastic Four:
4 Yancy Street #1! --Tom

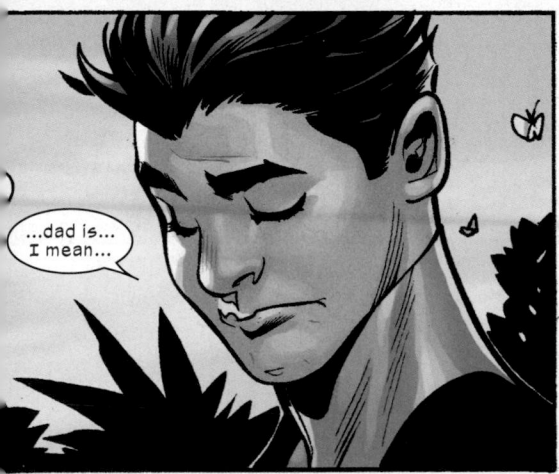

...dad is...
I mean...

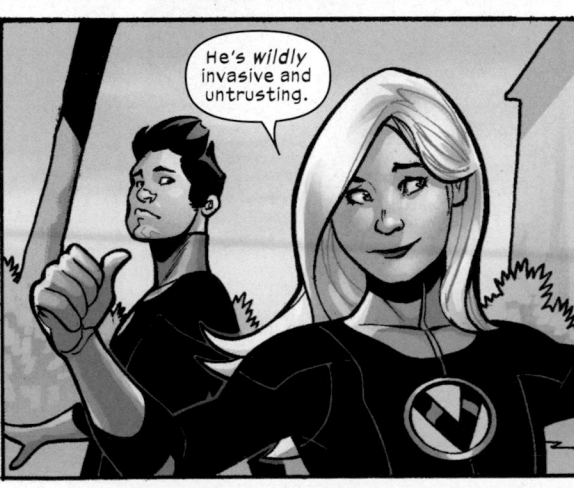

He's wildly
invasive and
untrusting.

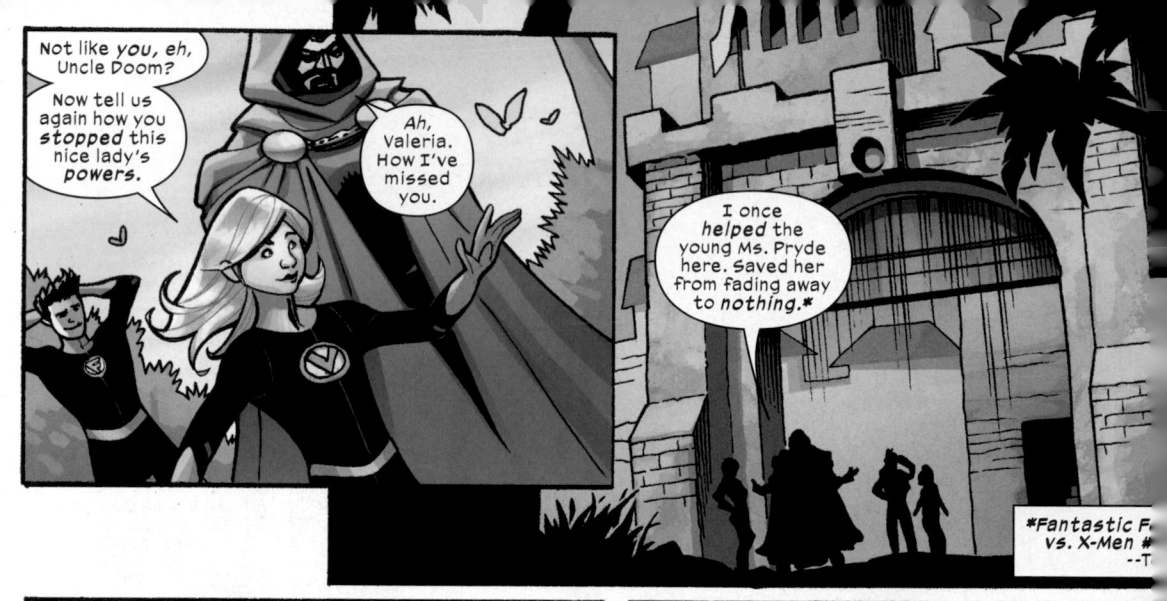

Not like *you*, eh, Uncle Doom?

Now tell us again how you *stopped* this nice lady's *powers*.

Ah, Valeria. How I've *missed* you.

I once *helped* the young Ms. Pryde here. Saved her from fading away to *nothing*.*

*Fantastic F[...] vs. X-Men # [...] --T[...]

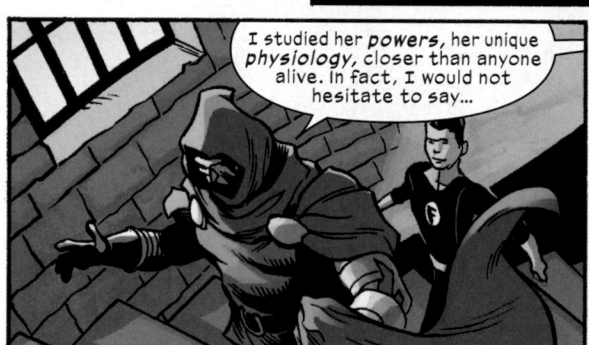

I studied her *powers*, her unique *physiology*, closer than anyone alive. In fact, I would not hesitate to say...

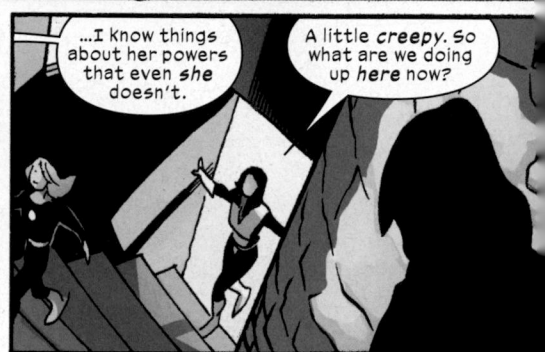

...I know things about her powers that even *she* doesn't.

A little *creepy*. So what are we doing up *here* now?

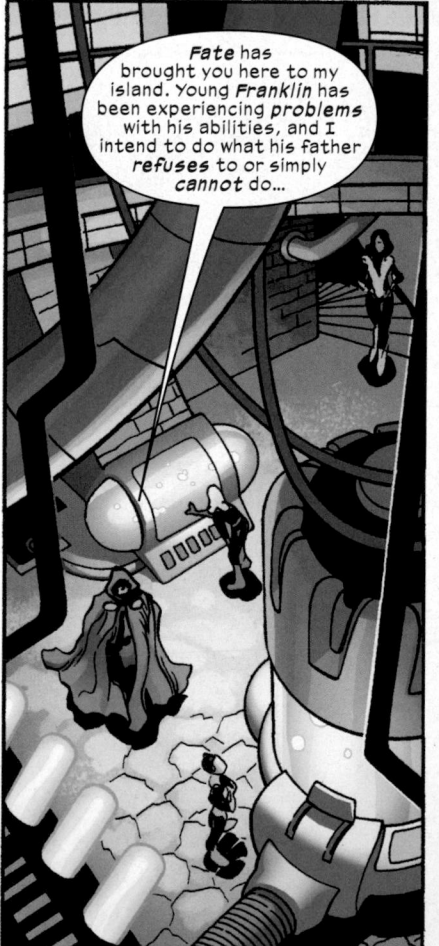

Fate has brought you here to my *island*. Young *Franklin* has been experiencing *problems* with his abilities, and I intend to do what his father *refuses* to or simply *cannot* do...

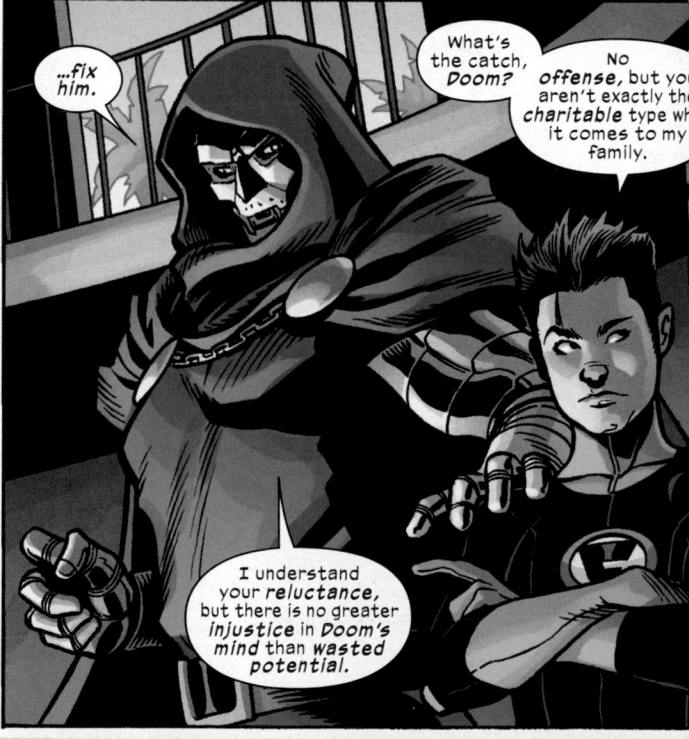

...*fix him*.

What's the catch, *Doom*?

No *offense*, but yo[u] aren't exactly the *charitable* type wh[en] it comes to my family.

I understand your *reluctance*, but there is no greater *injustice* in Doom's mind than *wasted potential*.

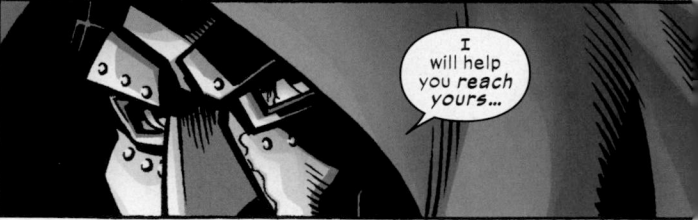

I will help you *reach yours*...

under
small
dition."
Stretch, I hope you got a plan to get us out of this!
Yes, Ben. It's to run. Fast.
We need to get to the Fantasticar before--
BAMF
Apologies, Doctor Richards, but you leave us no choice.
Nf!
Auf Wiedersehen!
BAMF
Oh, come on!
Ngh!
This isn't going to go the way you think it is.
Ya crumb bum! Let us go find our kids! We ain't--
Ben...

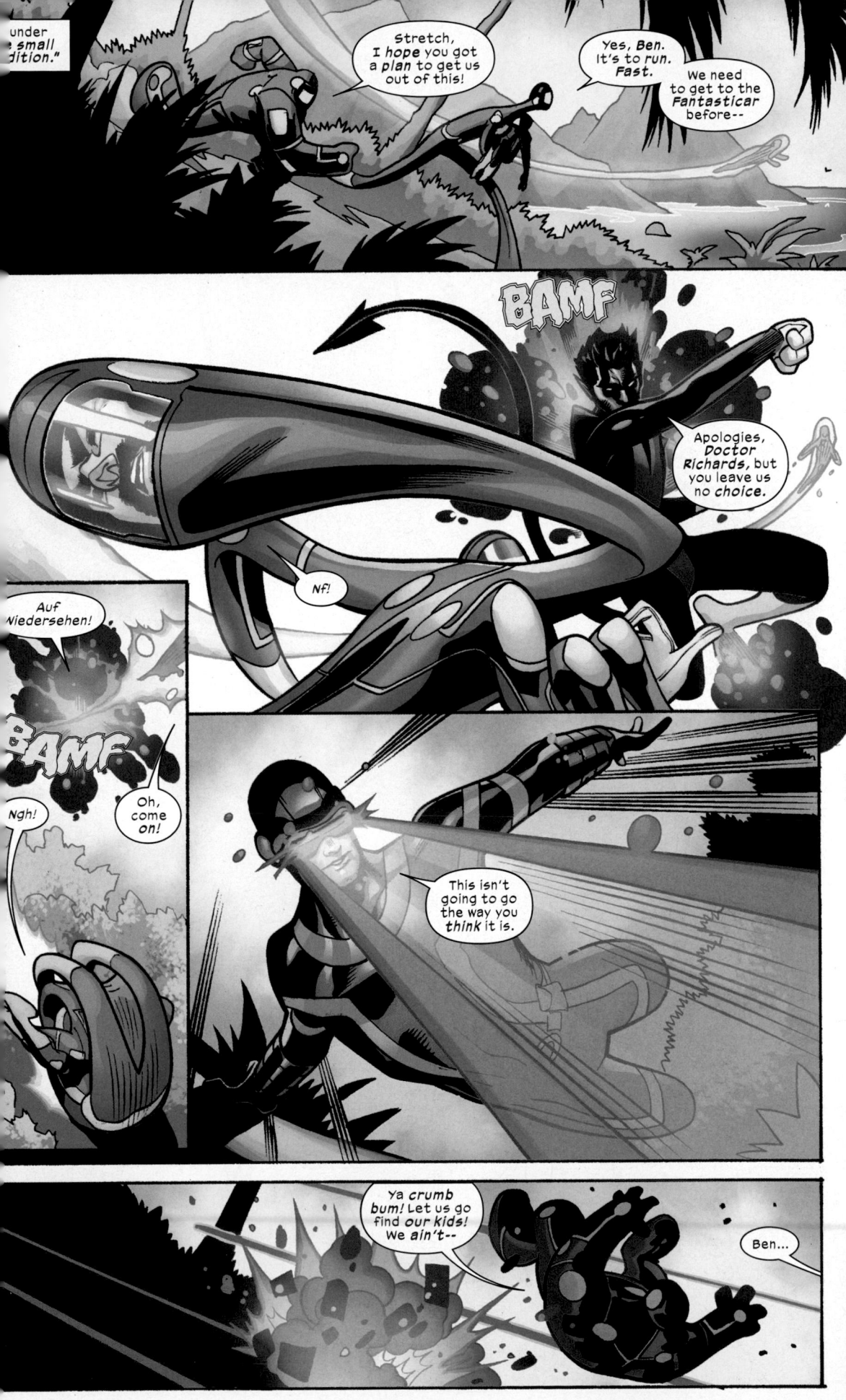

...we have *bigger* fish to *fry.*
Yikes. Was nice knowin' a *couple* of you guys...
Uh, Reed? *Reed?!*
Hold them back!
We need *Sue* to get us *out* of this!
Sue!
SUE!
Benjamin! You don't--*hnh!*
Nah, comrade. I *do.*
FWOOSH!
KTUNK!
Their *helm*
are blocking p
attacks

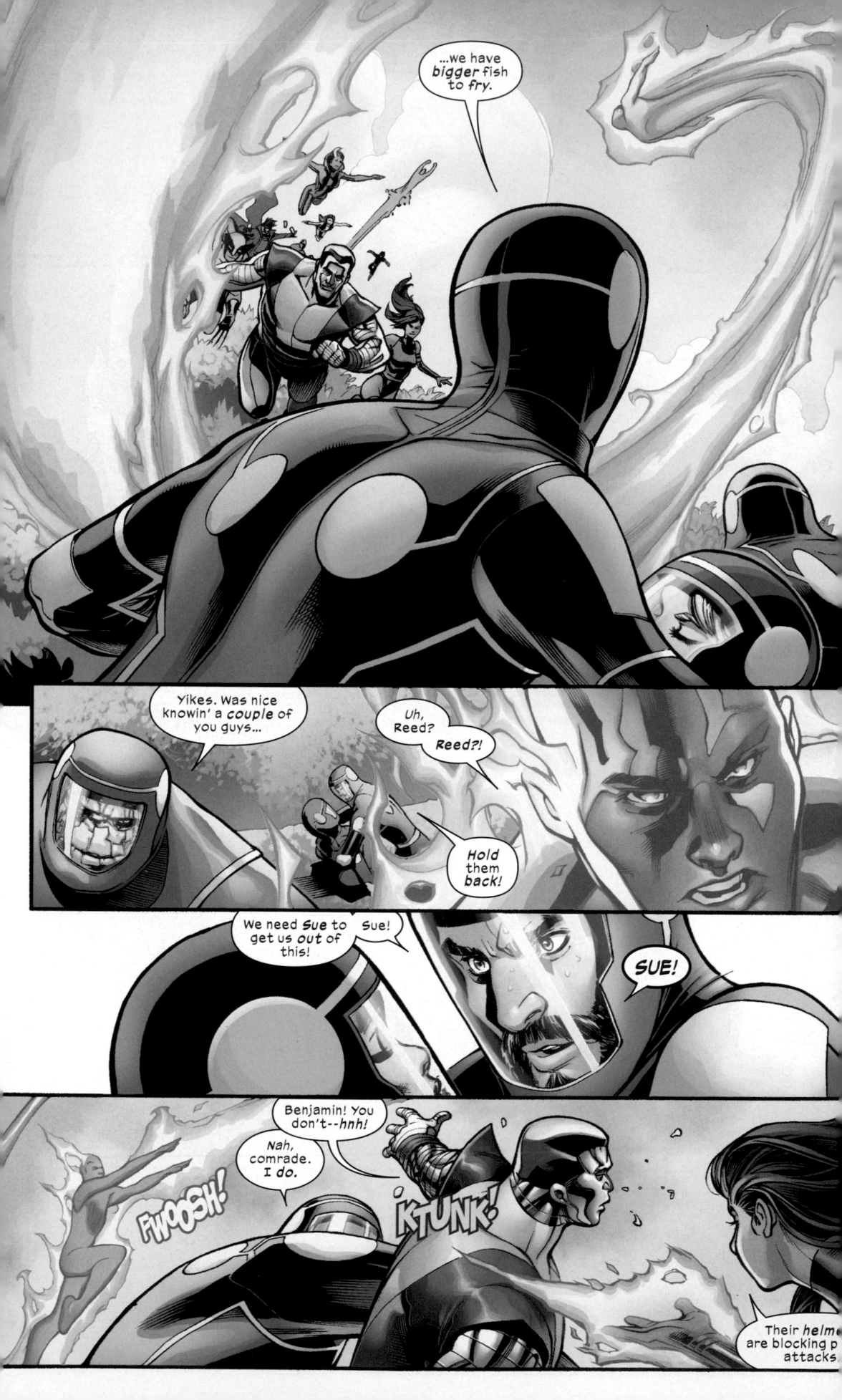

The helmets!
That's it!
PSH
Stretch...
...we're outta time and clobberin'!
Whatever you're gonna do, do it!
FSKOOM!
FSKOOM!
Come on, Sue, we just need a second to get you...
Someone broke through a helmet! I've got Susan!

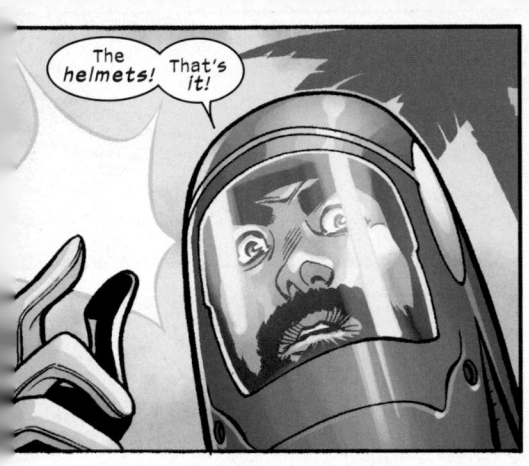

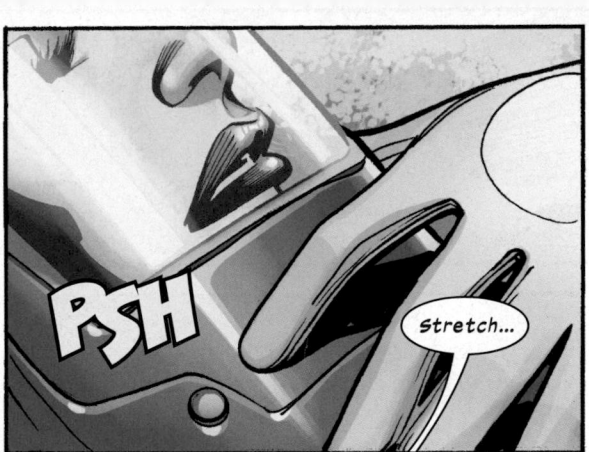

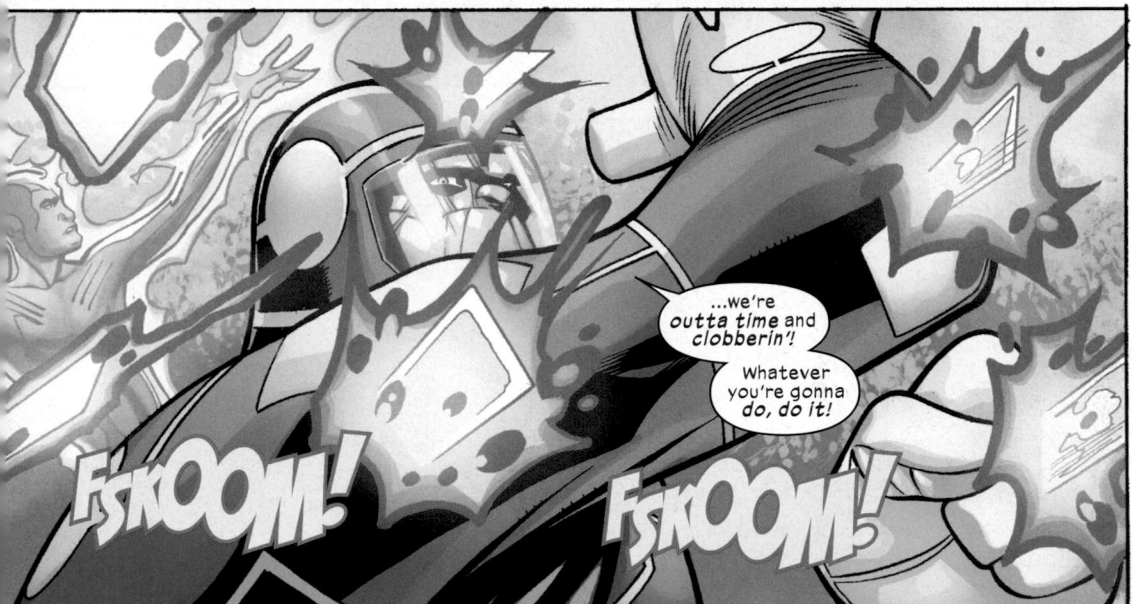

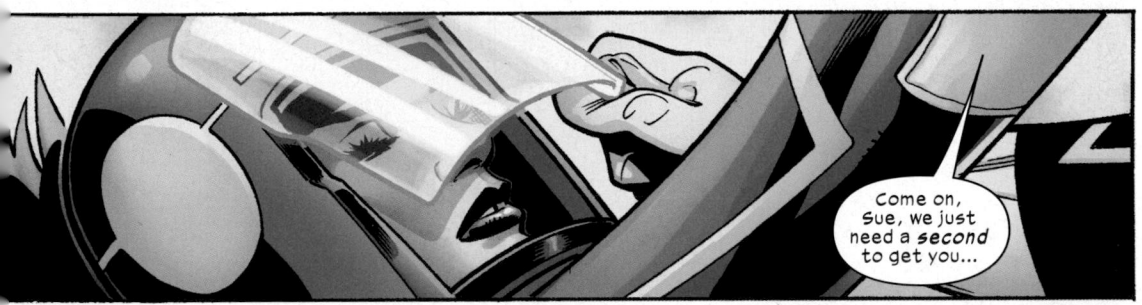

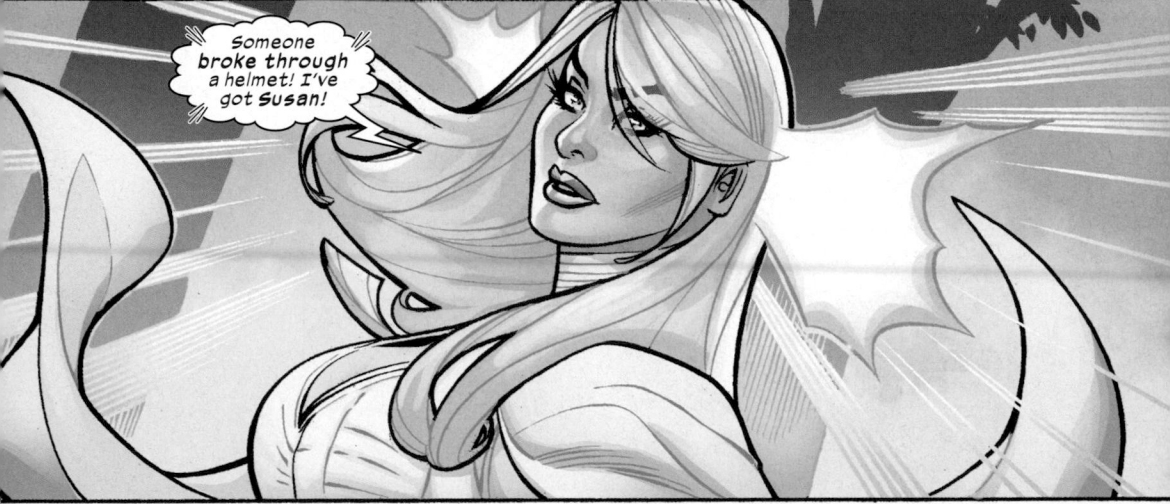

AAHH!
Nhhh... What--
SHNK!
I'm sorr honey. B we really n an assis here.
And you needed a ps jump-sta
RAHH! You little--
That's a warnin' shot, big guy. Stand down, or--
WOSHRAAAA
Got it.

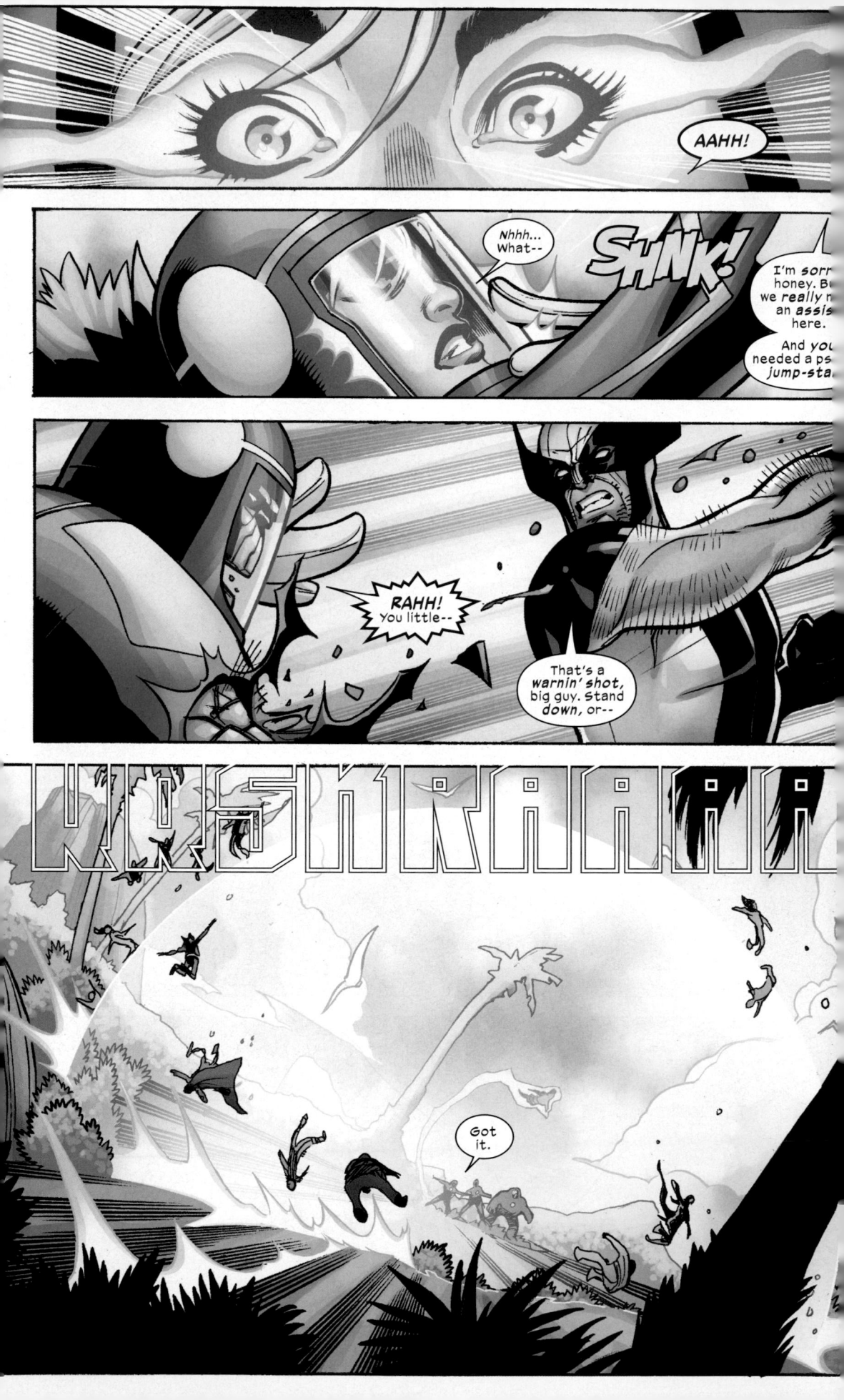

I love you.

I know.

Hey, hey. Let's get some *focus* here...

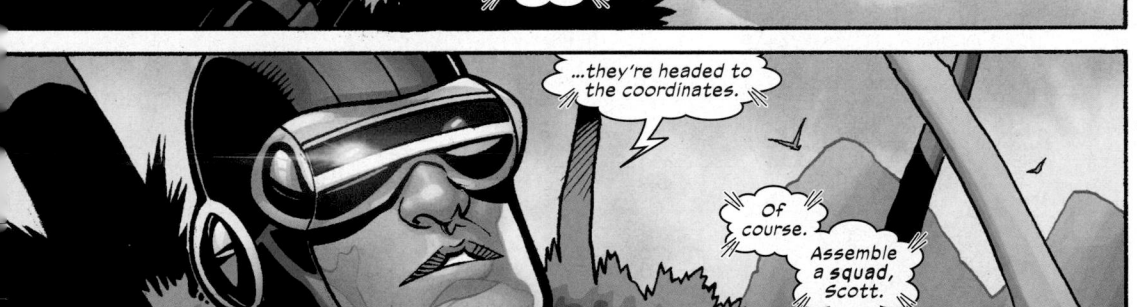

"...and go save the *kids!*"

Professor...

...they're headed to the coordinates.

Of course.

Assemble a squad, Scott.

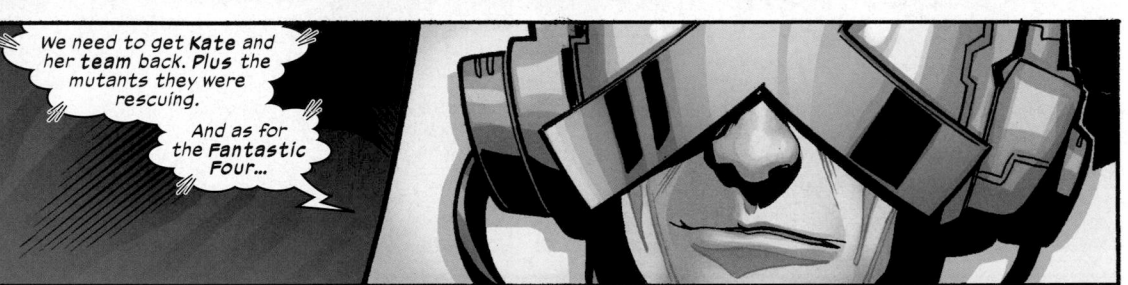

We need to get **Kate** and her **team** back. Plus the mutants they were rescuing.

And as for the **Fantastic Four...**

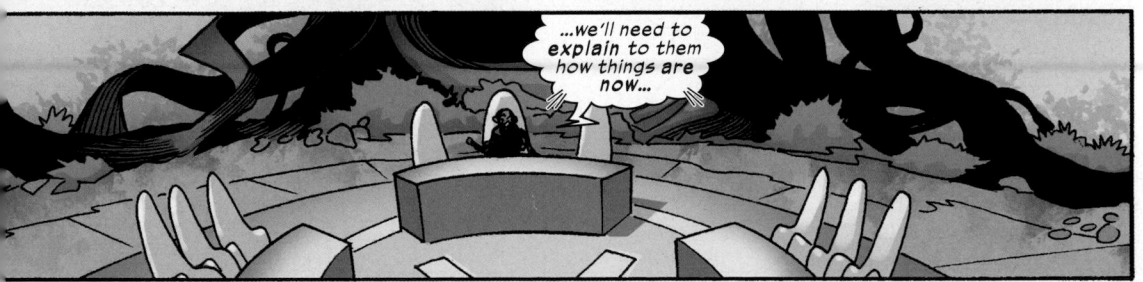

...we'll need to explain to them how things are now...

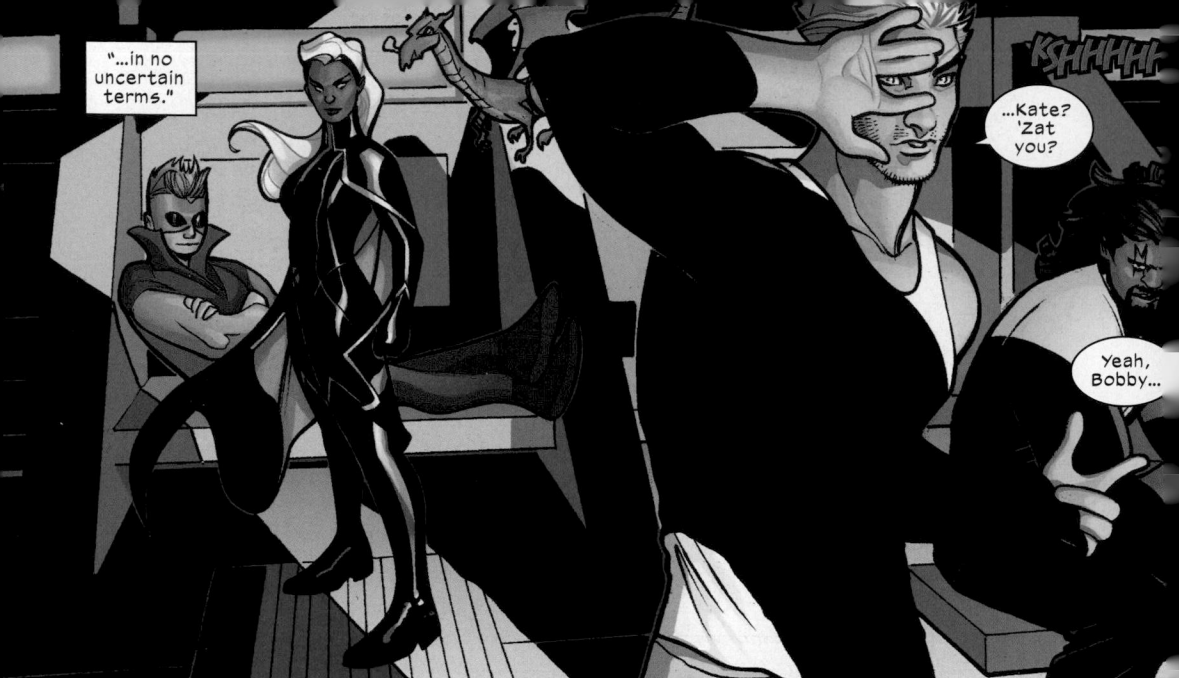

"...in no uncertain terms."

...Kate? 'Zat you?

Yeah, Bobby...

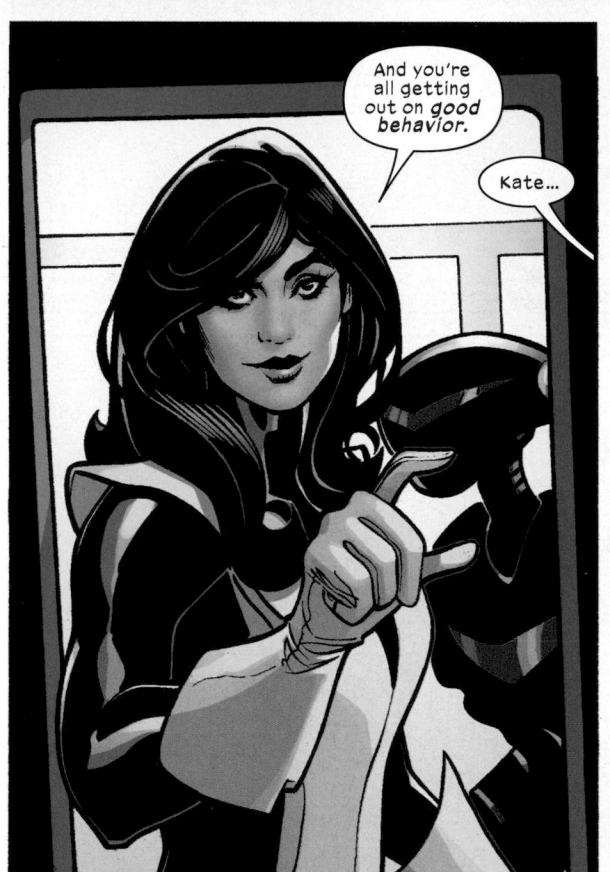

And you're all getting out on *good* behavior.

Kate...

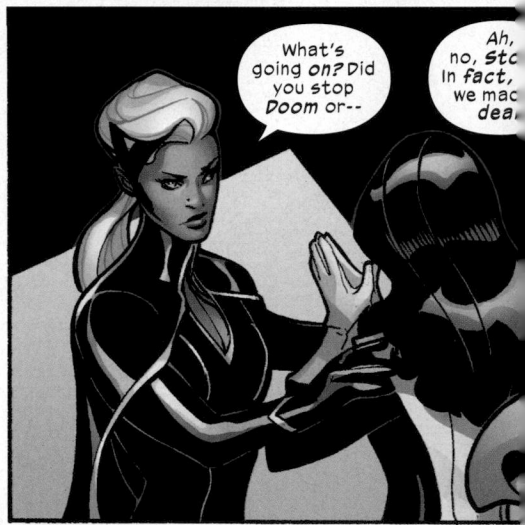

What's going *on?* Did you stop *Doom* or--

Ah, no, *Sto* In *fact,* we mac *dea*

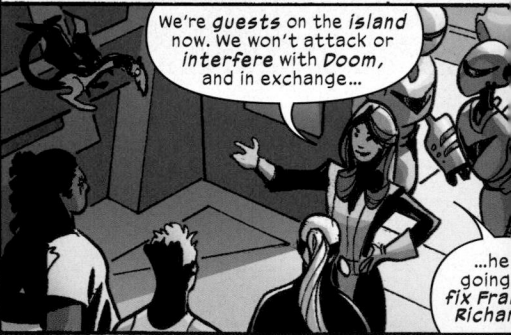

We're *guests* on the *island* now. We won't attack or *interfere* with *Doom,* and in exchange...

...he going fix Fra Richai

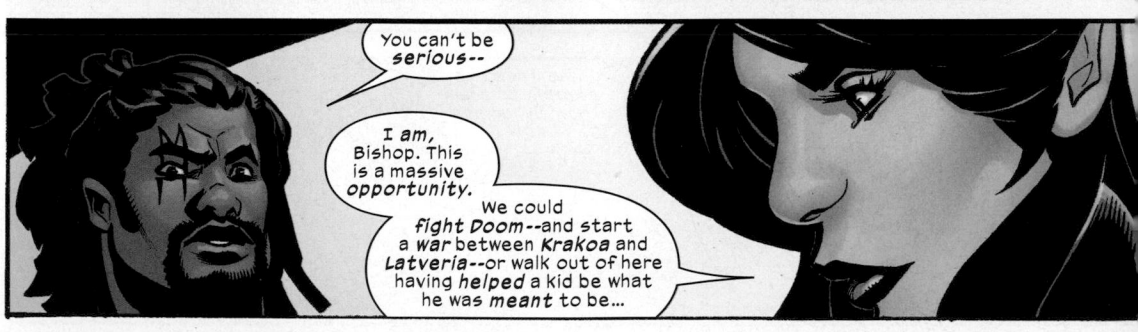

You can't be *serious--*

I *am,* Bishop. This is a massive *opportunity.*

We could *fight Doom*--and start a *war* between *Krakoa* and *Latveria*--or walk out of here having *helped* a kid be what he was *meant* to be...

world's most rful mutant."
Is this a good idea, Val?
I've heard worse.
Look, Victor Von Doom is historically a bad man, yes.
But he's got a soft spot for you and me. I genuinely think he'd never hurt us. Besides...
...he wouldn't pass up an opportunity to show Dad he's smarter...
Ah, Valeria. ould this be as simple as ego...
Master? Did you say something?
Nothing of concern, Victorious. How fares Latveria in my absence?
The rebuilding continues apace.
Are you...are you certain you don't want me on the island? It sounds like you're about to have many visitors...
Doom knows what he needs, my herald.
All he needs is preparation. And Doom...

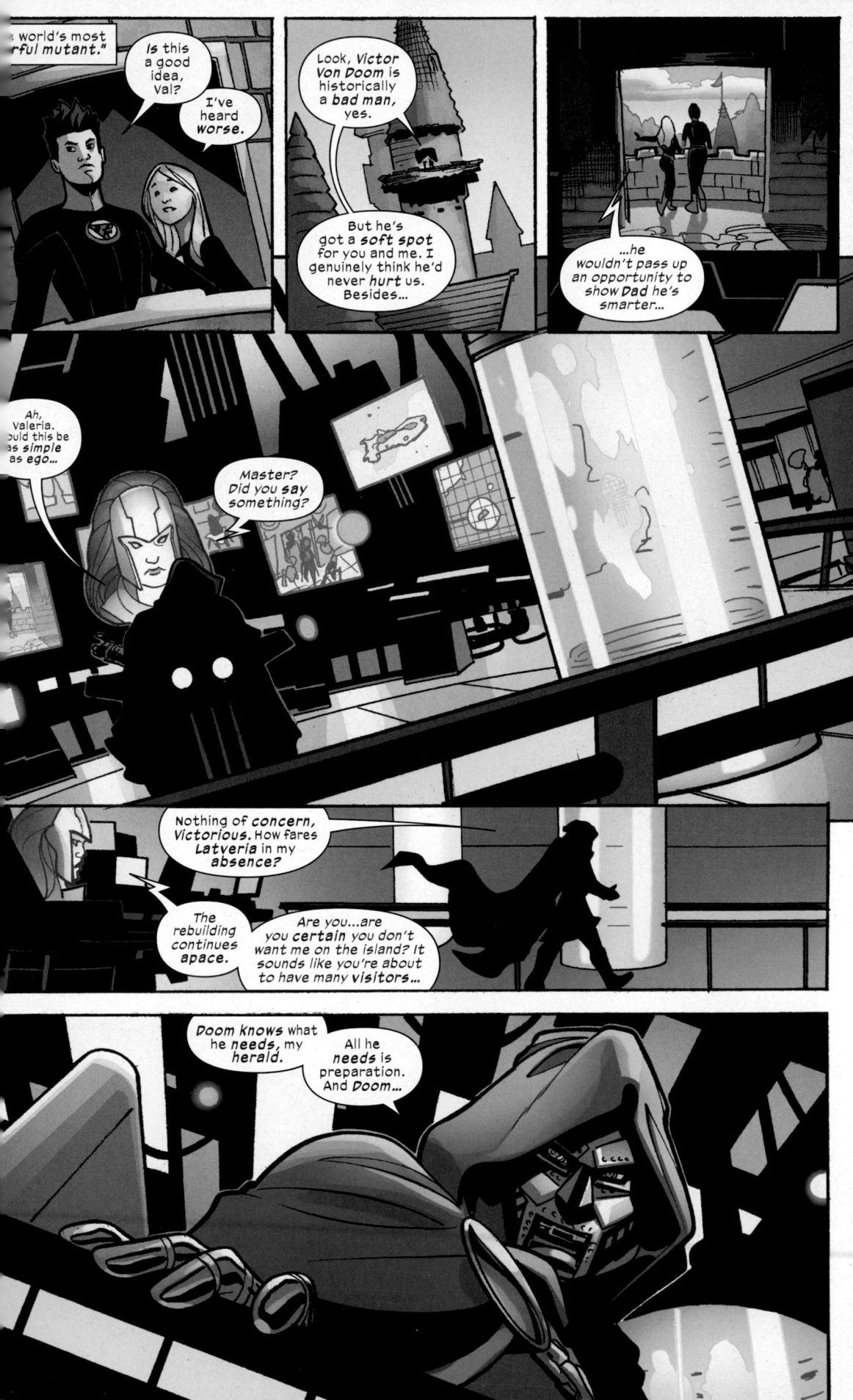

...is always prepared.

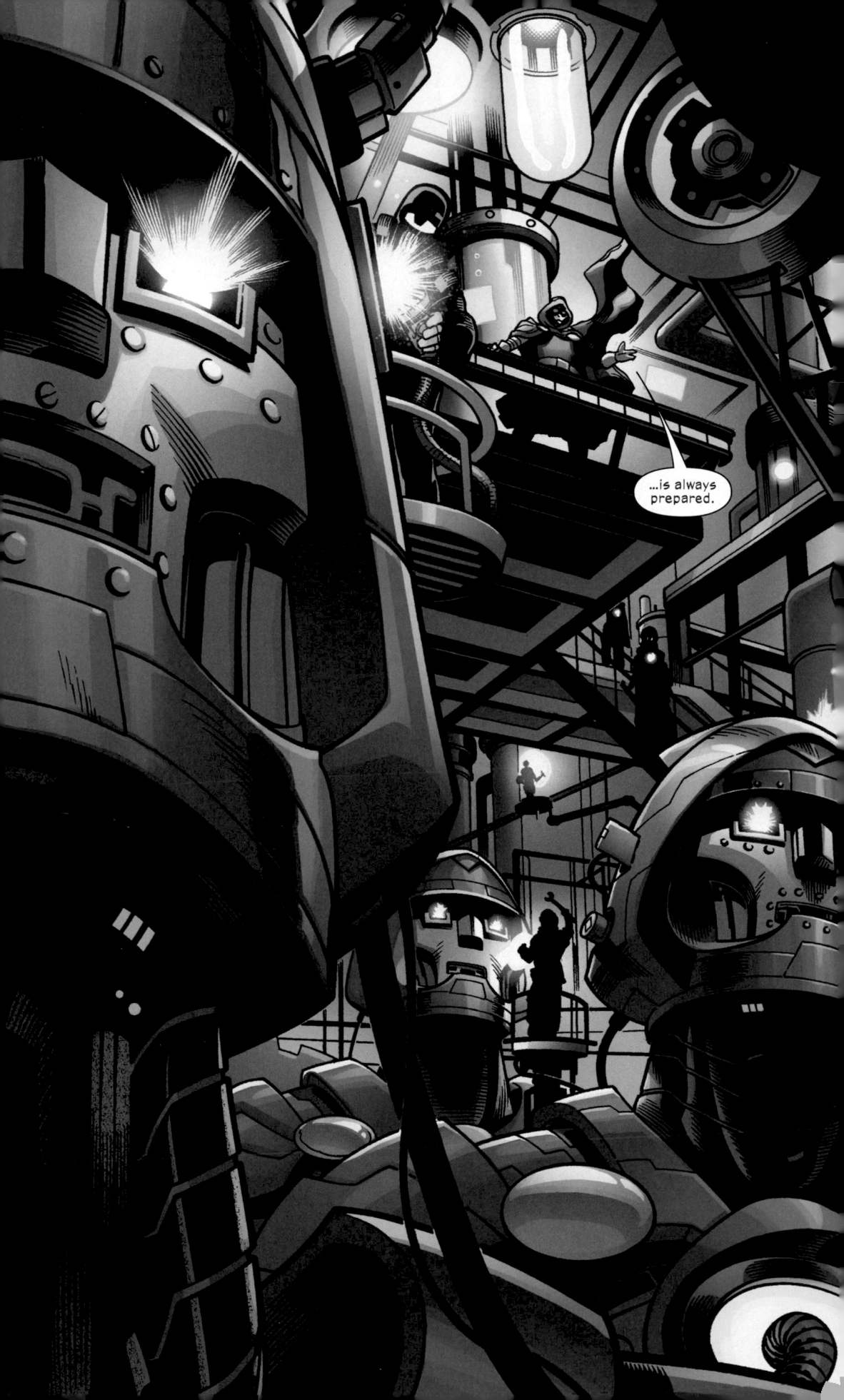

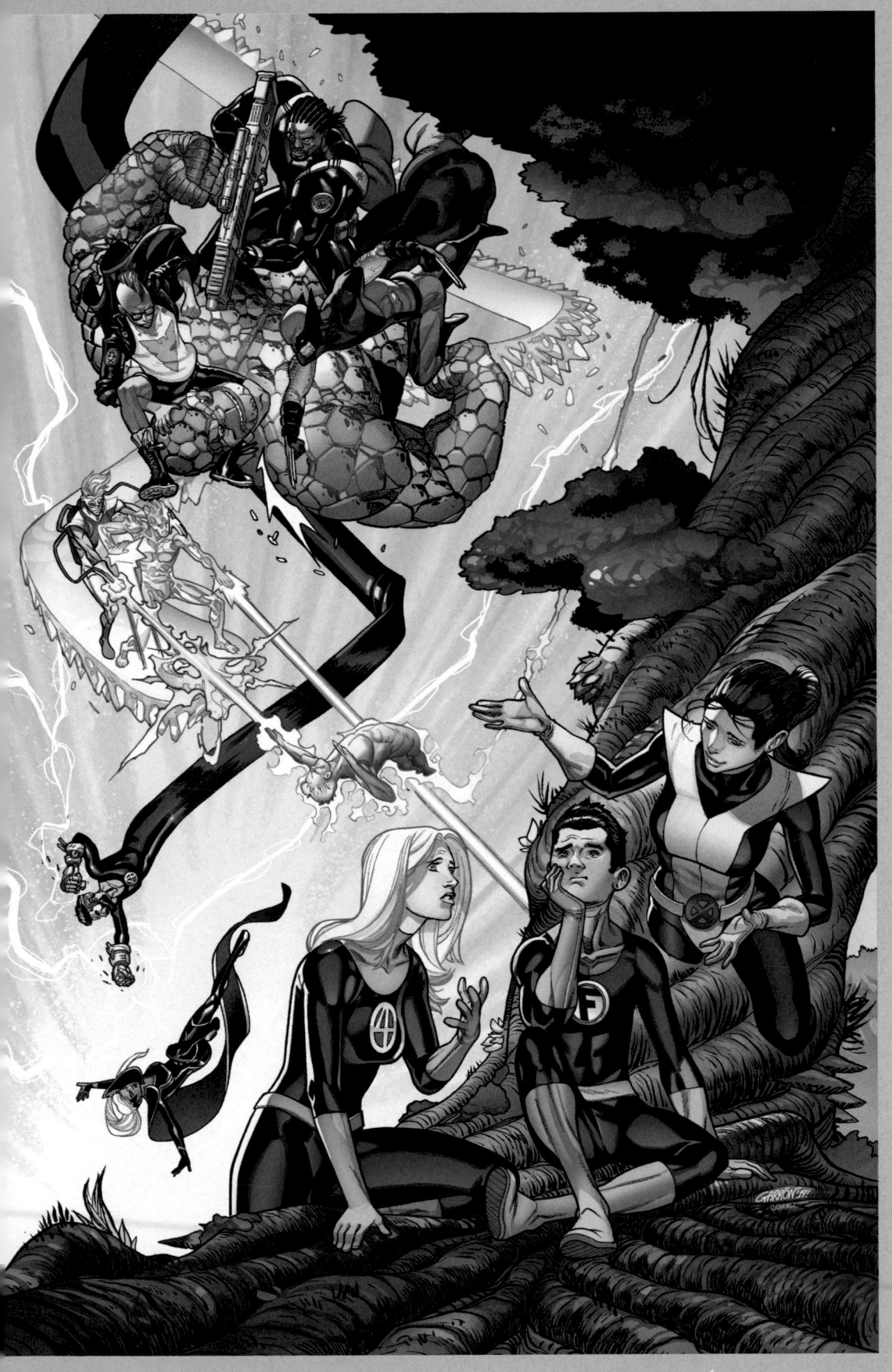

JAVIER GARRÓN + DAVID CURIEL

TERRY DODSON
RACHEL

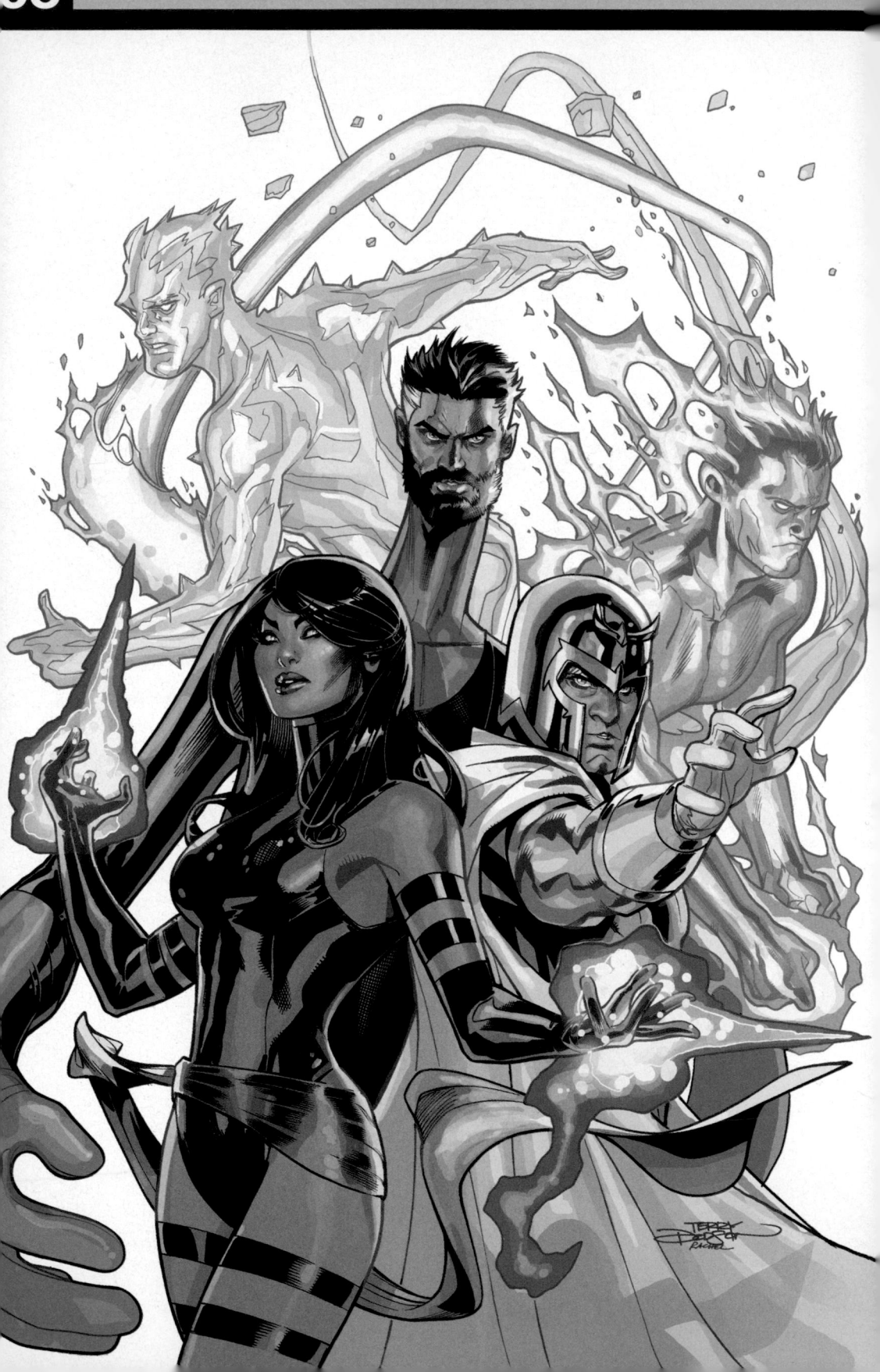

On them in 30 seconds. Could use you in the cockpit, *Cyclops*.

Coming, Beast.

Scott...

Be *careful*. This could lead to a *war* that we *do not want*.

Not today, *Professor*. Logan, what's the *situation*?

Grimm's *piloting*. Gonna need the *Summers touch* here, *Slim*.

...or else we can send *Rogue* to--

Logan, *please*. You know I'm the *best* there is at what I *do*...

CHK CHK

...and what I do is *precise*.

Ben! They're *on us!*
Yeah, I got *eyes, Stretch!* We're almost at the *coordinates!*
Those X-creeps sure ain't takin' kindly to our little *visit!*
Johnny! Keep *Sue's helmet sealed!* The *X-Men's telepaths* only need a *second* to grab *hold* of us!
Calm *down!* I just want to make sure my *sister* is all right!
I'm okay, Johnny... just winded.
Let's get you back to 100% so we can find the *kids* and head to--
Whoa! Maybe a bit more of a *gentle touch, rock hands?*
I'm doin' my *best*, ya *twerp!*
But it looks like they're playin' fer *keeps*--
ZARK ZARK ZARK

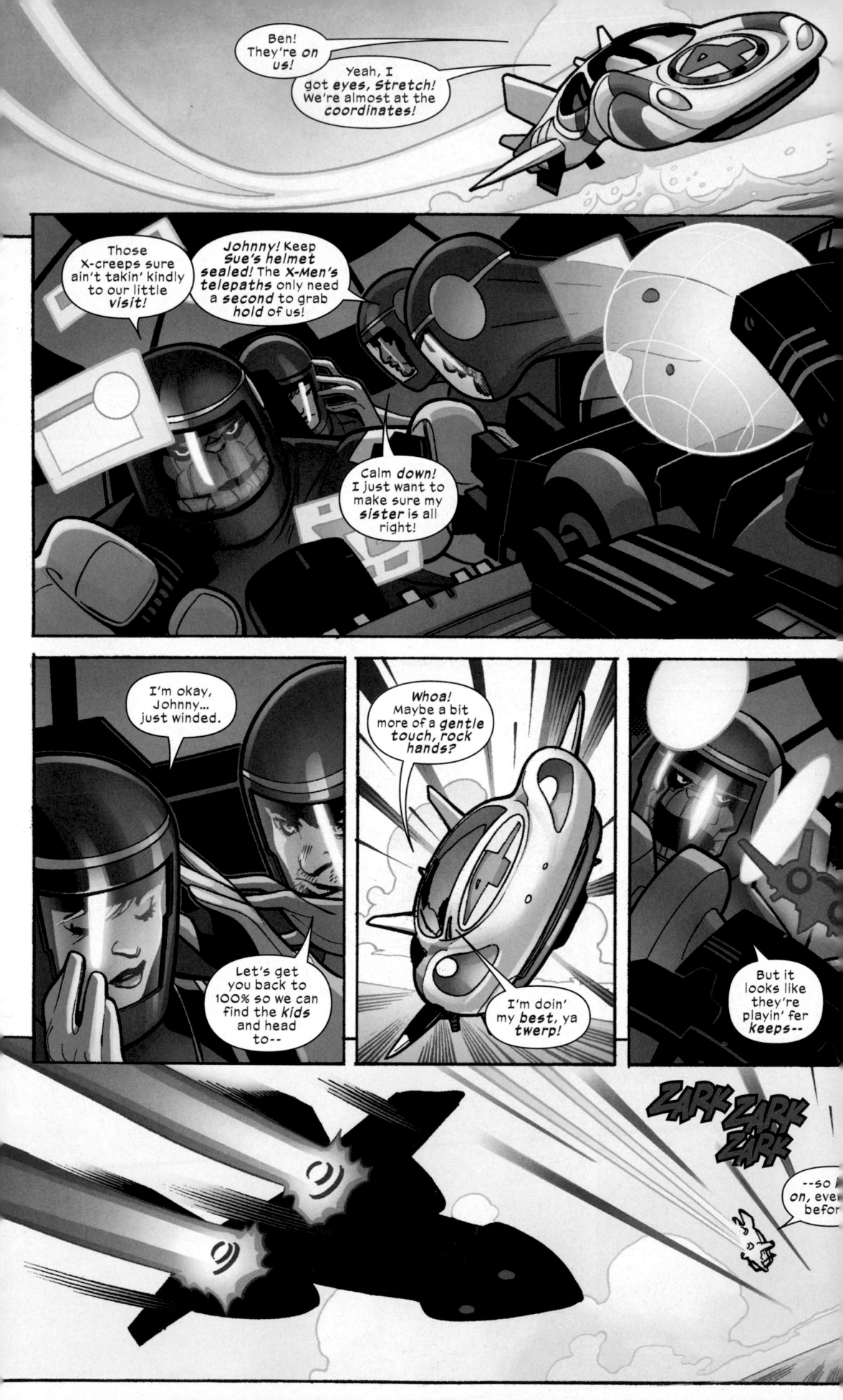

Got you.
SKRAA!
Good save, honey. Set us down on that island--
f!
KRNNNCH!
--and we'll figure out a way to talk them down from--
They ain't talkin', Reed!
FLAME ON!

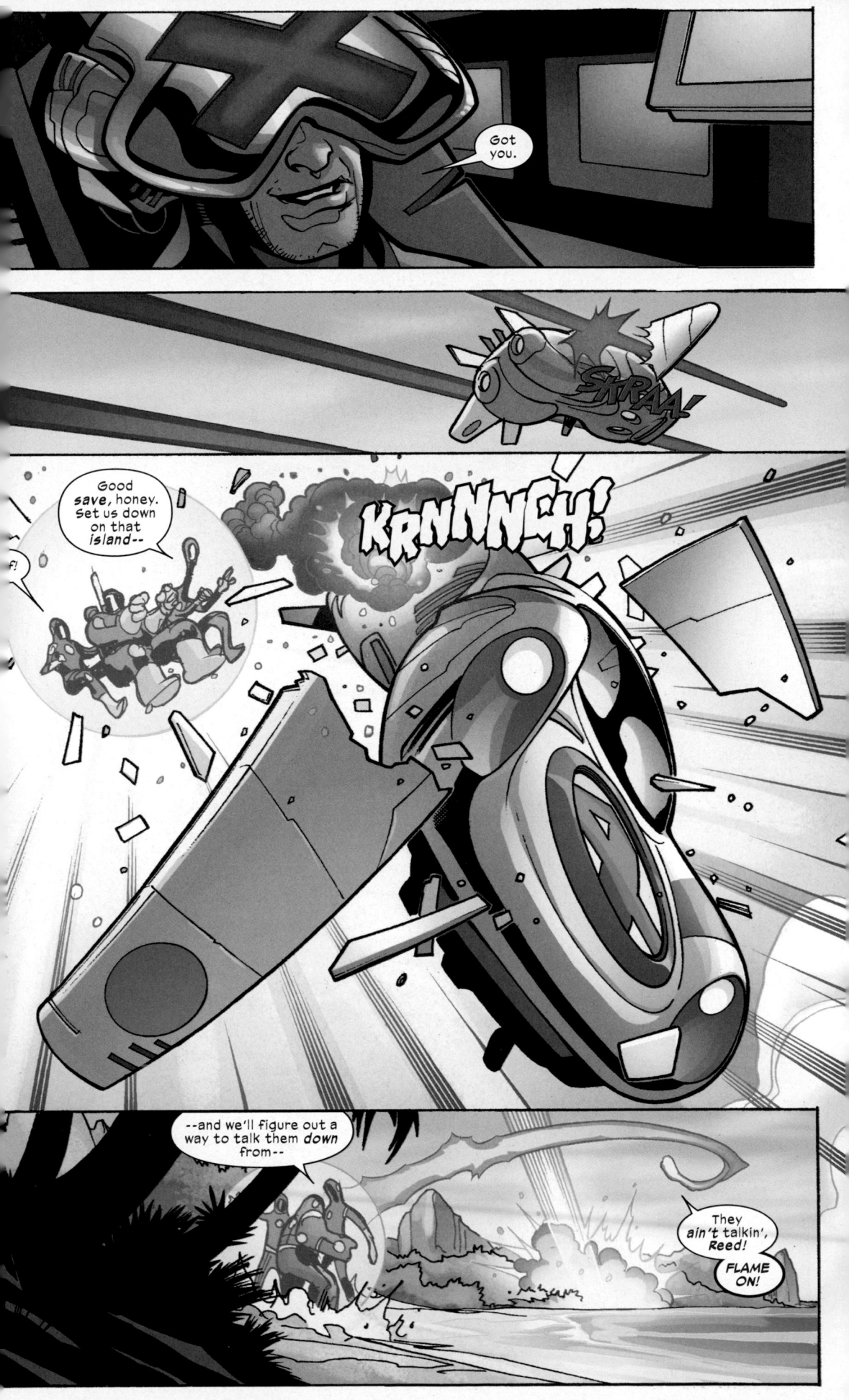

Surprise.
BAMF
AHHH
Ya can't just slip into a country and spy on it--
--without consequences!
Rogue, ya know it ain't-- nhh!
You know why we were there!
THOOOM!

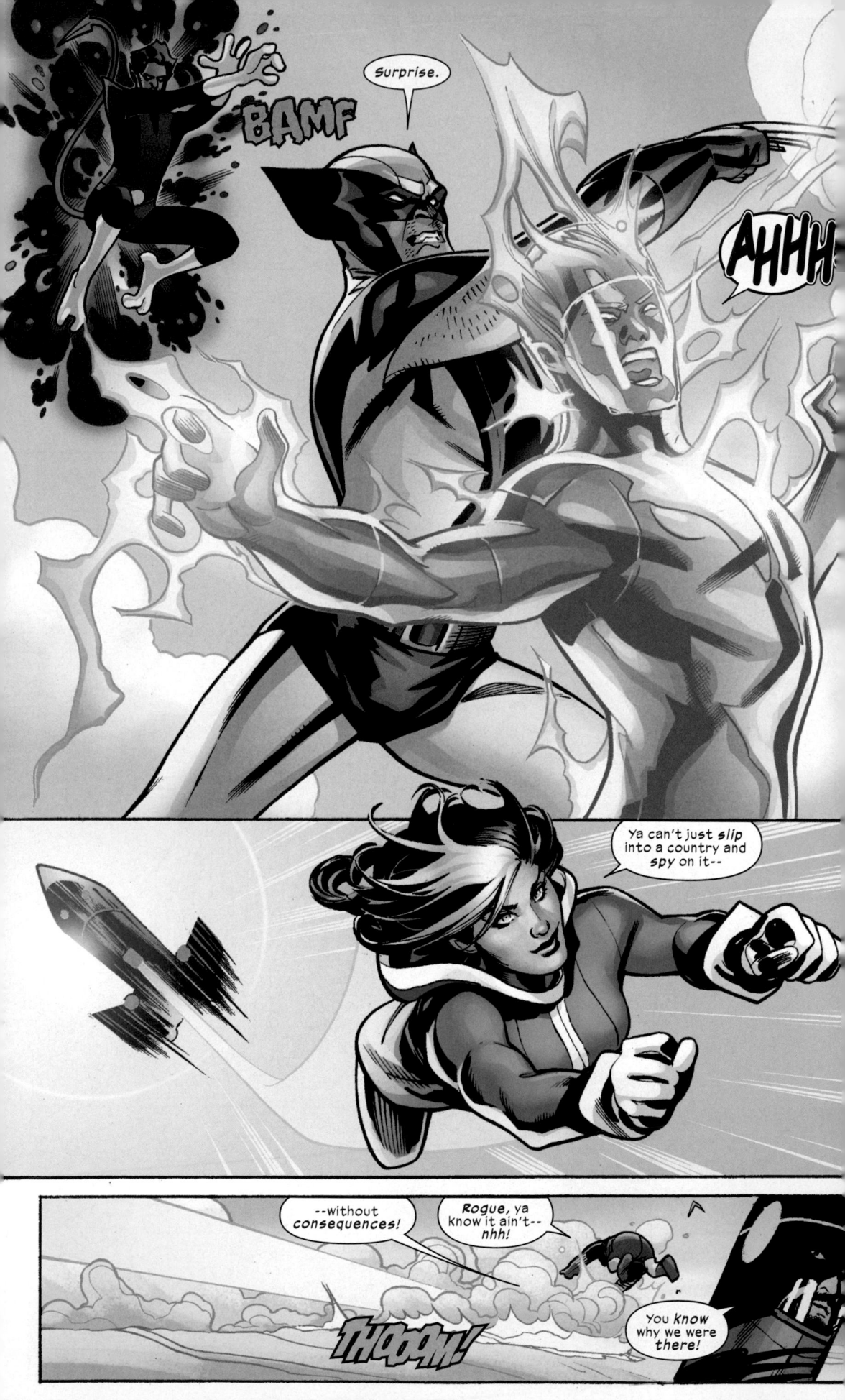

Are
out ta be
rphans--
--unless
ya--nhh!
You
didn't take
them...
...we know that now! Let's work together to find your people and--
Of course, dear...
...we'll get to that...
...but it seems like your brother's helmet has a leak now.
So let's first bring you to Krakoa for your espionage and illegal entry trial.

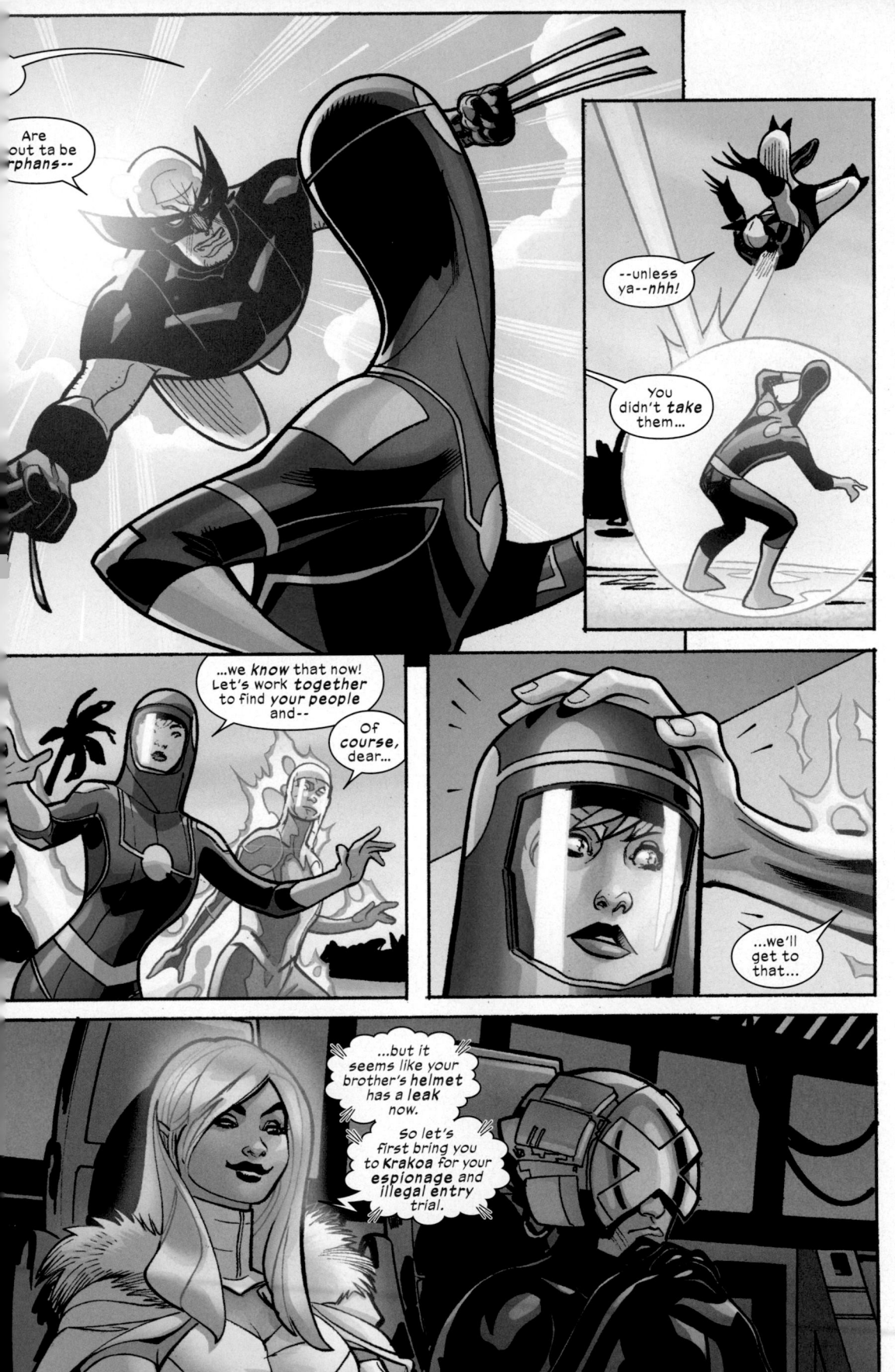

X-MEN /
FANTASTIC
FOUR

3 TO THE VICTOR

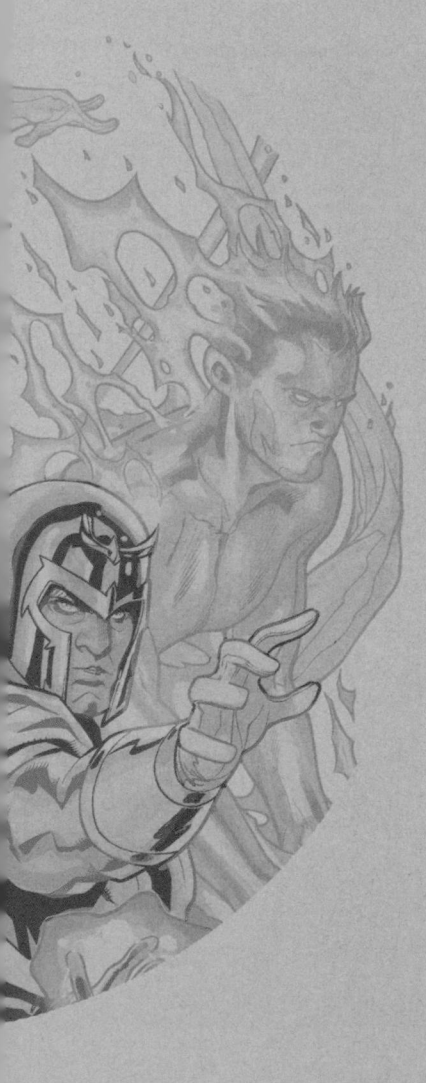

A "trial"? An interesting proposition...
...but a hypocritical one to make while illegally on Latverian soil.
Ms. Frost.
Wh-- Doom?!
What's going on here? What do you mean by--
Where are my children?
And where...
...are our X-Men?
Ah, Erik.
I can feel you attempting to manipulate my armor...
...but with you out in the world, I'd be a fool to rely on pure metal.
Unlike the little man with the metal bones. Why, Magneto could tear you apart, couldn't he?
In fact, I believe he has.
Answer before I get him to help push my claws as deep as they can go.
Where's Kate?!
It's okay, Logan...

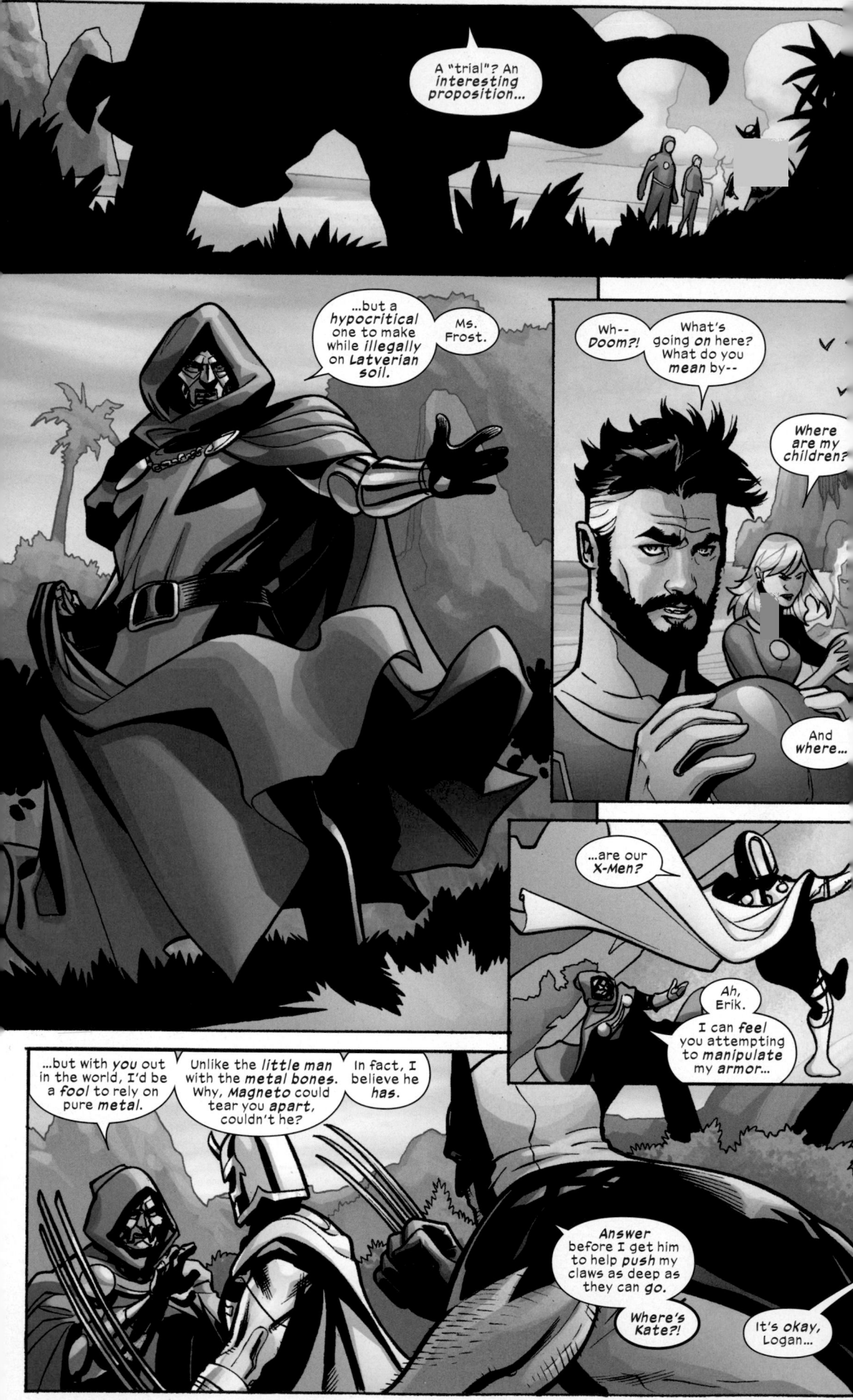

...we're fine.
I made a... a deal with Doom.
A fair deal.
Katherine came looking for mutants. They are safe here on Doom Island. Provided you respect my sovereignty and wishes and leave them be...
...I will restore your greatest mutant to his former glory.
Franklin! If you've so much as touched a hair on his head--
Susan. Those children mean the world to me.
I am simply doing...
...what his father could not.

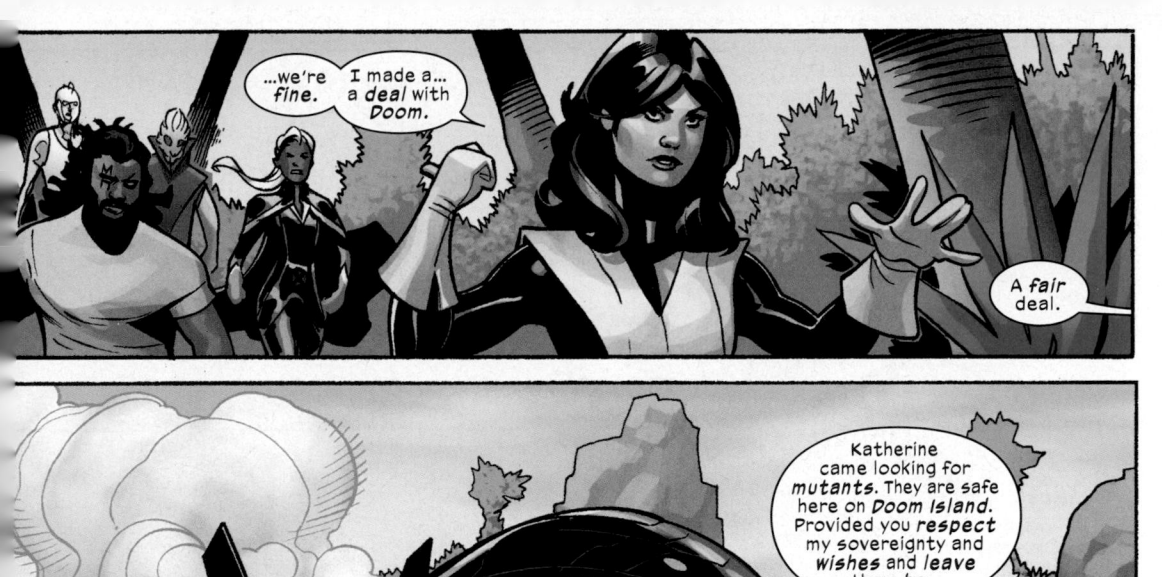

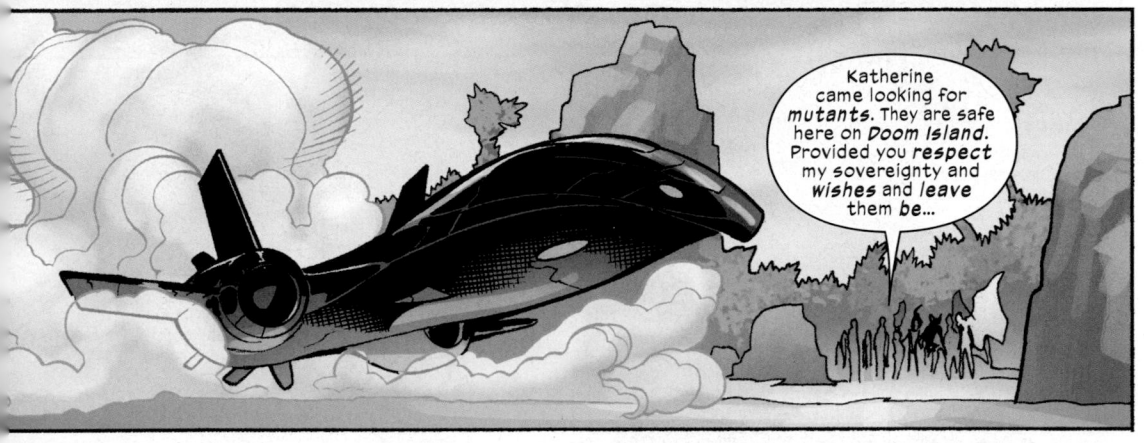

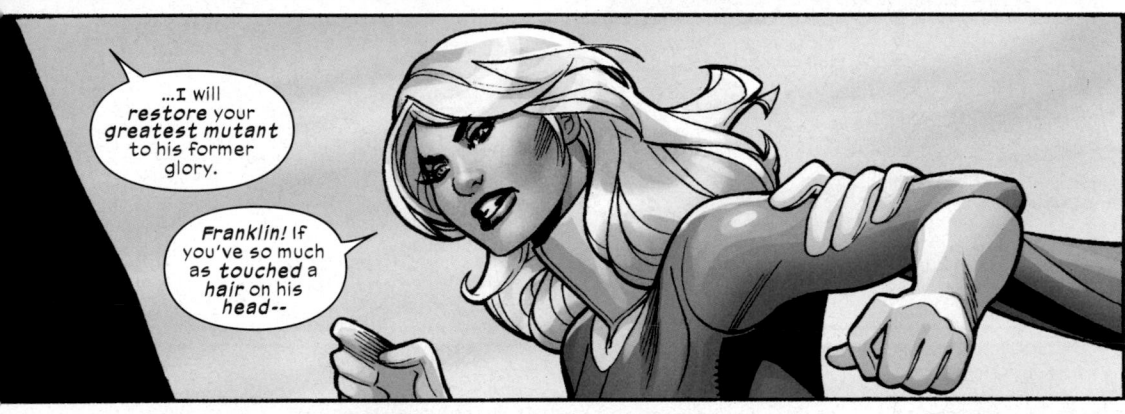

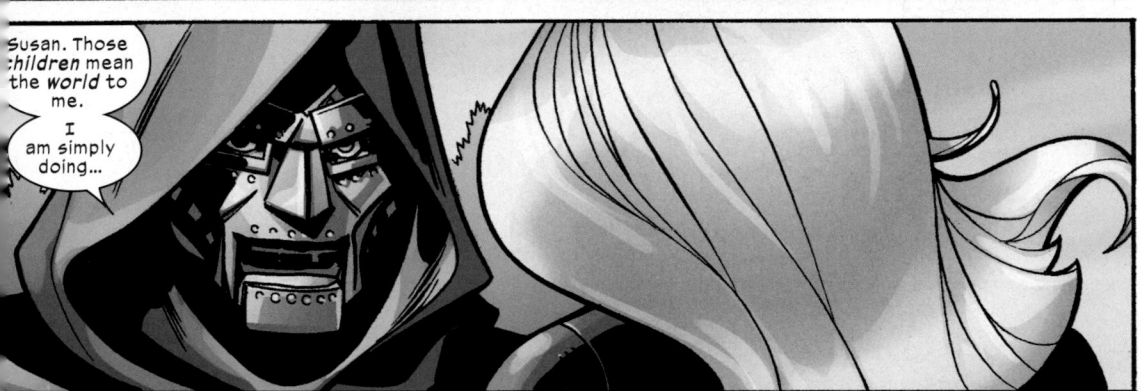

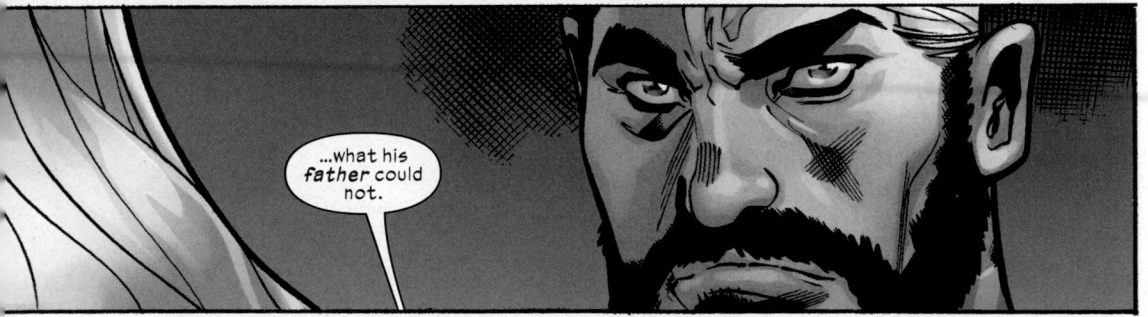

Unacceptable. Kate does not speak for Krakoa.
You don't get to--
I made an executive decision, Erik. My crew was in prison. Franklin wanted Doom's help...
I made the call.
Franklin's an Omega-level mutant and he needs our help!
And the mutants you came to rescue? You'd leave them to this despot? Should we--
It's fine, Erik.
Kate made the correct call.
No. She had zero right.
Our son isn't some sc
of bargainin
chip! He's-
His own man, Richards.
A piece of him is missing. You know how that feels, how that's felt for years.
You toss and turn at night, missing that sliver of intelligence that would put you on par with Doom.
If you are to stay, then no one is permitted to enter the island's town.
This island is Latveria. Here...
The majority of you shall wait here, and I will make you comfortable until the procedure is complete.

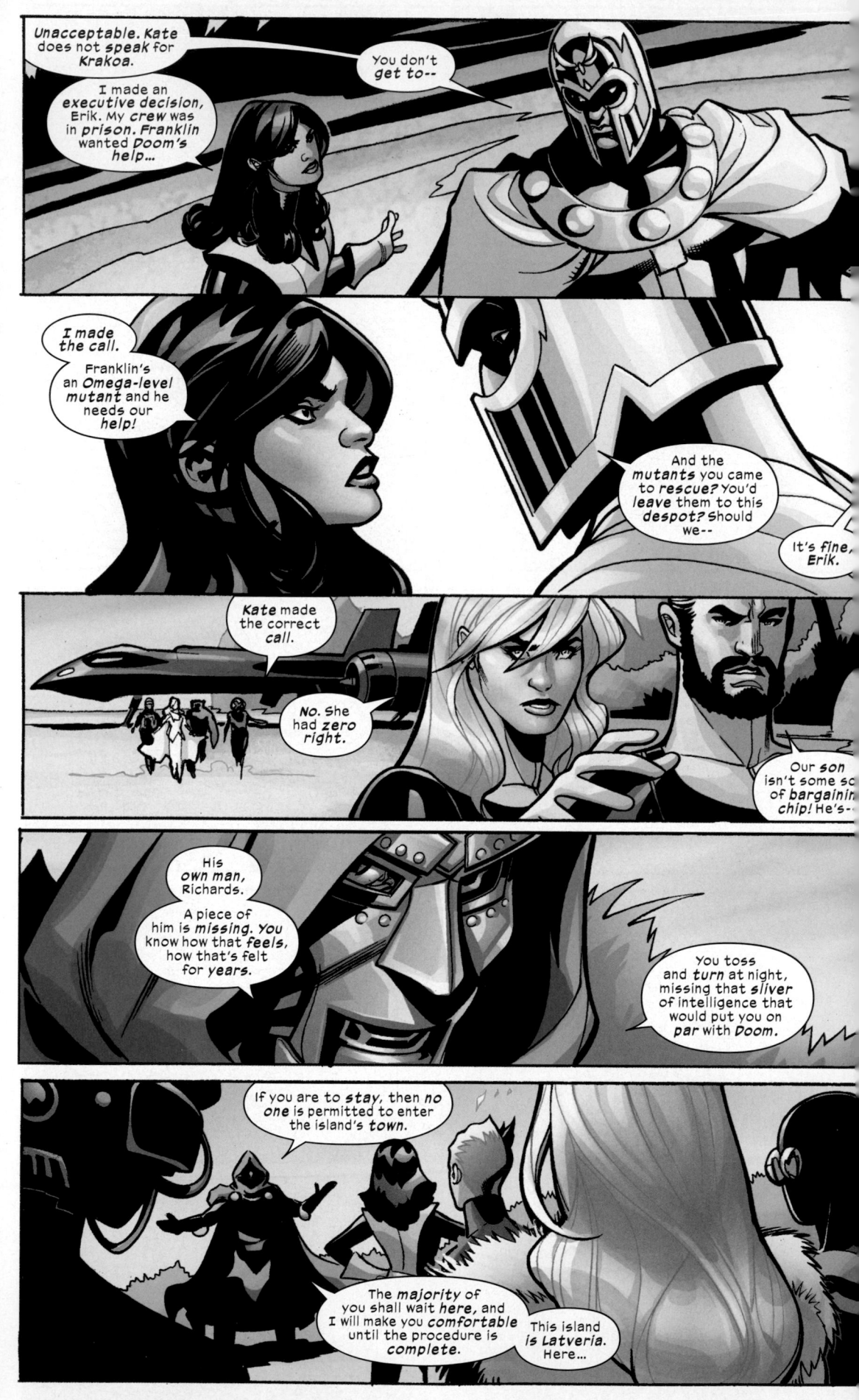

oom's
is law."
...but I don't think Uncle Victor is going to kill you, Franklin.
Great.
Do you think it will work, Val?
ok, biology ecessarily my lty...especially our gross biology...
No idea.
All I know is... you're unhappy.
And maybe this will help.
Val...
Look, Dad can't help, or maybe he just won't, so--
That's not true.
I wouldn't lie to you about that.
Sure...
...about that.
Glad you could make it, Dad. Did you find us through some more secret tracking chips you put in us?
It's time to come home. We'll talk more then.

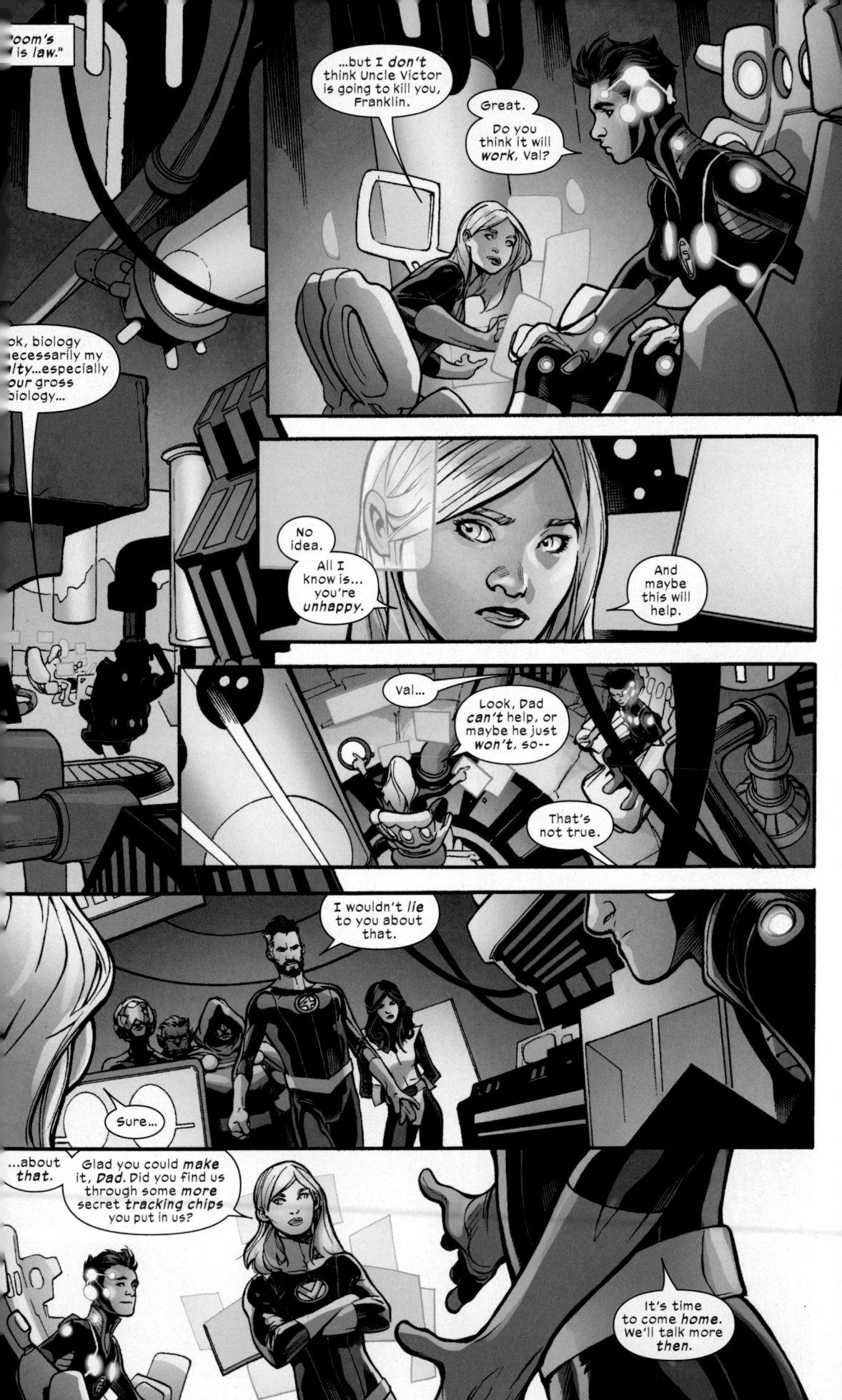

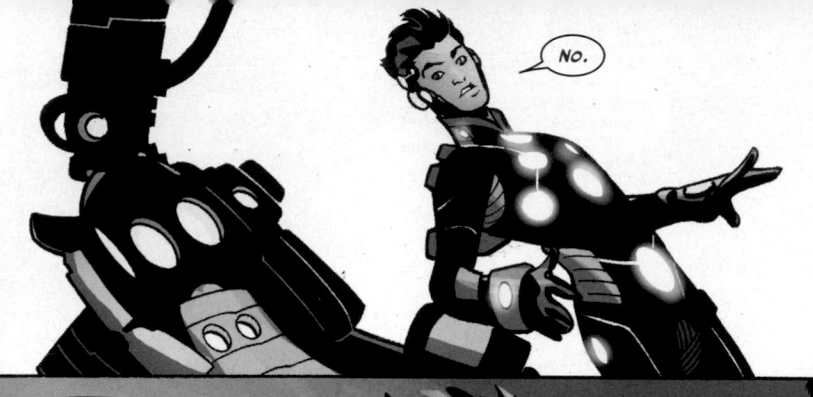

NO.

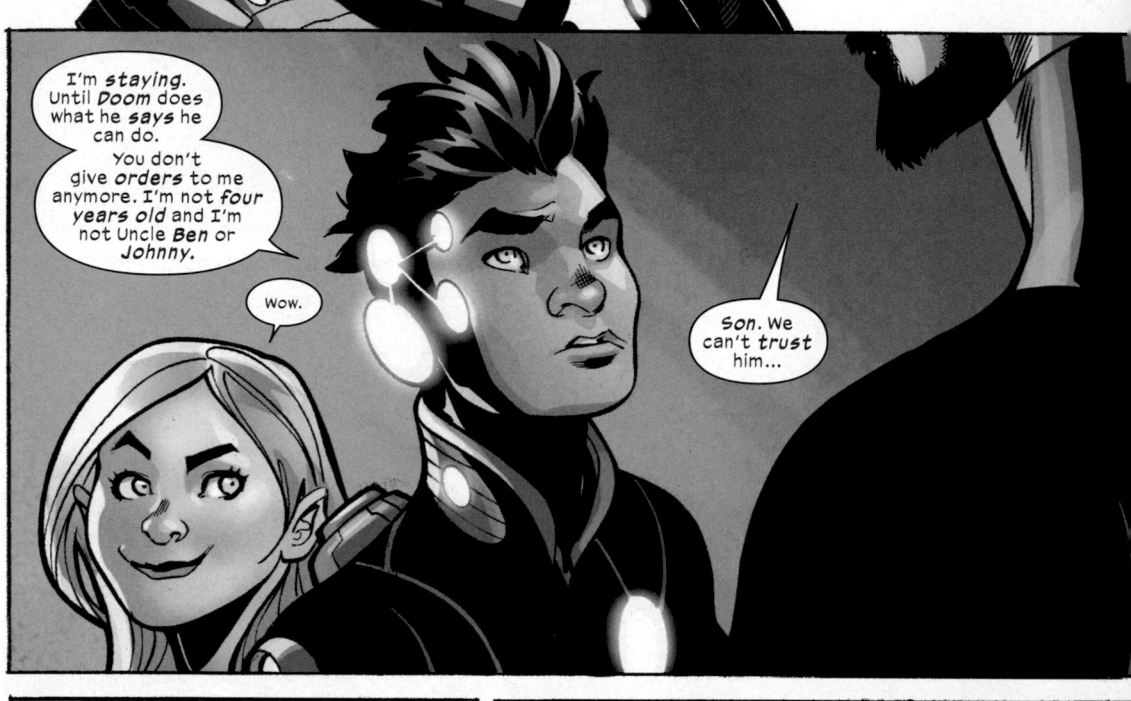

I'm *staying.* Until *Doom* does what he *says* he can do.

You don't give *orders* to me anymore. I'm not *four years old* and I'm not Uncle *Ben* or *Johnny.*

Wow.

Son. We can't *trust* him...

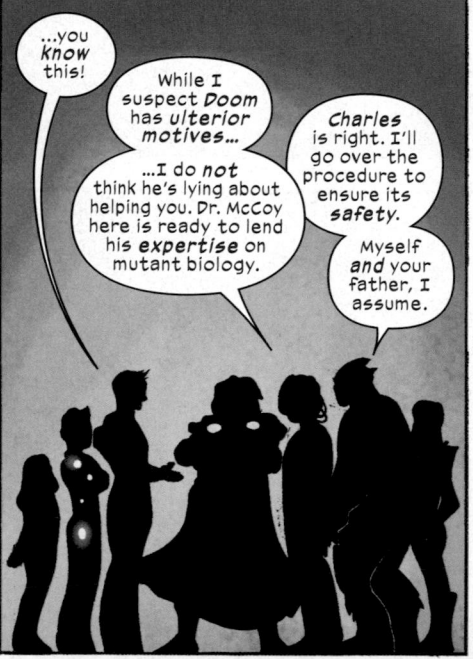

...you *know* this!

While *I* suspect *Doom* has *ulterior motives...*

...I do *not* think he's lying about helping you. Dr. McCoy here is ready to lend his *expertise* on mutant biology.

Charles is right. I'll go over the procedure to ensure its *safety.*

Myself *and* your father, I assume.

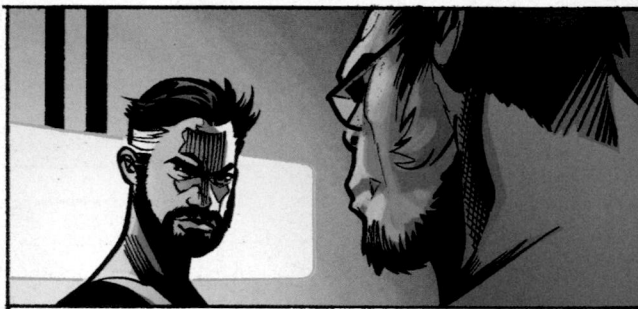

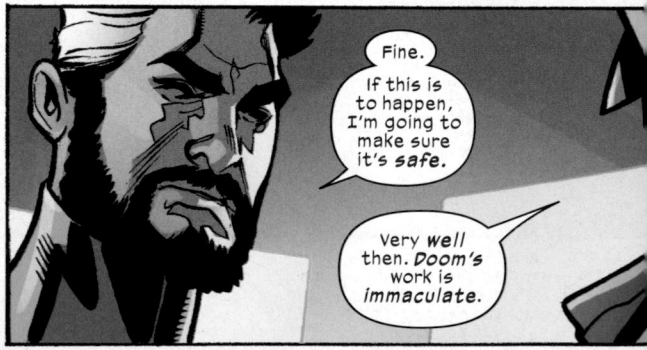

Fine. If this is to happen, I'm going to make sure it's *safe.*

Very *well* then. *Doom's* work is *immaculate.*

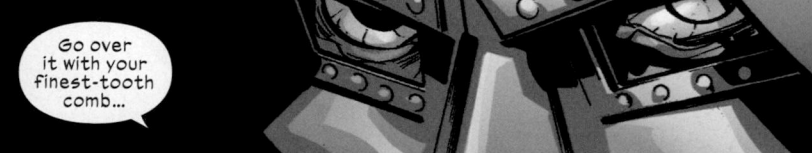

Go over it with your finest-tooth comb...

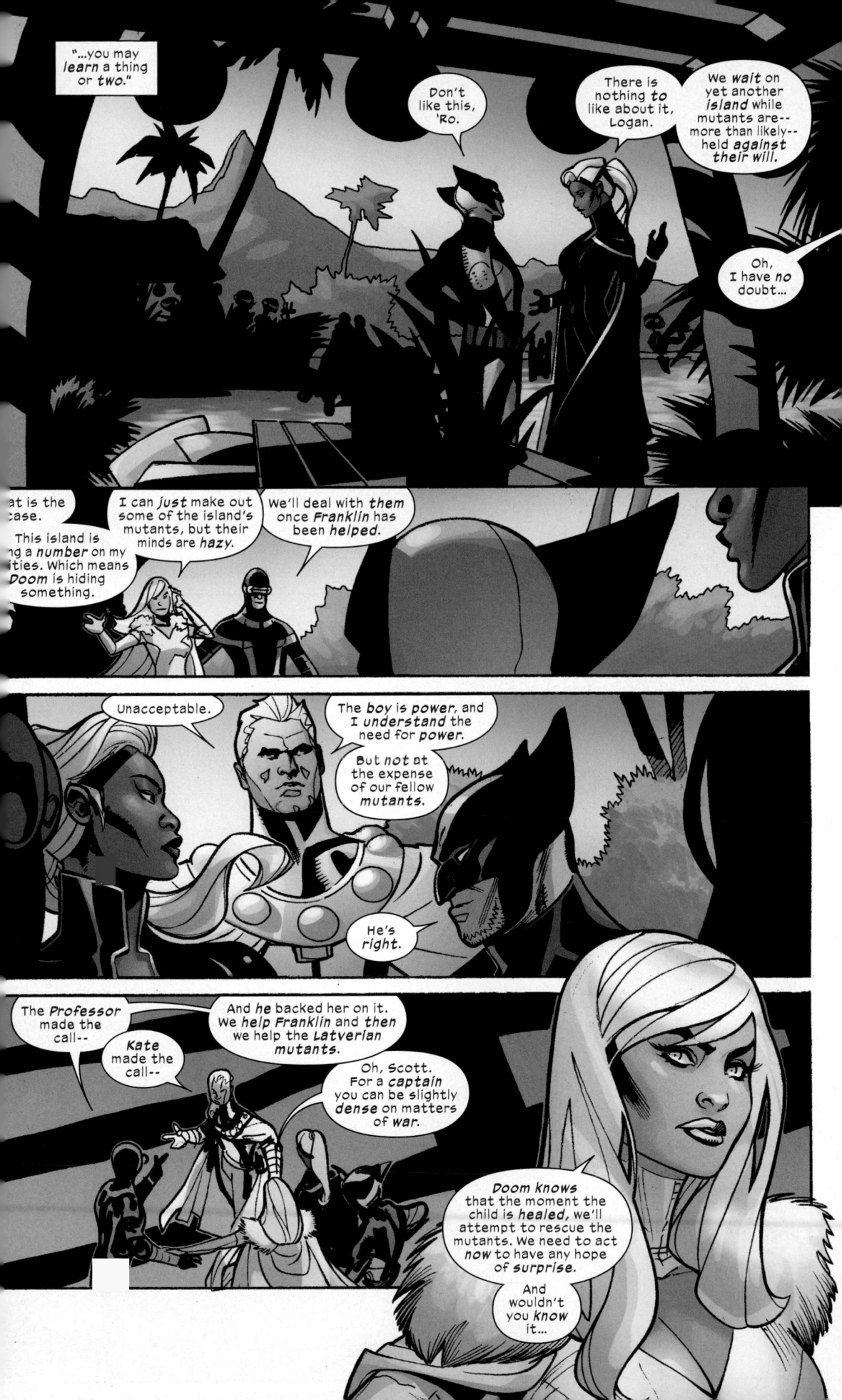

"...you may *learn* a thing or *two*."

Don't like this, 'Ro.

There is nothing *to* like about it, Logan.

We *wait* on yet another *island* while mutants are-- more than likely-- held *against* their *will*.

Oh, I have *no* doubt...

...at is the ...case.

This island is ...g a *number* on my ...ities. Which means ...Doom is hiding ...something.

I can *just* make out some of the island's mutants, but their minds are *hazy*.

We'll deal with *them* once *Franklin* has been *helped*.

Unacceptable.

The *boy* is *power*, and I *understand* the need for *power*.

But *not* at the expense of our fellow *mutants*.

He's *right*.

The *Professor* made the call--

Kate made the call--

And *he* backed her on it. We *help Franklin* and *then* we help the *Latverian mutants*.

Oh, Scott. For a *captain* you can be slightly *dense* on matters of *war*.

Doom knows that the moment the child is *healed*, we'll attempt to rescue the mutants. We need to act *now* to have any hope of *surprise*.

And wouldn't you *know* it...

...we have the Dior of surprise in our midst.
All right, provided she wants to even help...how we gonna do this so Doom's cabana boys don't know we're missin'?
I'll stay behind and obfuscate with a tropical storm.
I don't agree with this, but...I'll stay behind as well.
If they suspect you're gone and make any move to alert Doom, I'll take care of them.
We'll do this quickly.
And if it turns out Doom has been holding mutants against their will...
...then Latveria will suffer.

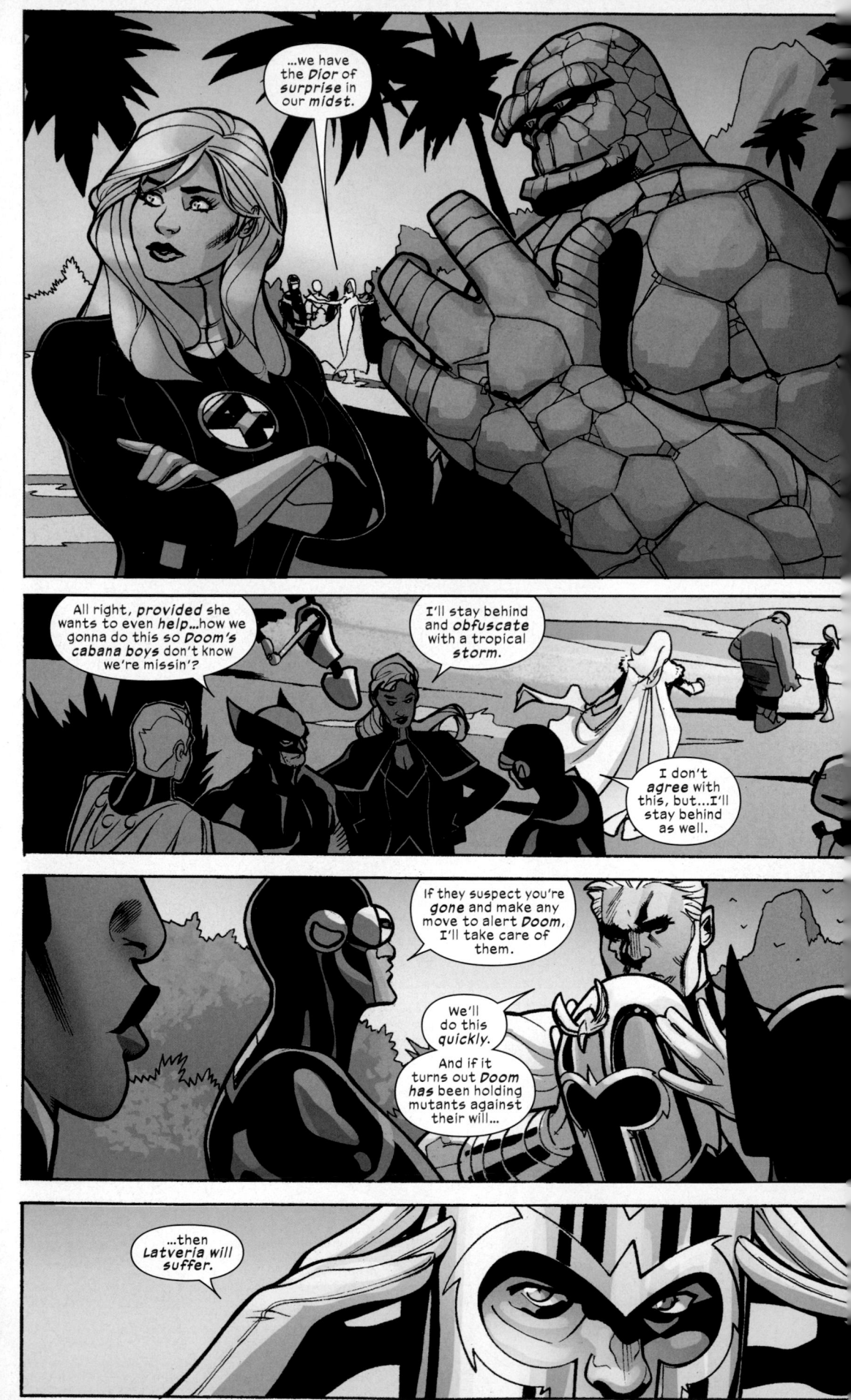

REED RICHARDS

Entry 662037a DOOM ISLAND

Initial Scan
Send–Susan Richards
      Johnathan Storm
      Benjamin Grimm
      Scott Summers

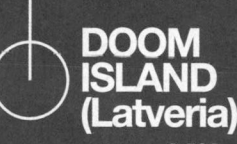

DOOM ISLAND (Latveria)
est. pop. 2,500

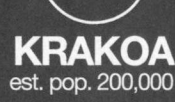

KRAKOA
est. pop. 200,000

HIGH
ELECTRICAL
READINGS

LANDING
PARTY

TOWER
DOOM

POPULATED
AREAS

This is an audacious piece of work, Victor...
...exploding the body's mitochondria to open a... channel?
It appears that alongside the fuel of adenosine triphosphate, Franklin's body is creating a secondary type of energy.
That's not unique to Franklin...
...it's true of all of you with "powers."
Mutant, superhuman...anyone who expends more power than they can seemingly generate has this energy type flowing through them.
I call them "Von Doom Particles."
Of course you do.
And if these schematics are any indication, you don't think they're being generated by us, but rather...
Traveling through conduits within the mitochondria, yes.
One would presume from another dimension, an unlimited power source.
The scientist Dr. Rachna Koul has already been working on finding that source...
...which she calls "godpower."
Von Doom Particles.
Once Doom is able to travel to this dimension, it will be claimed as Latveria's.
Victor...

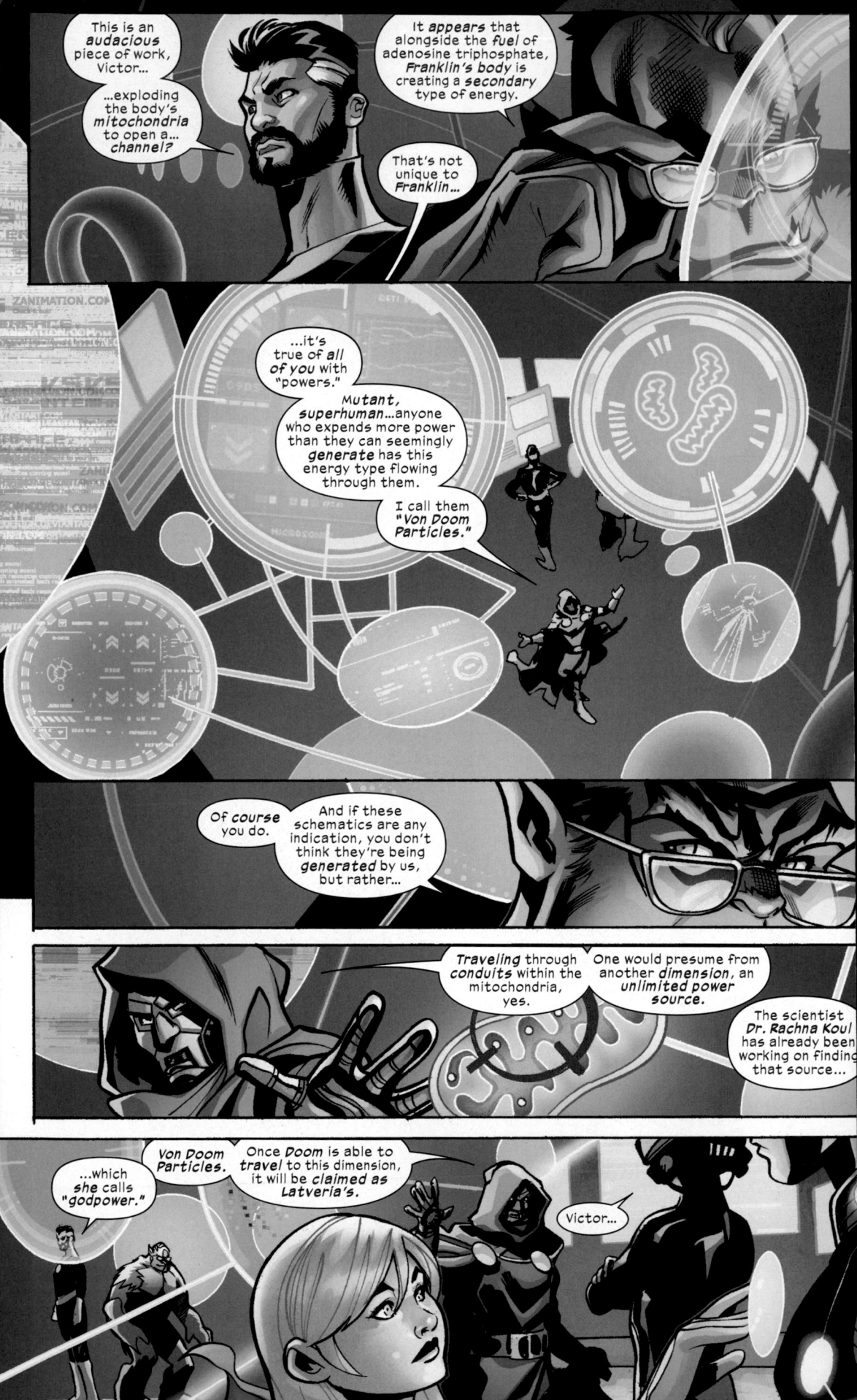

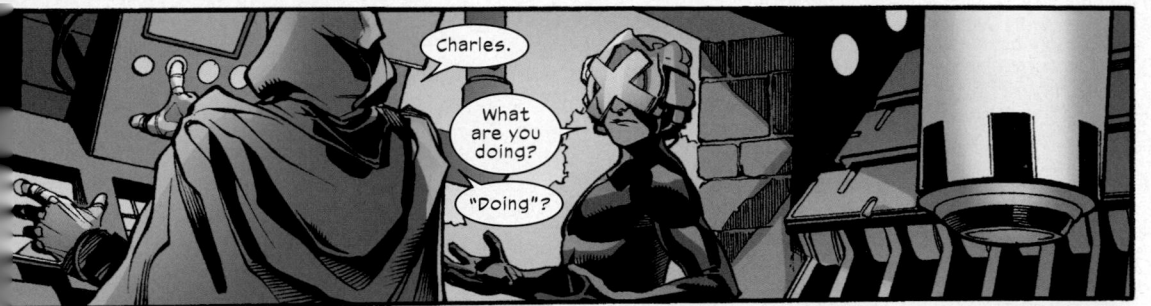

Charles.

What are you doing?

"Doing"?

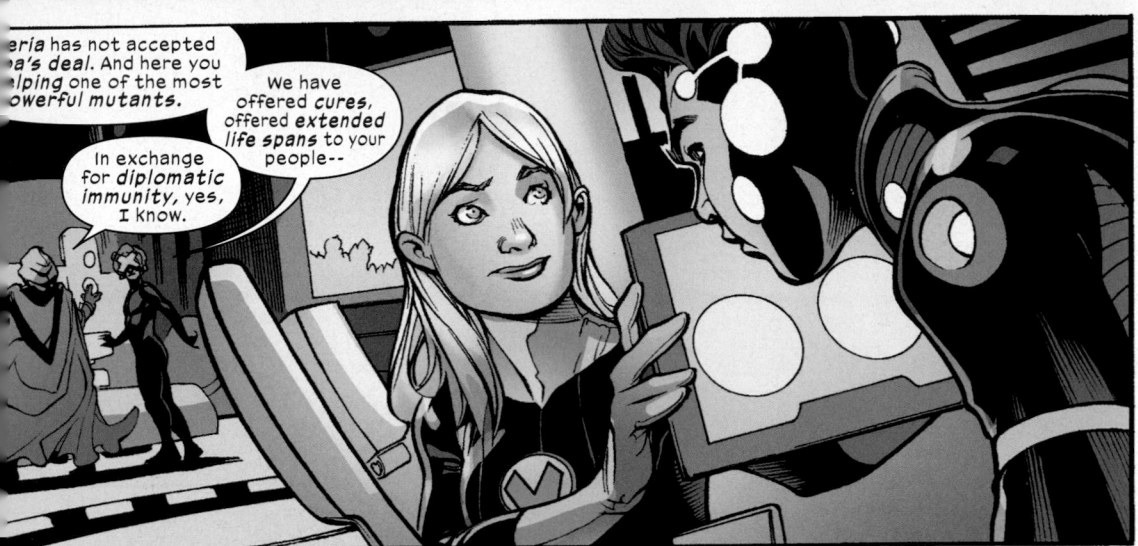

...eria has not accepted ...a's deal. And here you ...lping one of the most ...owerful mutants.

In exchange for *diplomatic immunity*, yes, I know.

We have offered *cures*, offered *extended life spans* to your people--

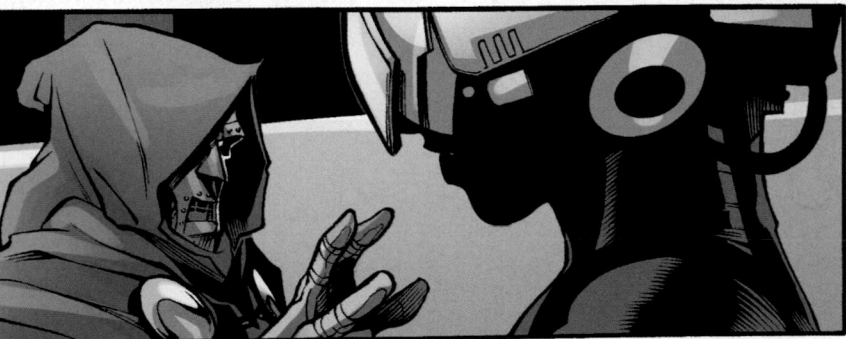

While I have little ...espect for traditional ...plomats," *Doom* at least ...cognizes that they are ...e supposed *exceptional examples* of an underwhelming populace.

You, however, have decided to make *all* your citizens free to do what they *will* in countries that come *begging* for your *plants*.

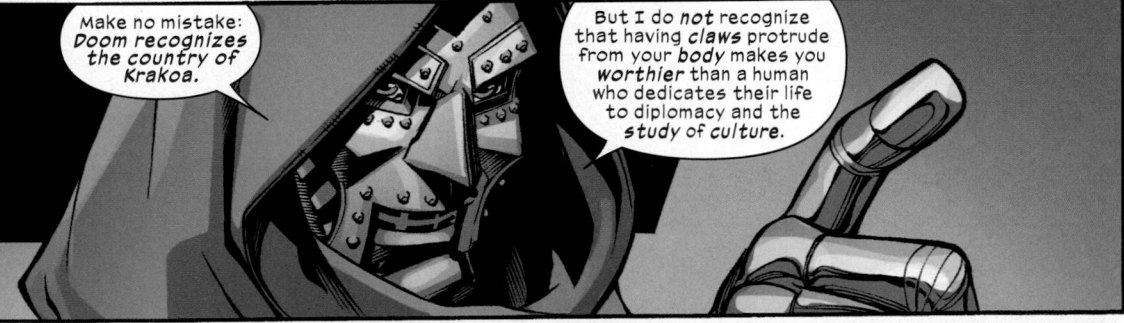

Make no mistake: *Doom recognizes the country of Krakoa.*

But I do *not* recognize that having *claws* protrude from your *body* makes you *worthier* than a human who dedicates their life to diplomacy and the *study* of *culture*.

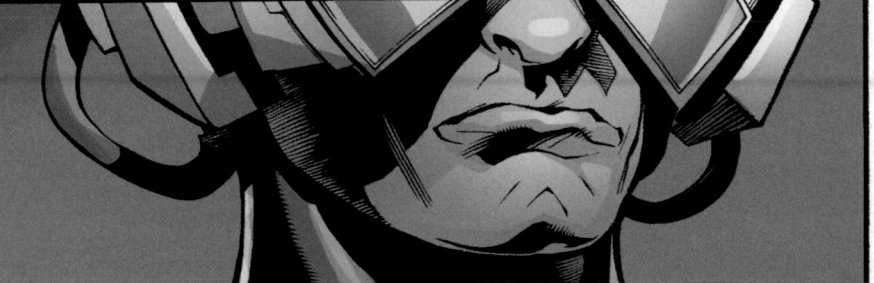

It is *insulting.* You are insulting, Charles, with this pretence of superiority.

Doom will *help* this young man because it is what *Doom* wishes to do with his *power*, power that he has *earned*...

"...while you were simply born with it."
What're you pickin' up, Emma?
I... There appear to be two mutants within that building over there... but things are still cloudy for me.
I know we have not seen... eye to eye so far, Susan...
...but the nation of Krakoa appreciates--
Shut up.
The Fantastic Four helps people because it's right.
You should try it sometime.
Children, quiet.
‹Wh-who--?›*
‹Y-you're Krakoans--›
‹Please, do not scream. We're not here to harm you. Do you know who we are?›
*Translated from Latverian.
‹Enemies of Latveria!›
‹You will not harm me or my brother! Nothing can get past my shell!›

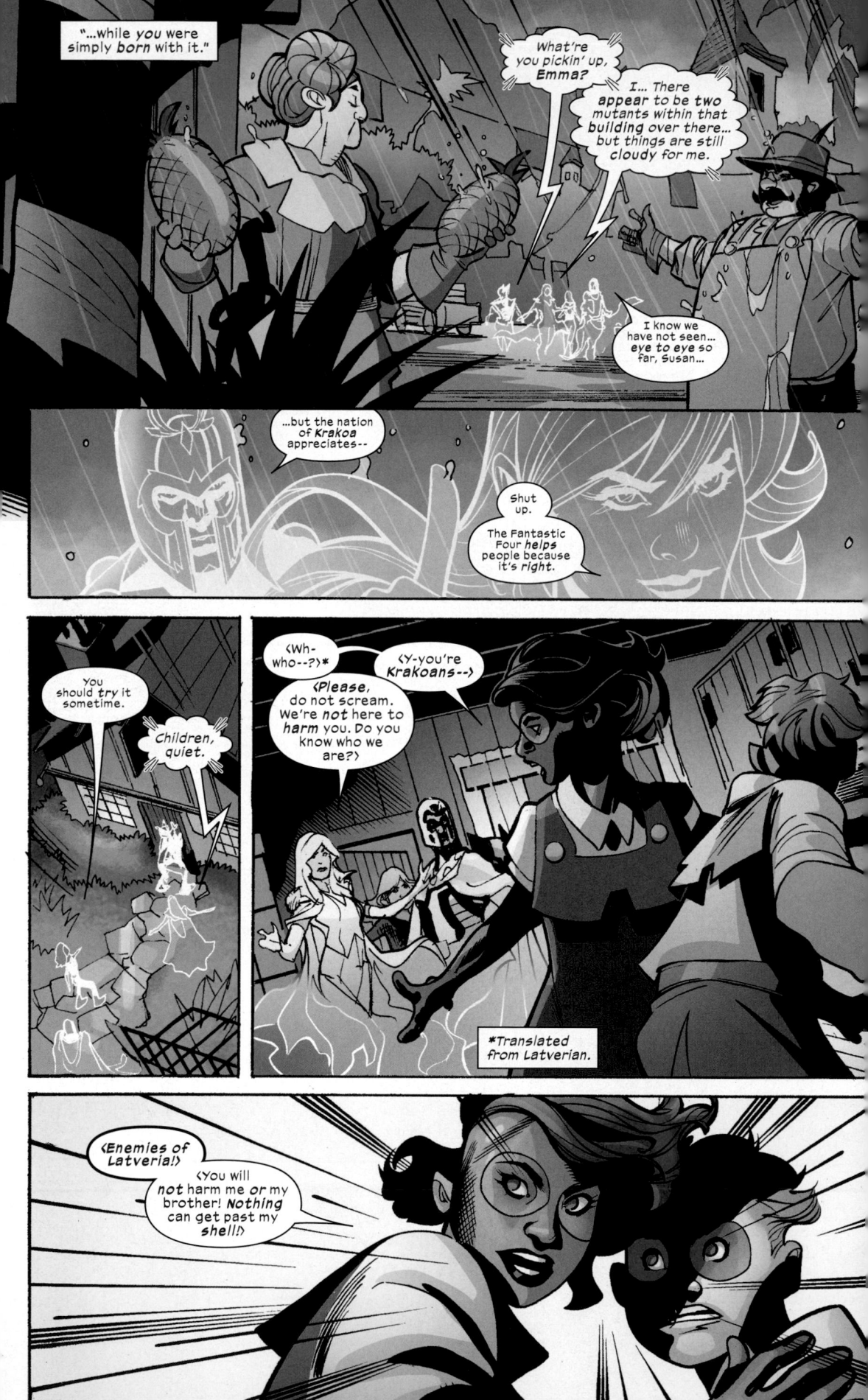

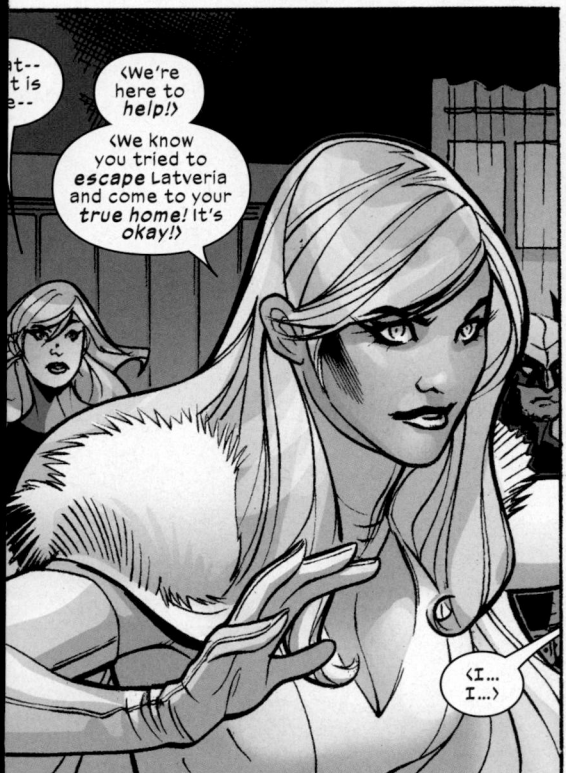

‹...at-- is e--›

‹We're here to help!›

‹We know you tried to escape Latveria and come to your true home! It's okay!›

‹I... I...›

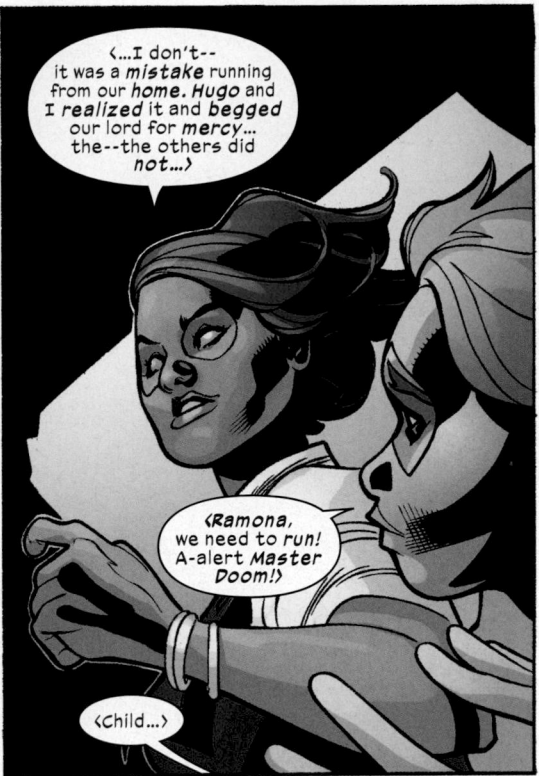

‹...I don't-- it was a mistake running from our home. Hugo and I realized it and begged our lord for mercy... the--the others did not...›

‹Ramona, we need to run! A-alert Master Doom!›

‹Child...›

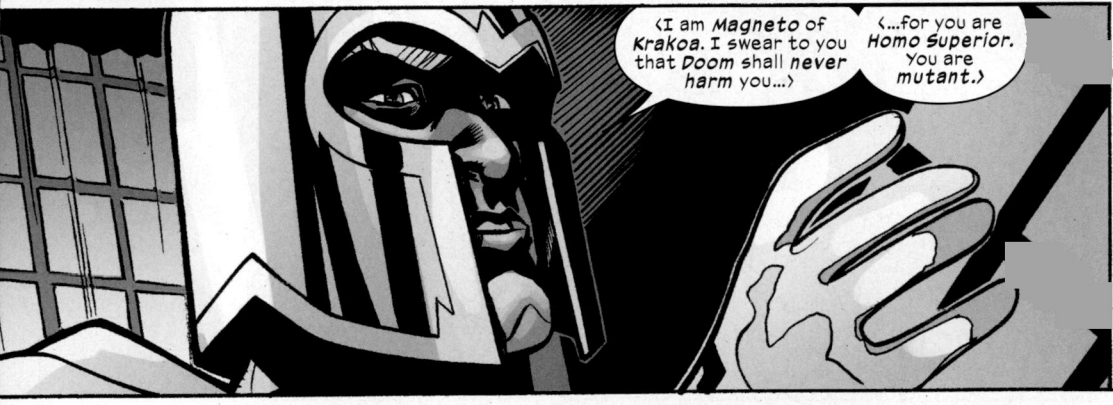

‹I am Magneto of Krakoa. I swear to you that Doom shall never harm you...›

‹...for you are Homo Superior. You are mutant.›

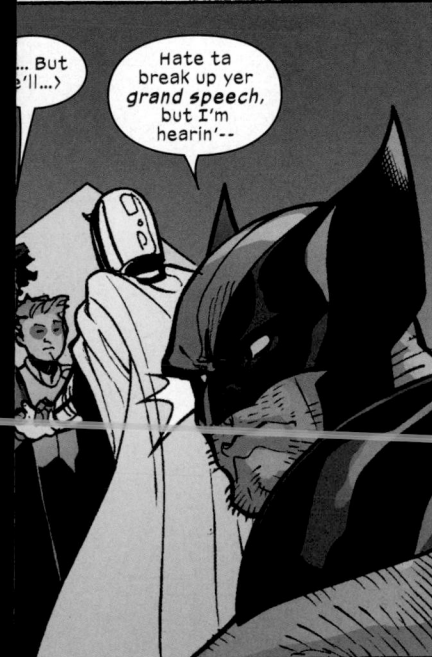

‹...But e'll...›

Hate ta break up yer grand speech, but I'm hearin'--

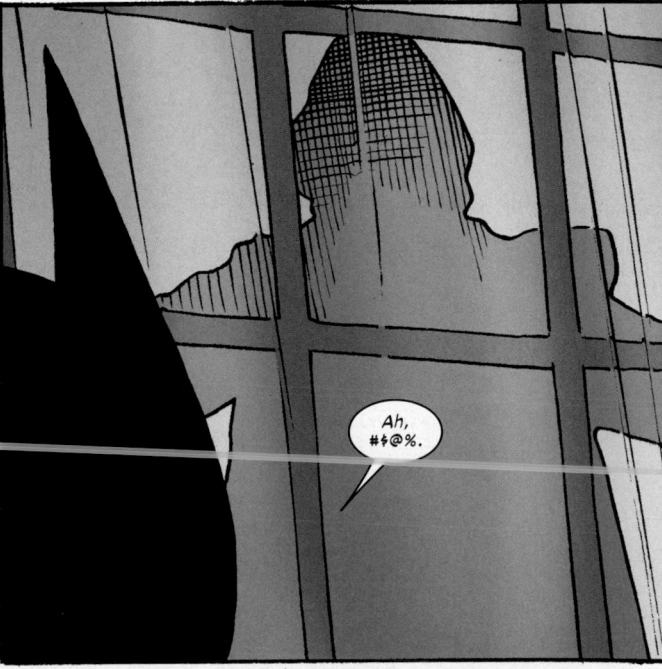

Ah, #$@%.

LOGAN!

SNIKT

gRk

SKRAKOOM!

SNI

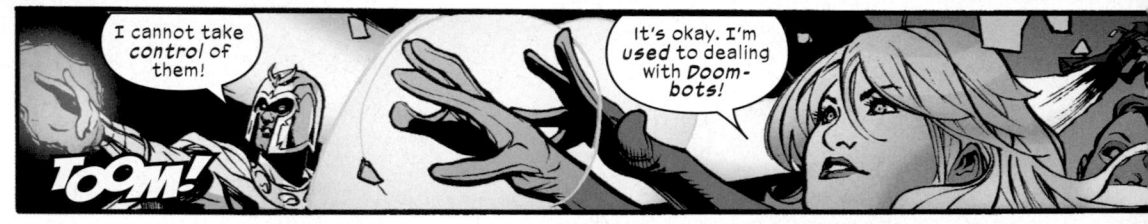

I cannot take control of them!

It's okay. I'm used to dealing with Doom-bots!

TOOM!

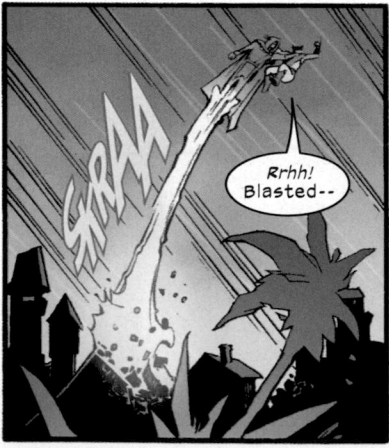

STRAA

Rrhh! Blasted--

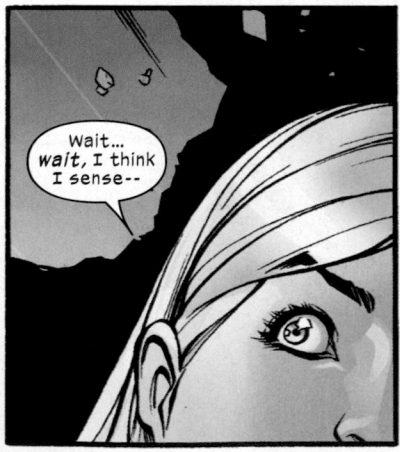

Wait... wait, I think I sense--

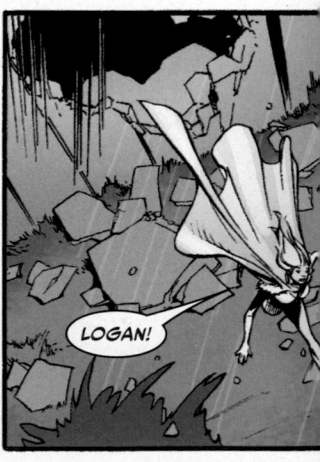

LOGAN!

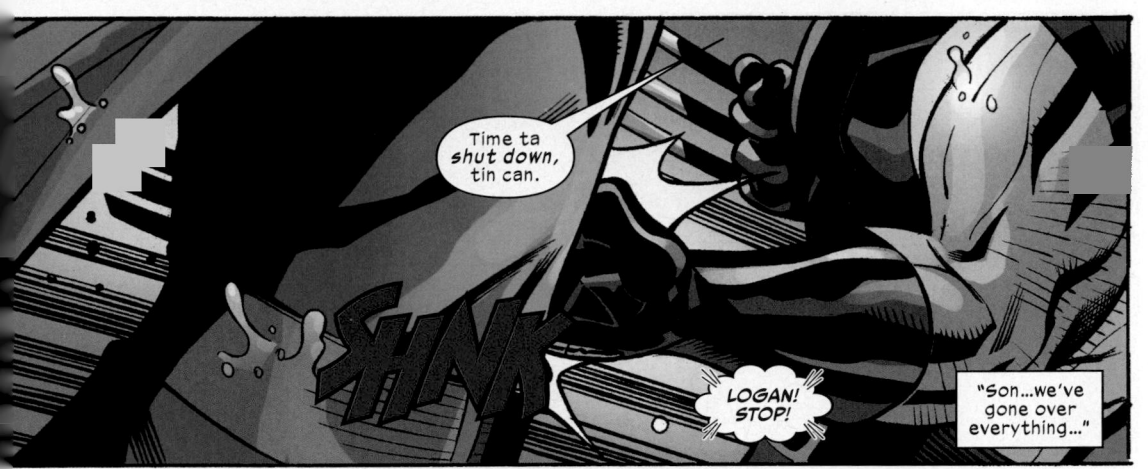

Time ta **shut down**, tin can.

SHNK

LOGAN! STOP!

"Son...we've gone over everything..."

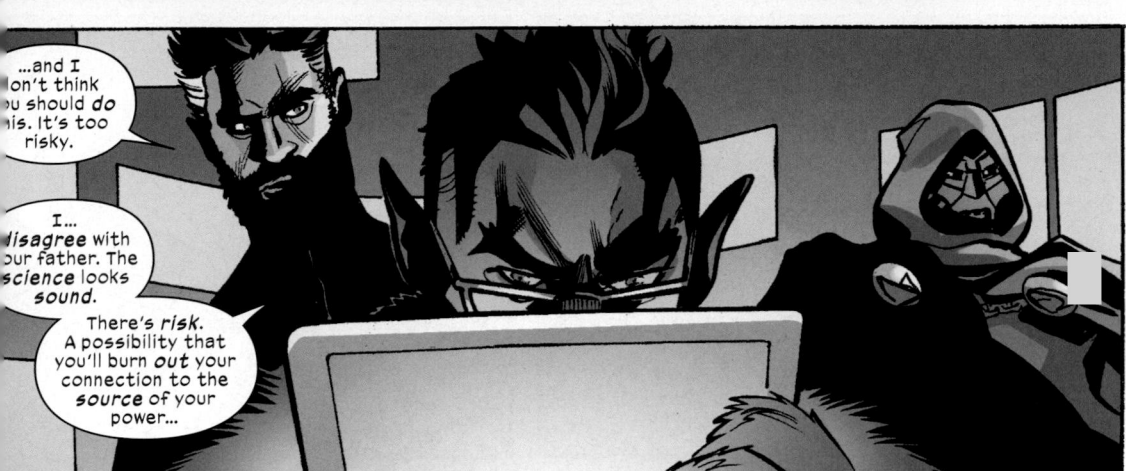

...and I don't think you should **do** this. It's too risky.

I... **disagree** with your father. The **science** looks **sound**.

There's **risk**. A possibility that you'll burn **out** your connection to the **source** of your power...

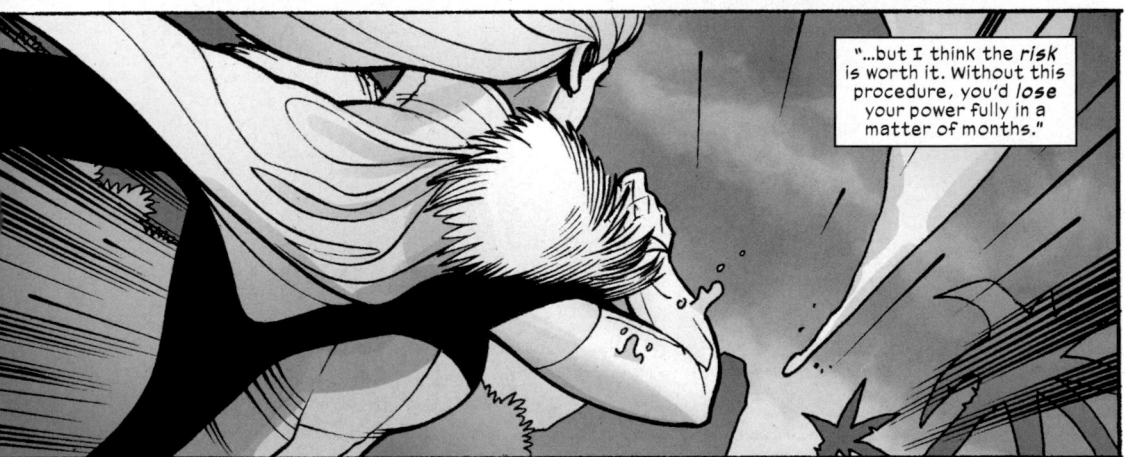

"...but I think the **risk** is worth it. Without this procedure, you'd **lose** your power fully in a matter of months."

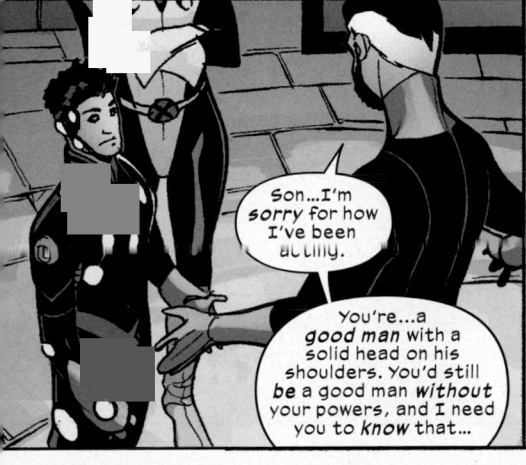

Son...I'm **sorry** for how I've been acting.

You're...a **good man** with a solid head on his shoulders. You'd still **be** a good man **without** your powers, and I need you to **know** that...

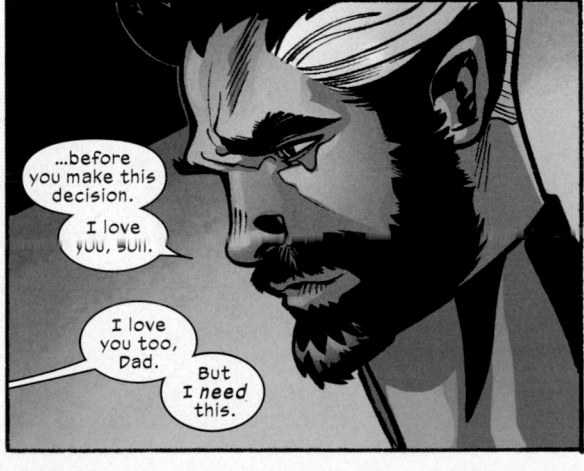

...before you make this decision. I love you, son.

I love you too, Dad. But **I need** this.

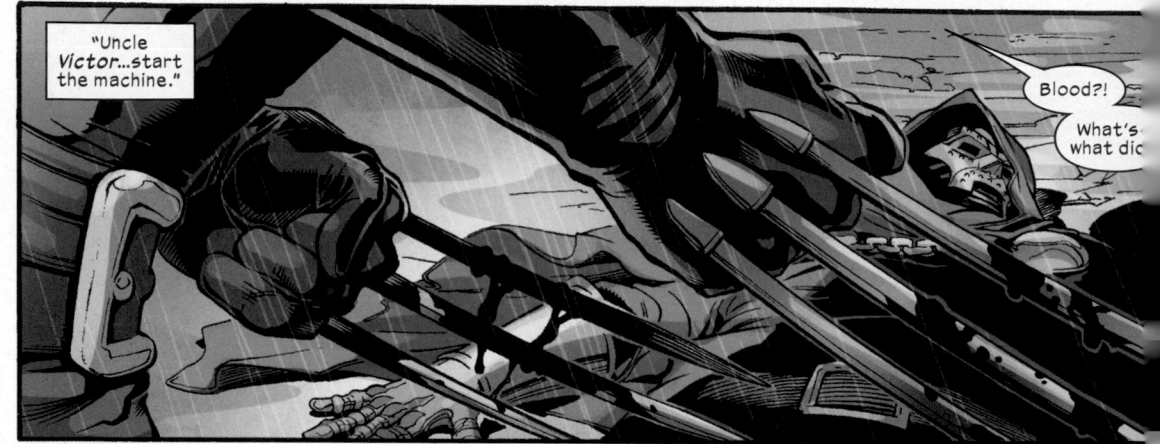

"Uncle *Victor*...start the machine."

Blood?!

What's
what di[d]

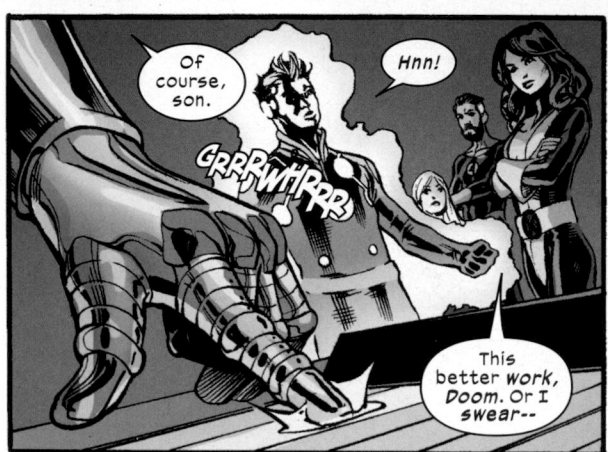

Of course, son.

Hnn!

GRRRWHRR!

This better *work*, *Doom*. Or I swear--

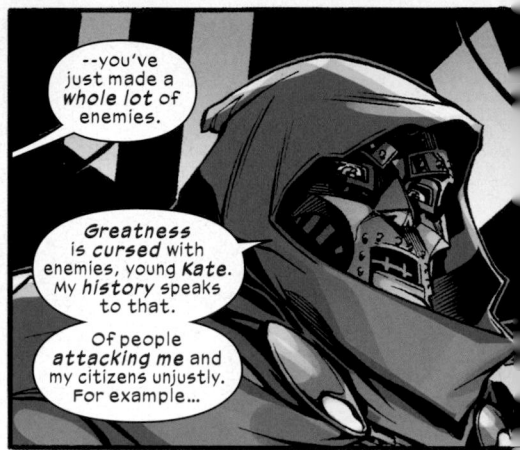

--you've just made a *whole lot of* enemies.

Greatness is *cursed* with enemies, young *Kate*. My *history* speaks to that.

Of people *attacking me* and my citizens unjustly. For example...

"...it appears y[ou]
fellow *mutan[ts]*
disobeyed m[y]
request. Not o[nly]
that..."

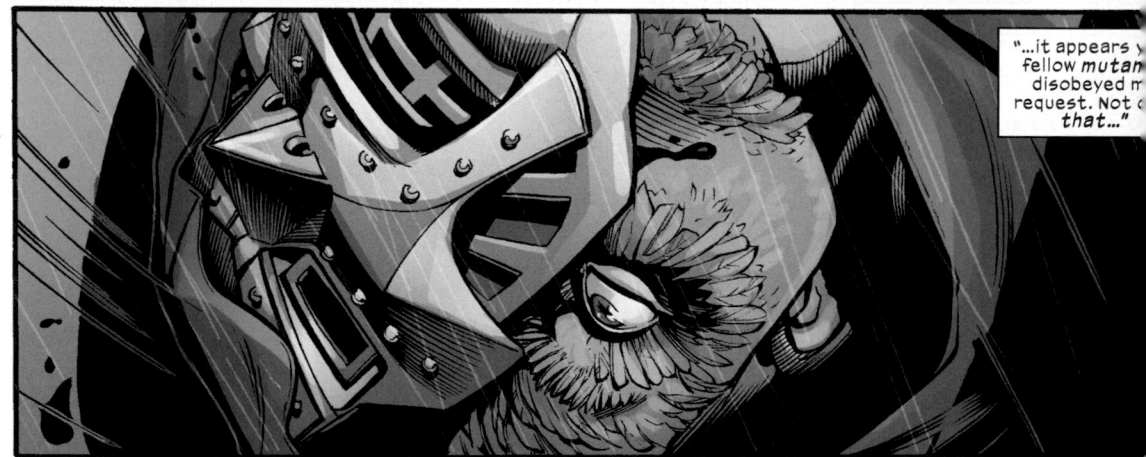

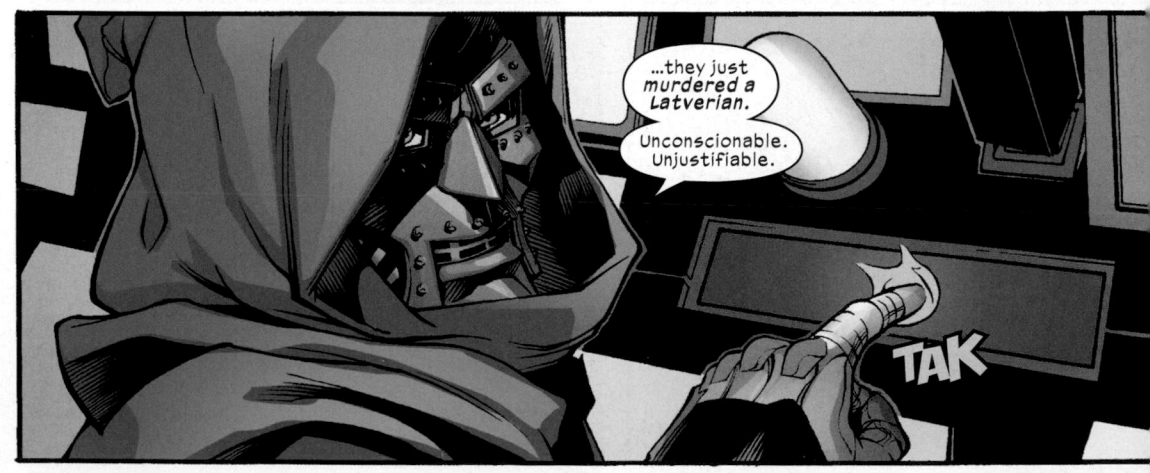

...they just *murdered* a *Latverian*.

Unconscionable. Unjustifiable.

TAK

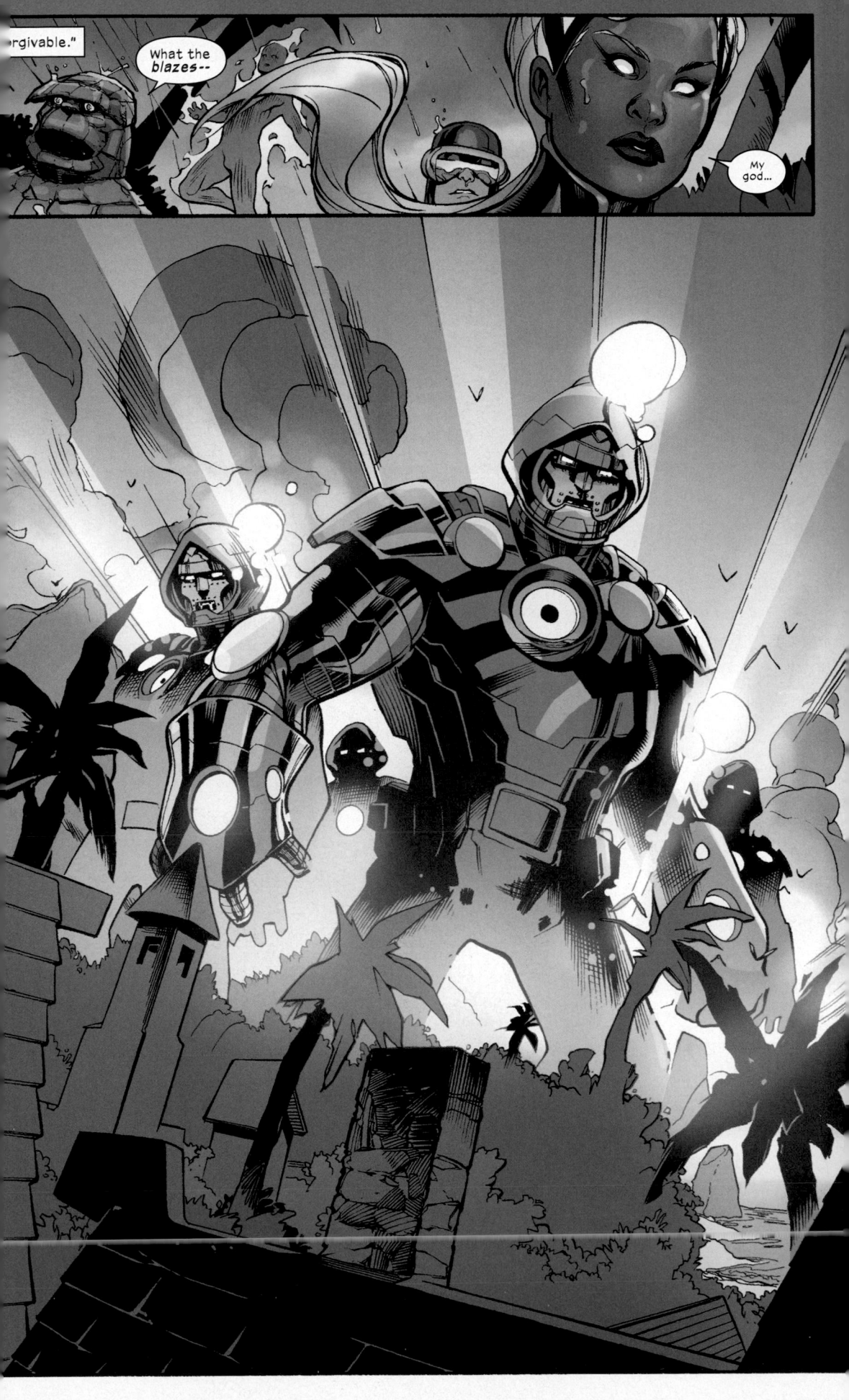

TERRY
DODSON
RACHEL

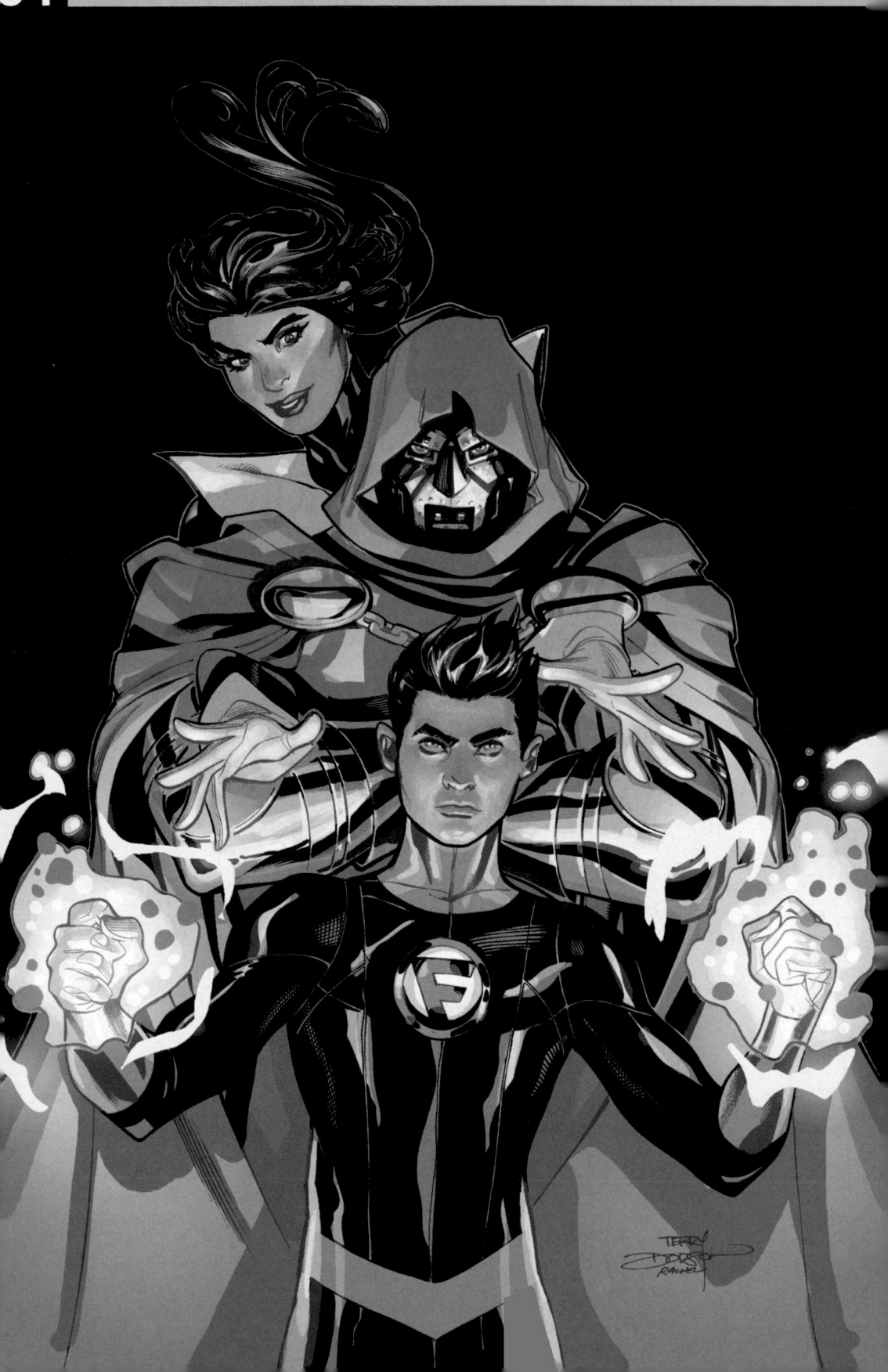

KRA-BOOM!
Oh, Uncle Doom.
You just can't help yourself from making things worse, can you?
Dear Valeria...
...the Krakoans did that all on their own.
I extended hospitality despite their illegal entry, and to repay my kindness...
FZWAAH!
...they ignored my orders and murdered a Latverian mutant.
Nhhh... What's--what's happening...?
Victor...what have you done?
My God...
...I'll tell you what he's done...

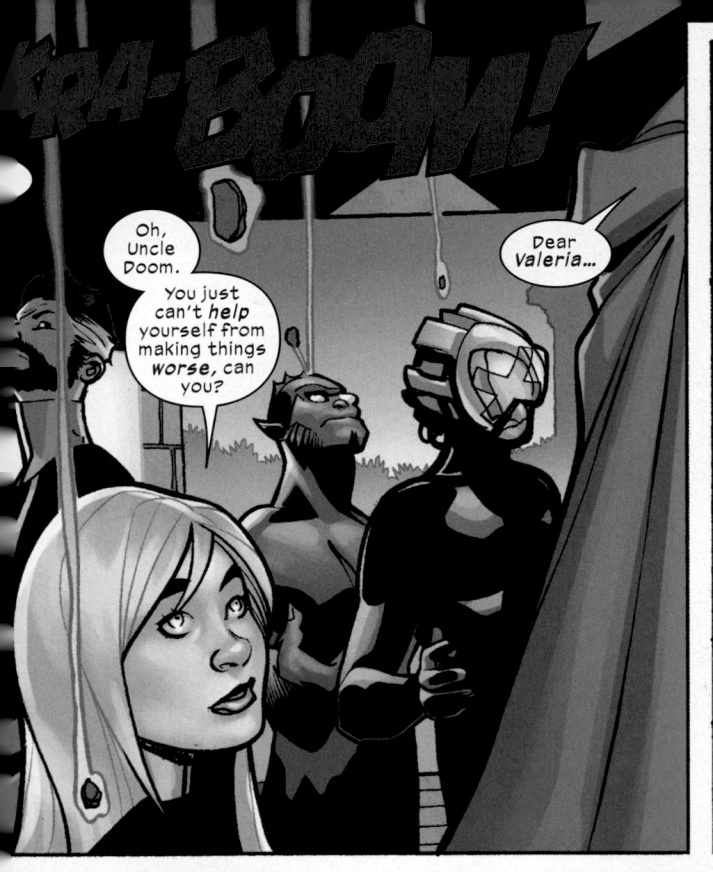

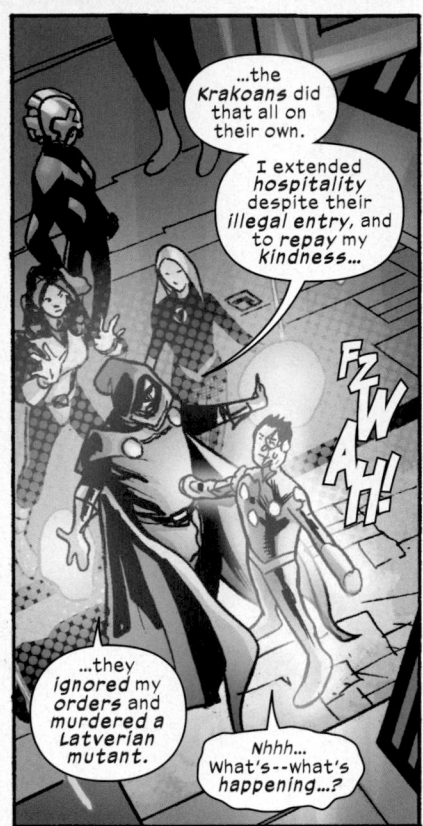

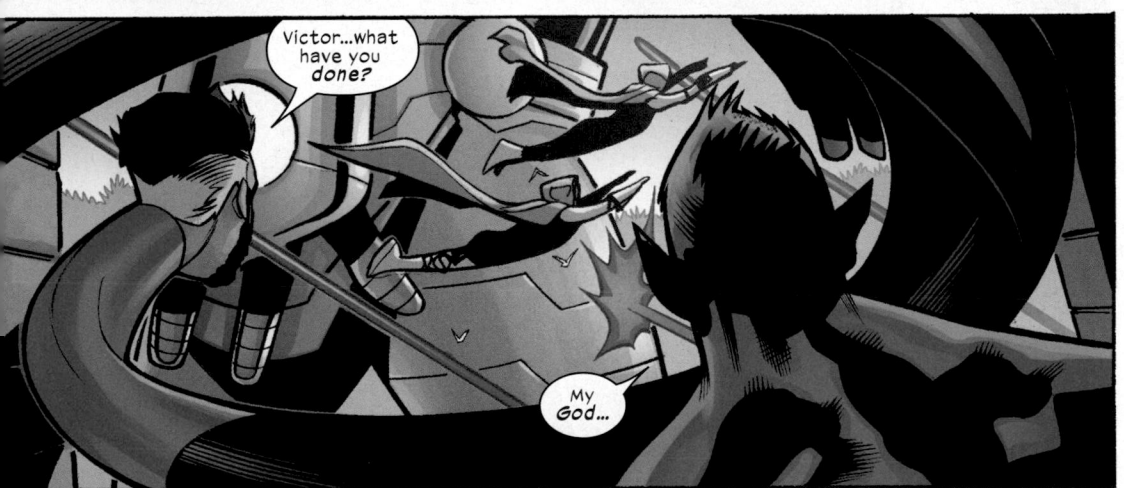

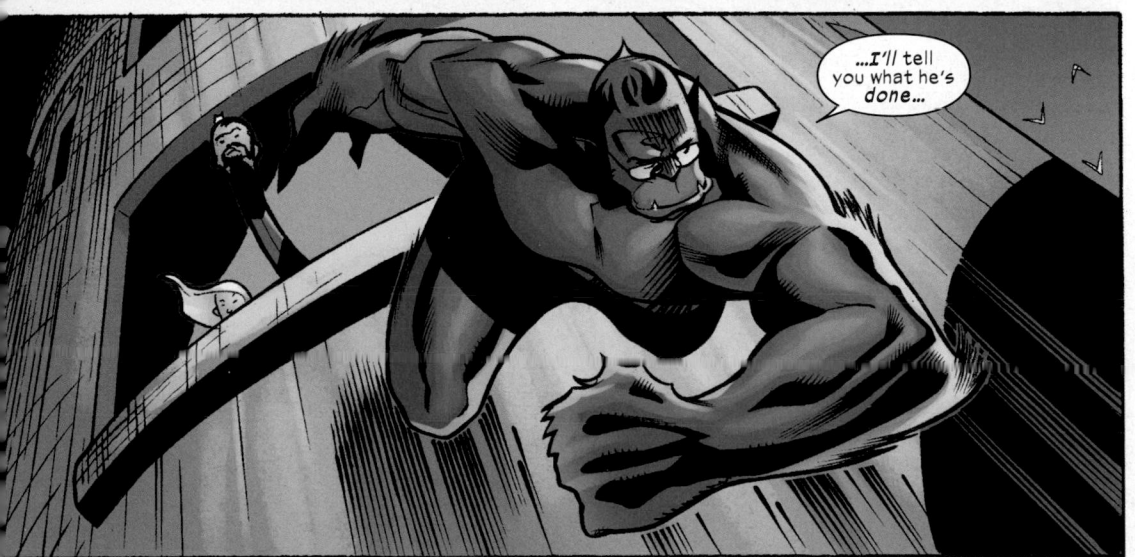

"...Doom's declared war on mutants."

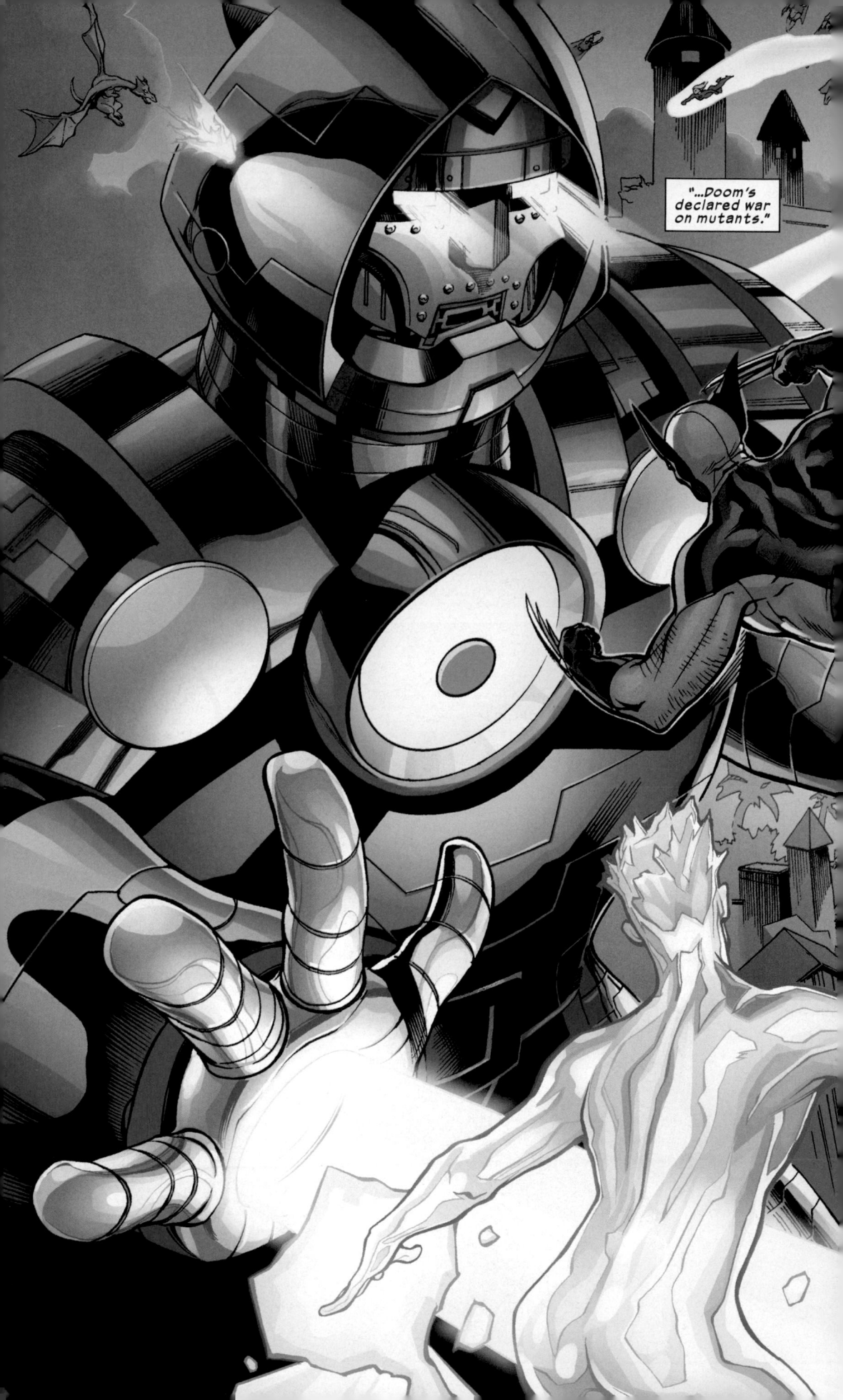

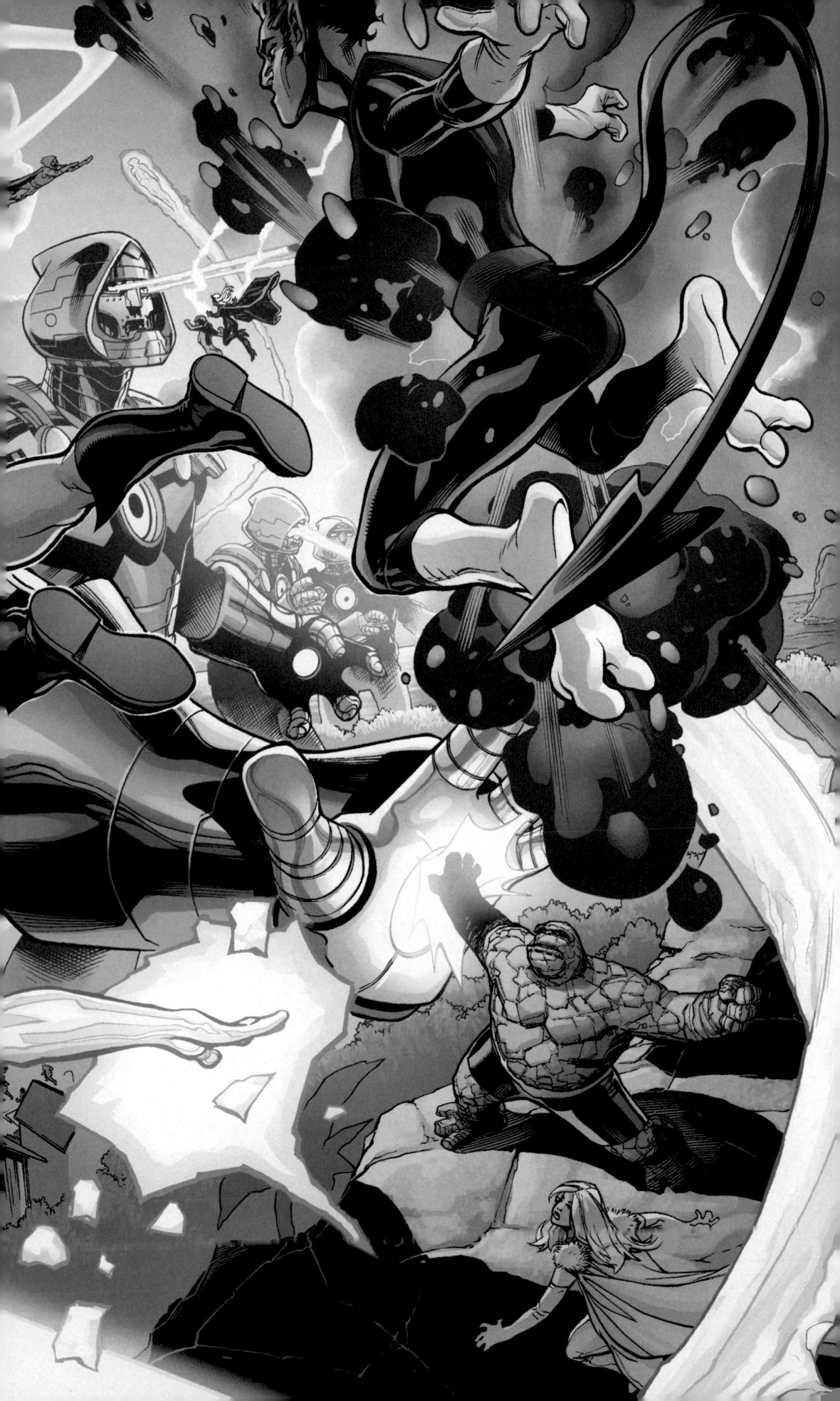

X-MEN /
FANTASTIC
FOUR

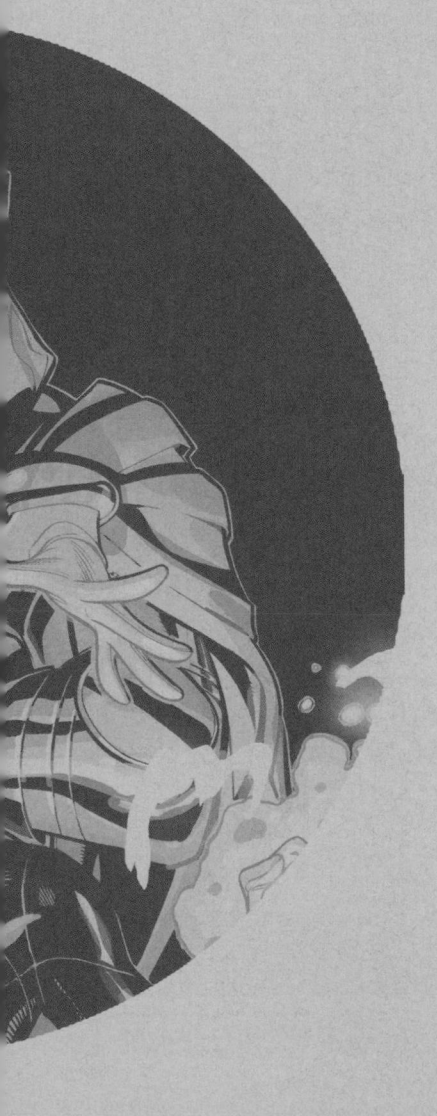

4 WELCOME TO THE NEW WORLD

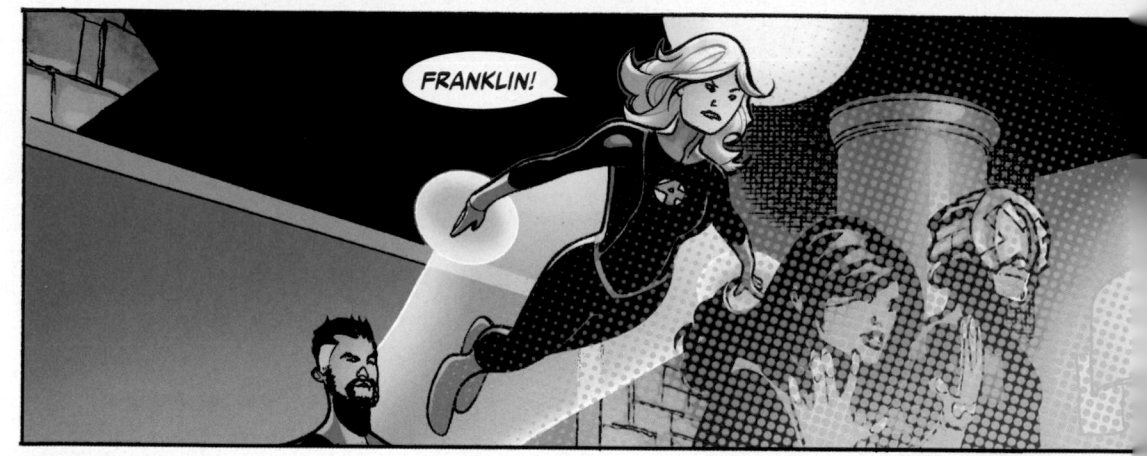

FRANKLIN!

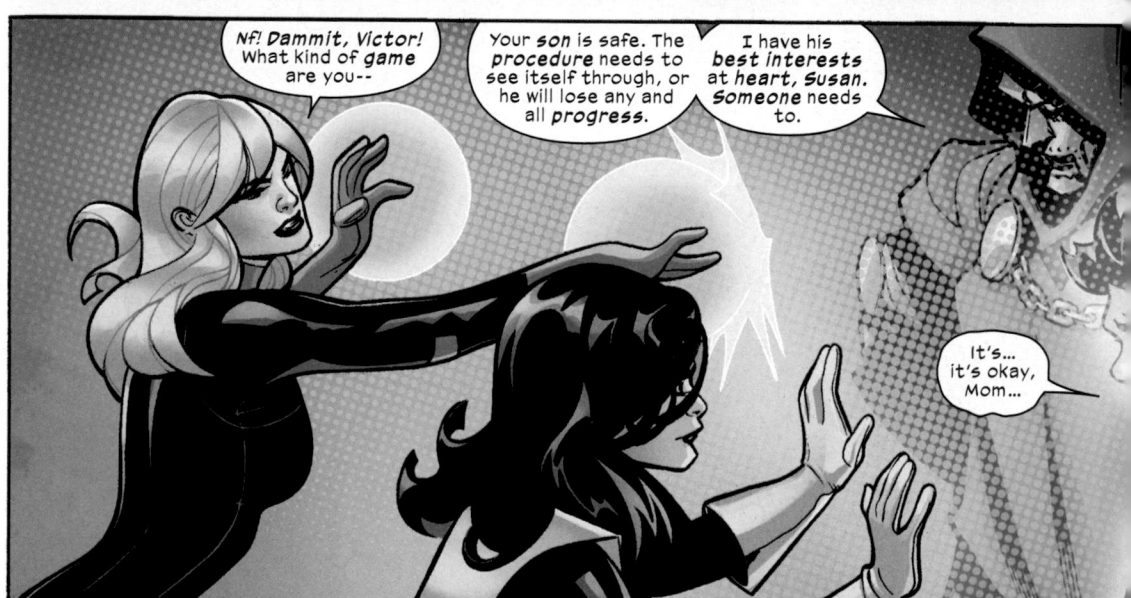

Nf! Dammit, Victor! What kind of **game** are you--

Your **son** is safe. The **procedure** needs to see itself through, or he will lose any and all **progress.**

I have his **best interests** at **heart, Susan. Someone** needs to.

It's... it's okay, Mom...

...I need to... to see this through...

Nh! I'm-- w-with you... Frank... Franklin...

...until the...the **end of the line.**

Looks like... like **I overrode** your **control** of my **powers, Doom.**

Drop the **force-field** or I'll **phase** through you and **fry** your armor.

Oh, Katherine... I **warned** you...

...I know your **powers** even **better** than you do.

What

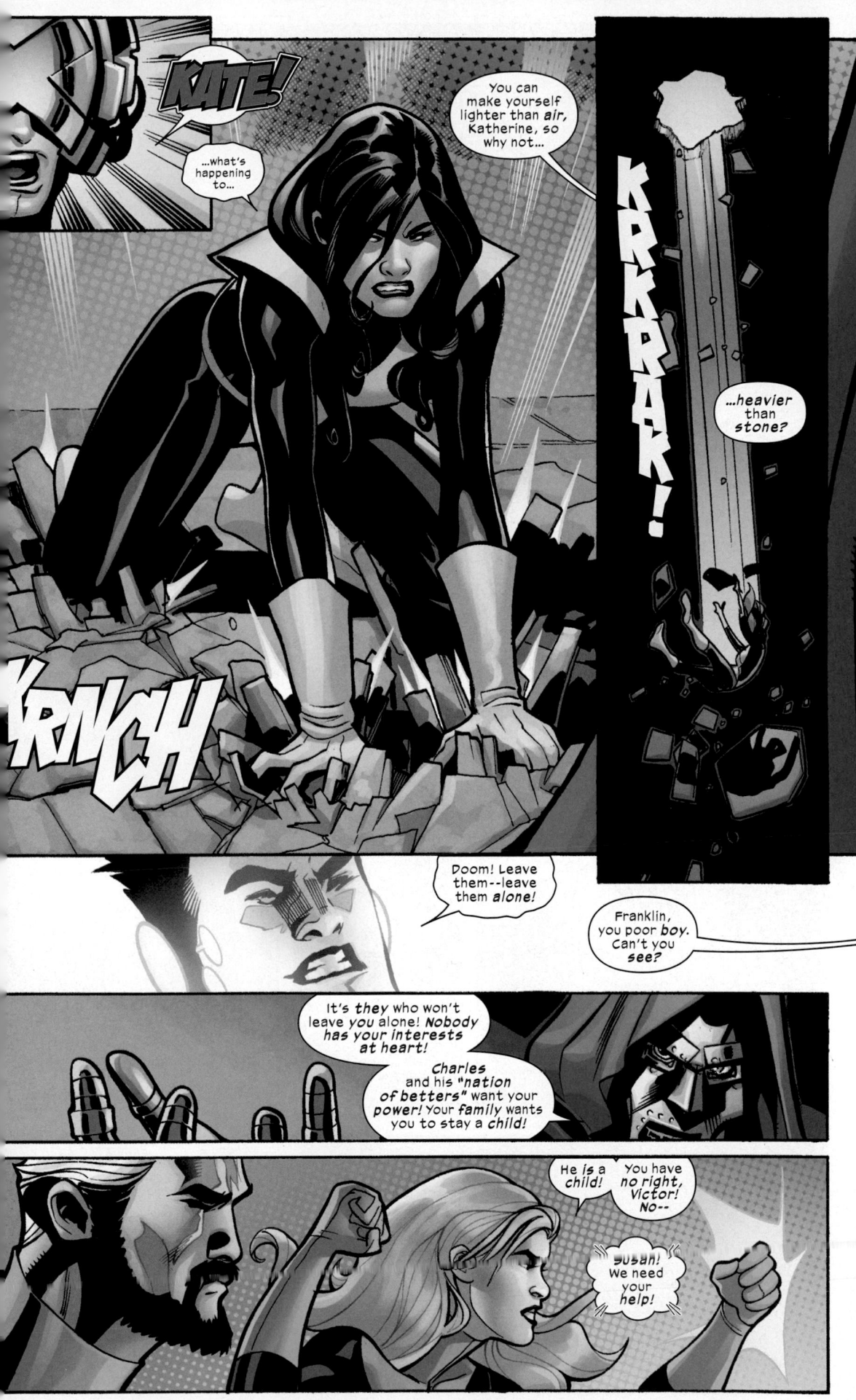

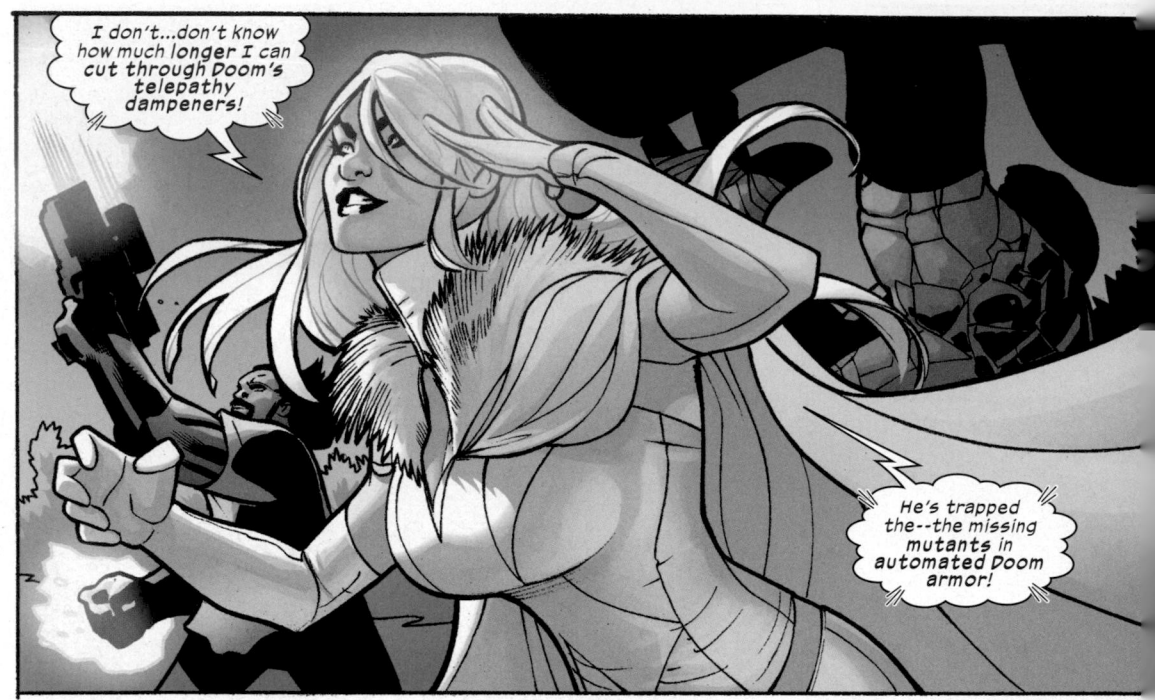

I don't...don't know how much longer I can cut through Doom's telepathy dampeners!

He's trapped the--the missing mutants in automated Doom armor!

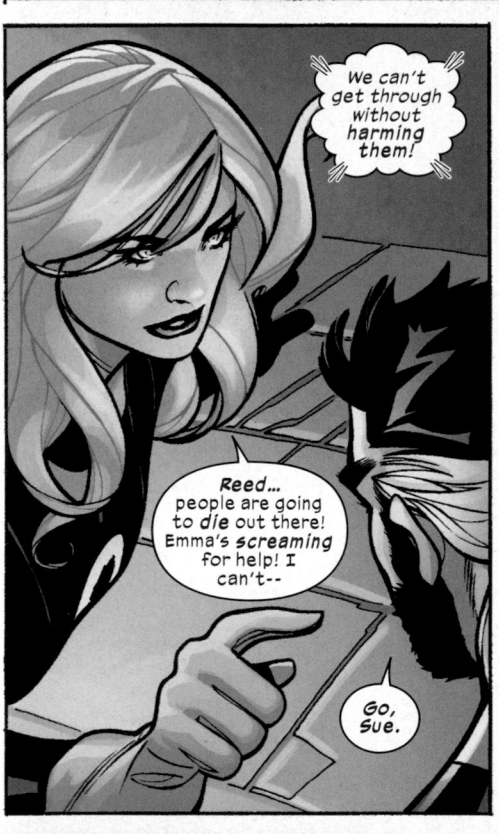

We can't get through without harming them!

Reed... people are going to die out there! Emma's screaming for help! I can't--

Go, Sue.

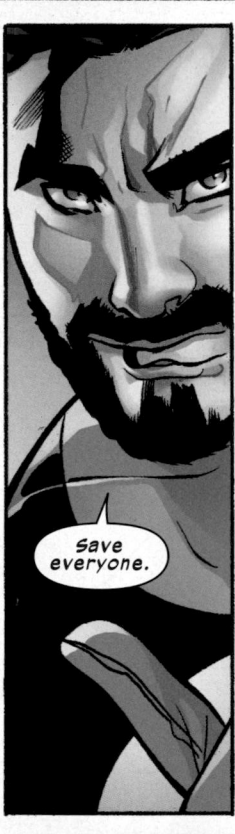

Save everyone.

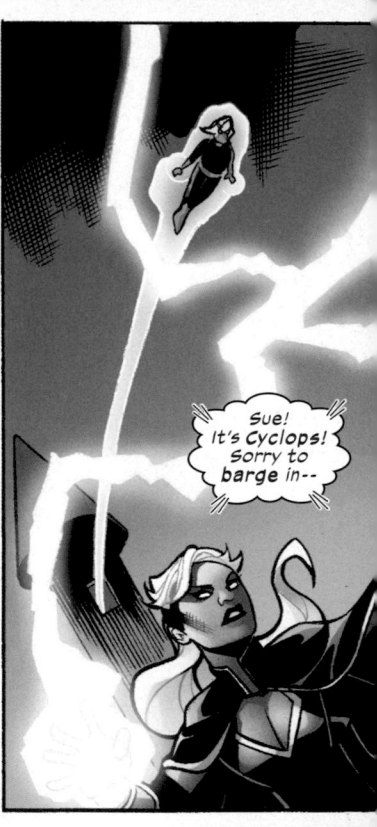

Sue! It's Cyclops! Sorry to barge in--

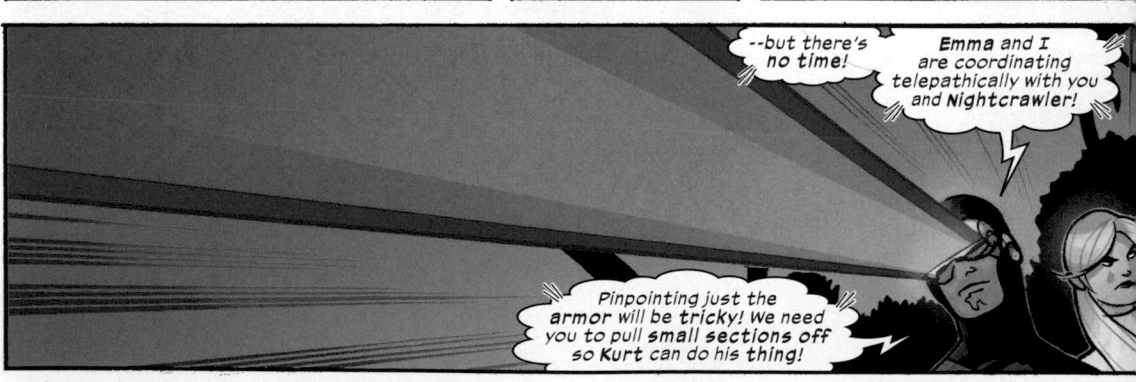

--but there's no time!

Emma and I are coordinating telepathically with you and Nightcrawler!

Pinpointing just the armor will be tricky! We need you to pull small sections off so Kurt can do his thing!

To get this right, ou'll need to t us direct oth of you before--
Just do it.
BAMF
Isn't it grand...
...when we--
BAMF
--come together--
BAMF
BAMF
--to fight evil?

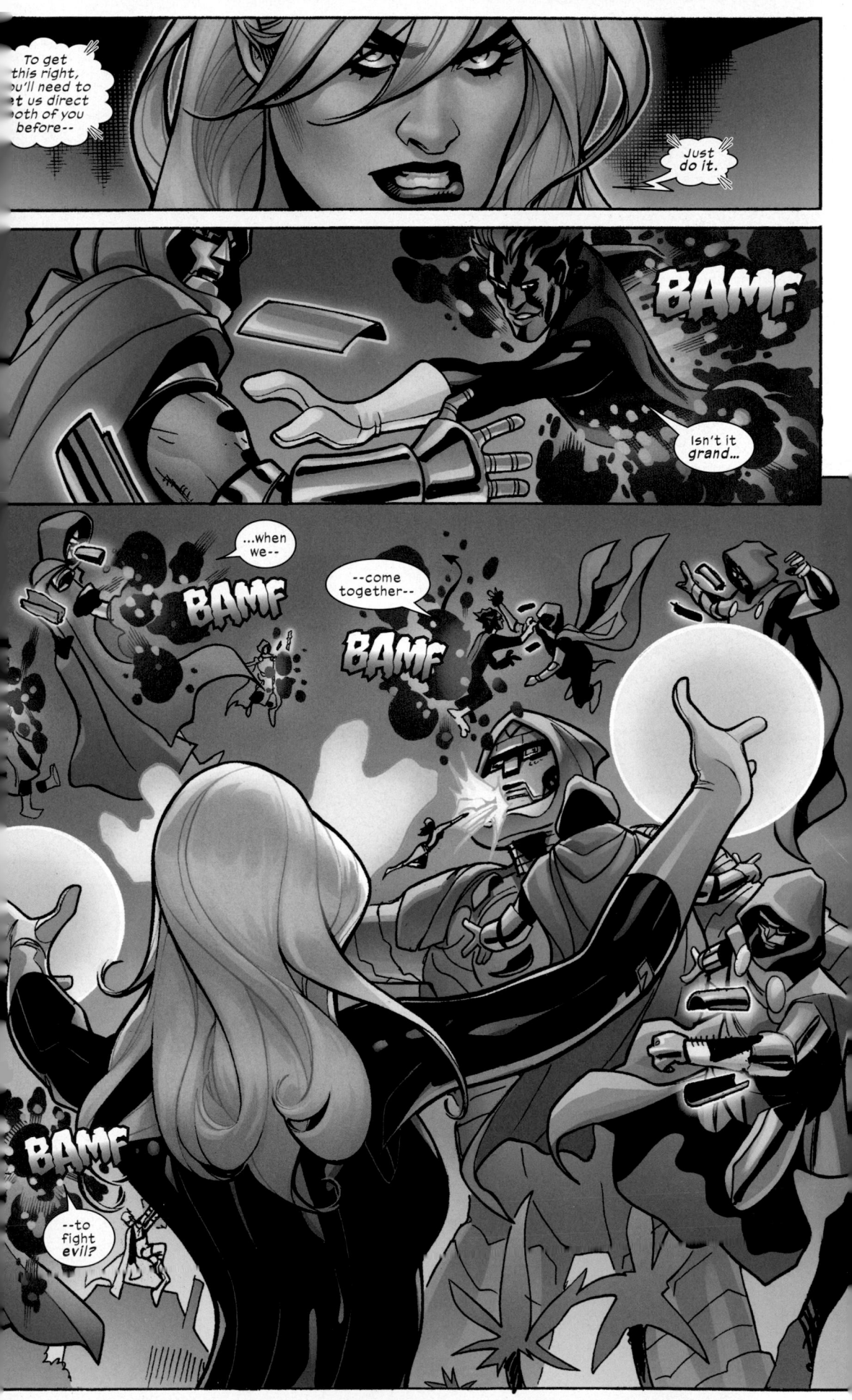

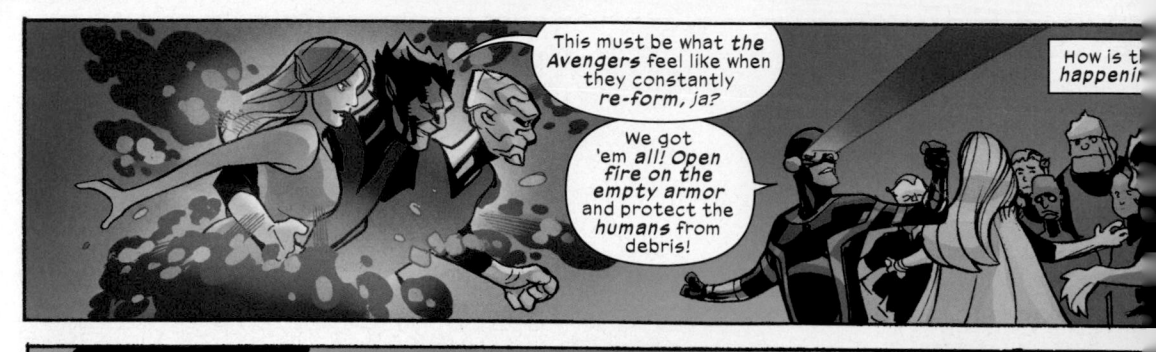

This must be what *the Avengers* feel like when they constantly re-form, ja?

We got 'em *all! Open fire* on the *empty* armor and protect the *humans* from debris!

How is t happenir

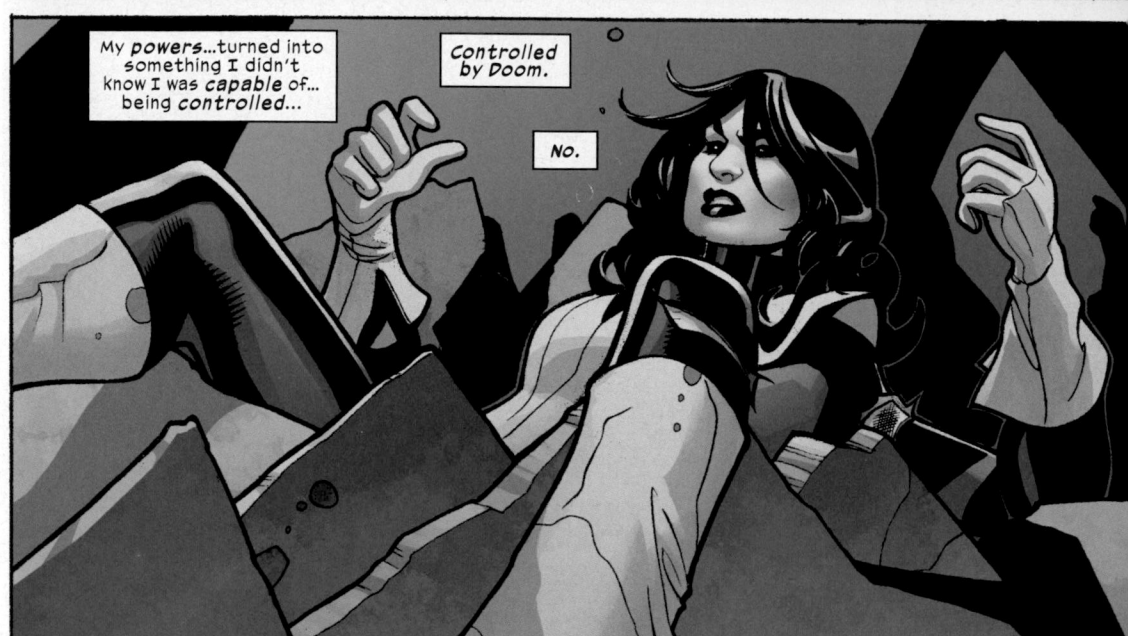

My *powers*...turned into something I didn't know I was *capable* of... being *controlled*...

Controlled by Doom.

NO.

I won't let him.

And I won't let him control *Franklin.*

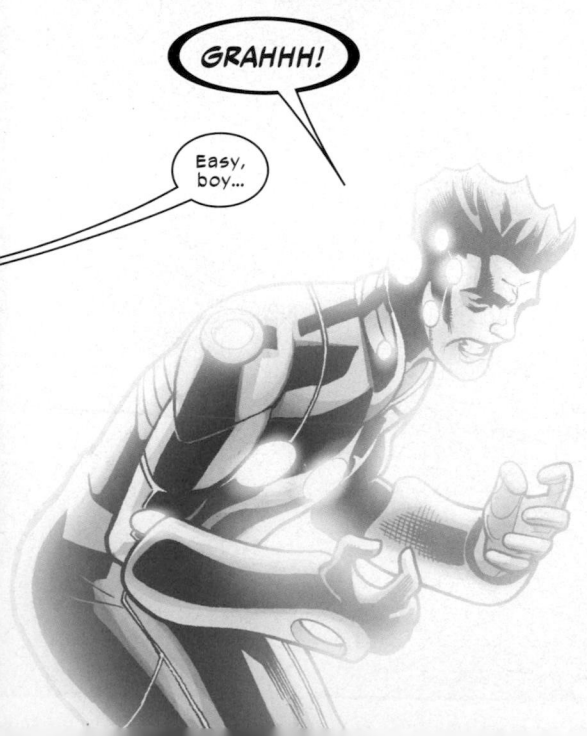

GRAHHH!

Easy, boy...

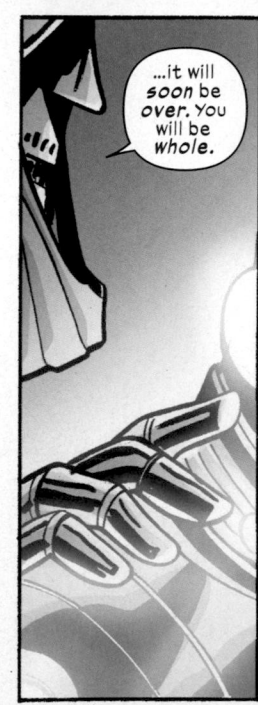

...it will *soon* be *over.* You will be *whole.*

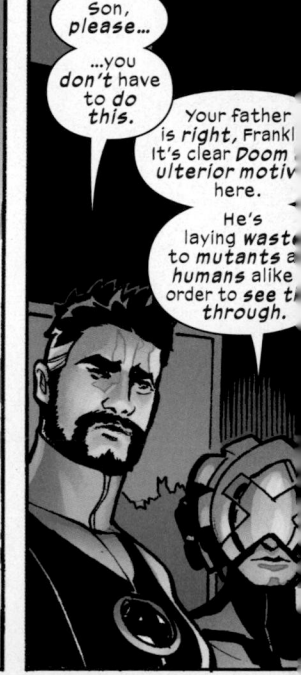

Son, please...

...you *don't* have to *do* this.

Your father is *right*, Frankl It's clear *Doom* ulterior *motiv* here.

He's laying *wast* to *mutants* a *humans* alike order to *see t* through.

people are...
U-Uncle Doom...s-stop ...stop the p-process...
No! I refuse to stop! You don't see what you can become! What we can--
You're just like the rest of them...
...you don't care about anyone's autonomy, Doom.
Grah!
FZZT!
...she went out and h-helped everyone...
...people are in t-trouble... I'm...
...I want to go with her...

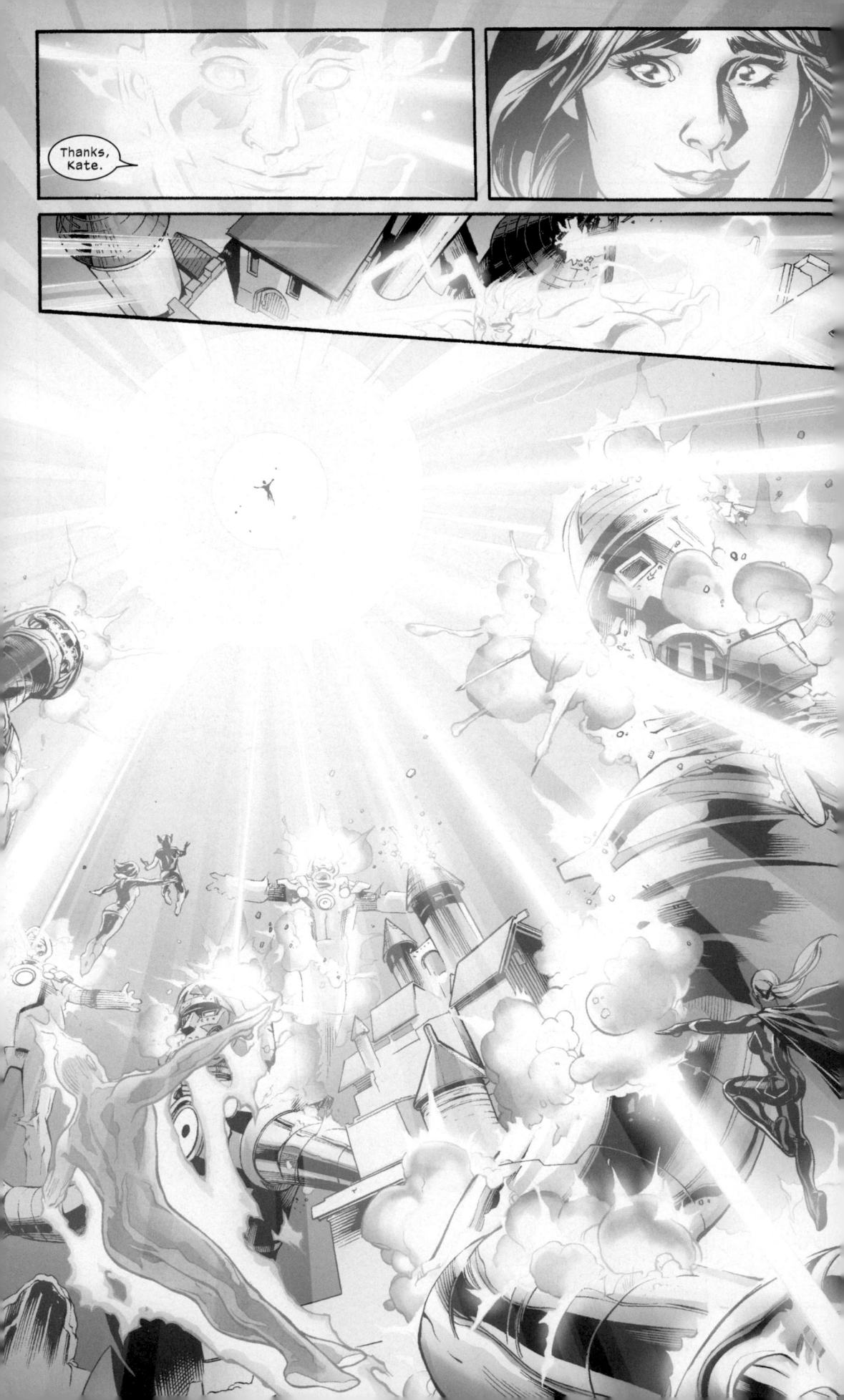

Well, ah'll be...
Wh--Did we... did we save everyone...?
No, Franklin...
...you did.

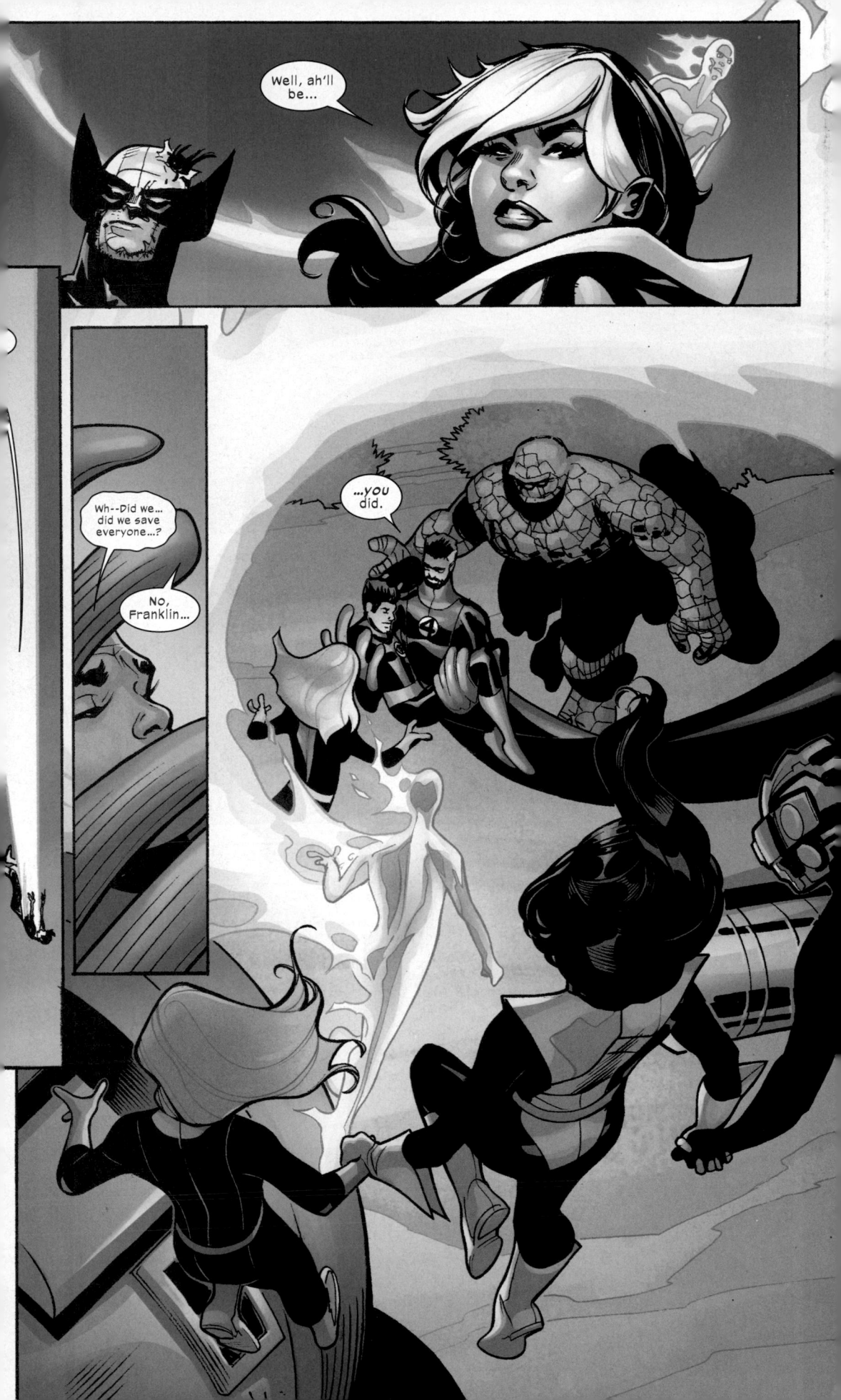

Oh, my darling... you're okay...
"Okay"?
He is far from okay!
The boy may be irreparably damaged from halting Doom's immaculate process!
Franklin Richards is as foolhardy as his father!
You've got a lot of nerve, Doom.
Faux Sentinels? The death of a mutant?! You will pay dearly--
He will...
...but not today, I suspect.
You have driven Doom from Latverian soil with your attacks. The number of laws you have broken with your intolerable superiority is astonishing.
You ignored my conditions, trespassing among my citizens!
You murdered a Latverian mutant whom I was protecting!
And do not deign to draw comparisons to palt speciest Sentinels My Latviathans ma no distinction betwe mutant and humar They protect Latveria!

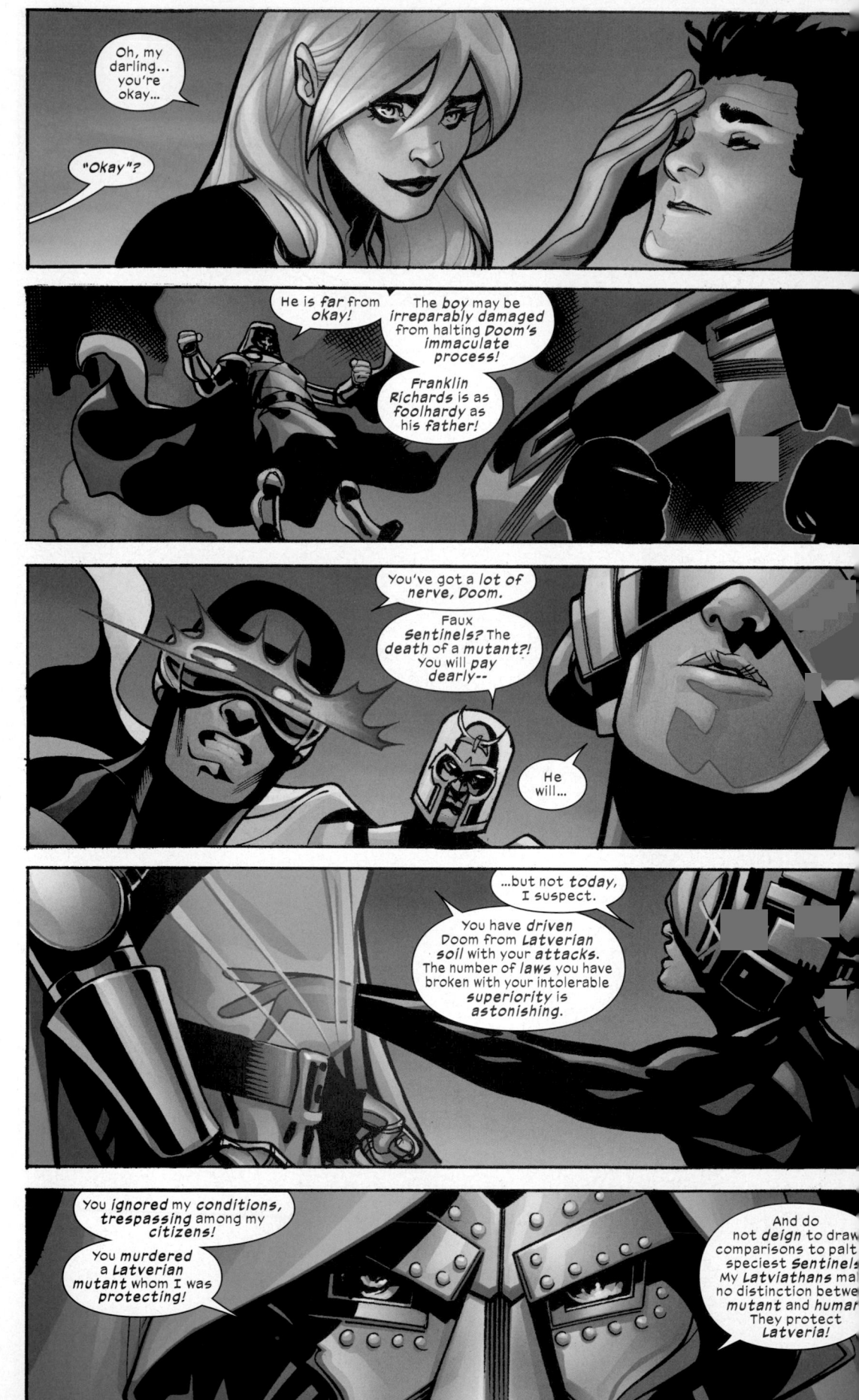

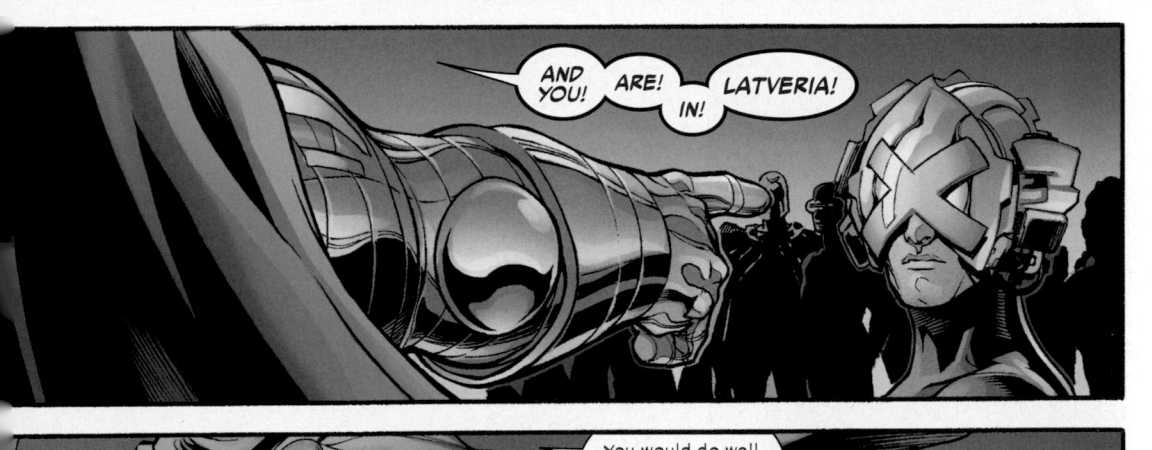

AND YOU! ARE! IN! LATVERIA!

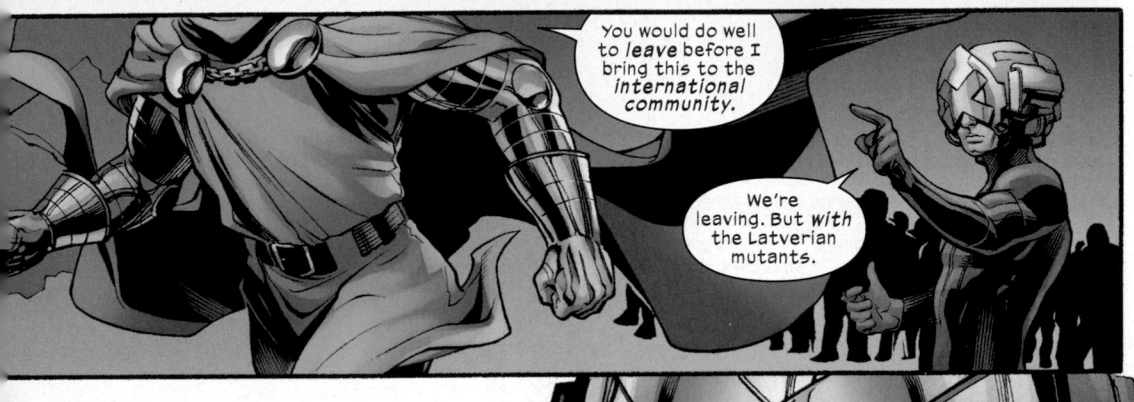

You would do well to *leave* before I bring this to the *international community.*

We're leaving. But *with* the Latverian mutants.

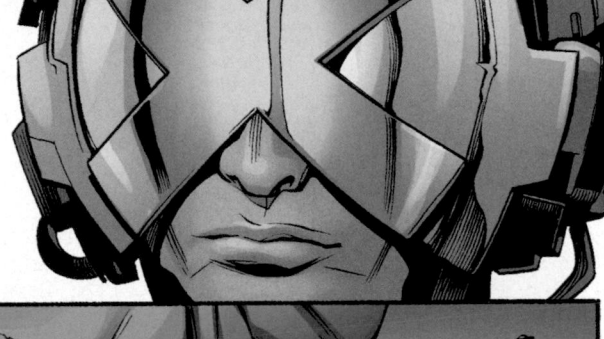

our story as hollow the *armor* u trapped ose poor souls in.

Their minds have been *tampered* with, their freedoms *limited.*

You *planned* this. That death is on *your* hands. But there will be *no more.*

They are Krakoan.

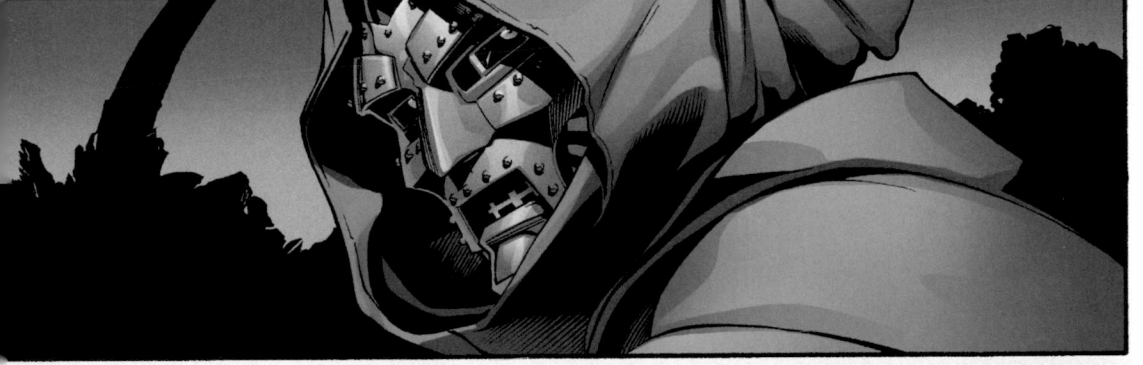

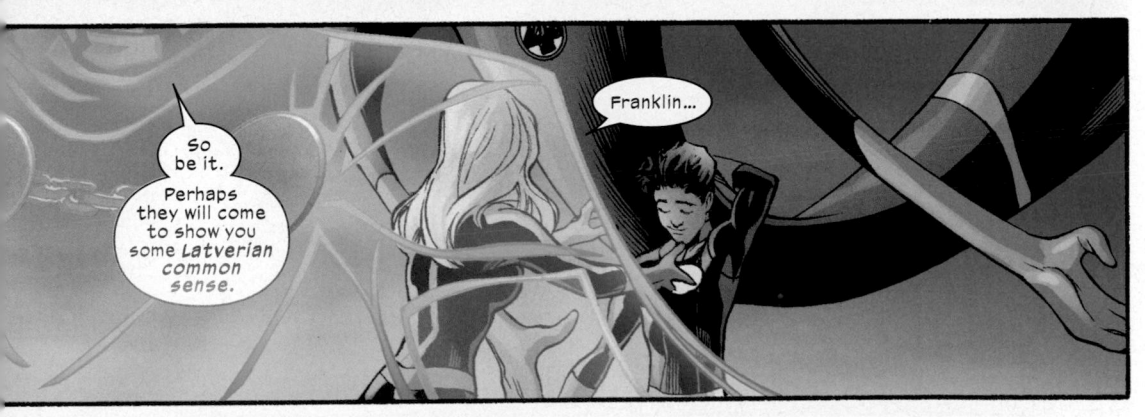

So be it. Perhaps they will come to show you some *Latverian common* sense.

Franklin...

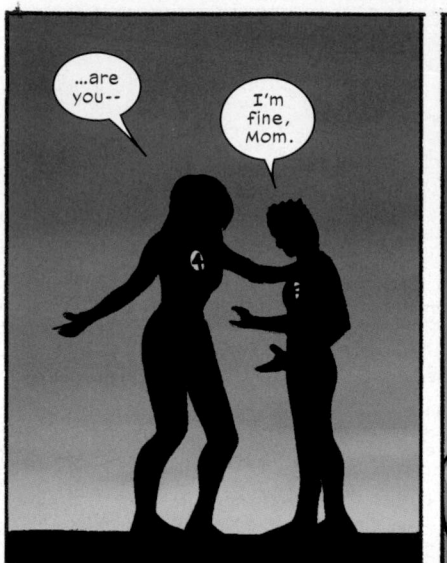

...are
you--

I'm
fine,
Mom.

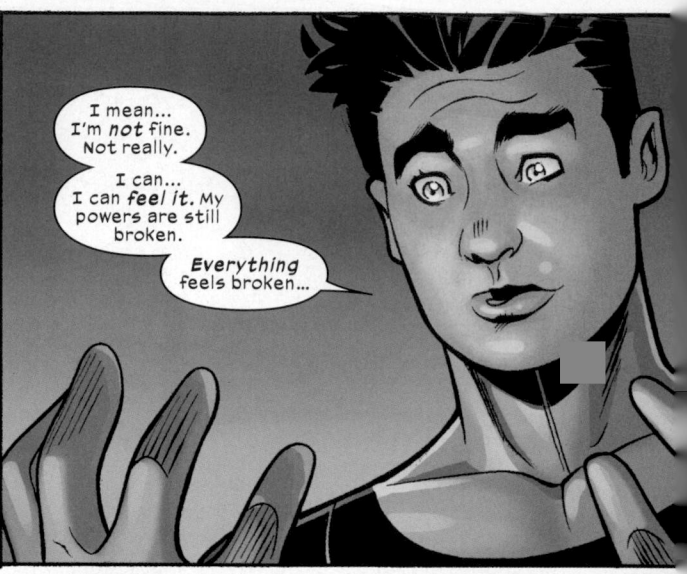

I mean...
I'm *not* fine.
Not really.

I can...
I can *feel it*. My
powers are still
broken.

Everything
feels broken...

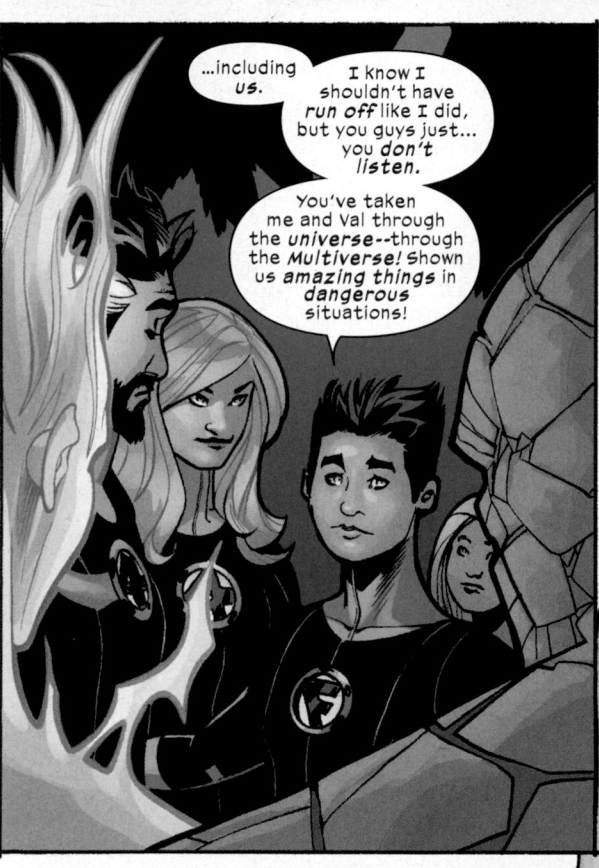

...including
us.

I know I
shouldn't have
run off like I did,
but you guys just...
you *don't*
listen.

You've taken
me and Val through
the *universe*--through
the *Multiverse!* Shown
us *amazing things* in
dangerous
situations!

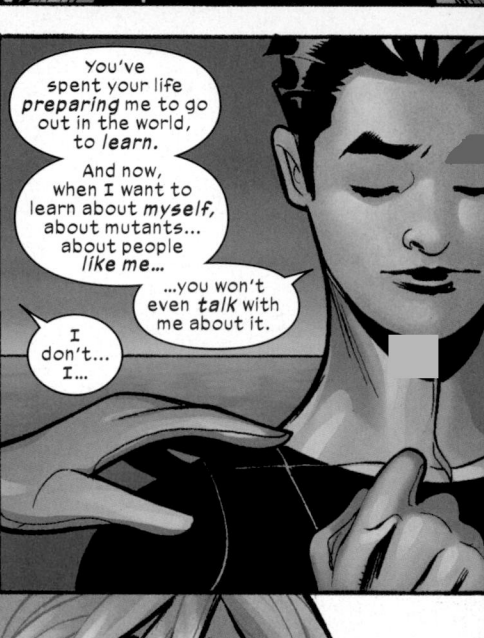

You've
spent your life
preparing me to go
out in the world,
to *learn.*

And now,
when I want to
learn about *myself,*
about mutants...
about people
like me...

...you won't
even *talk* with
me about it.

I
don't...
I...

...you
father and
so proud c
Of the *man*
becoming
just..

It's hard fc
me to *accept*
you're not our
boy anymore

Charles...
I know you've
dedicated your *life* to
helping young mutants.
Teaching is in your
blood, *protecting*
mutants is who
you *are*...

I'm sorry
I reacted the way
I did. I may not...
agree with some of the
ways you're bringing
your vision into
this world...

...but you
were here *freeing*
your people, *saving*
the island's humans
from *Doom's*
recklessness...

...being
heroes.

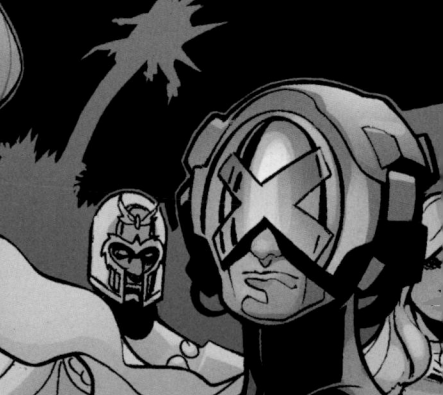

nd I...could
ve been more
tful in offering
nklin a home
on Krakoa.

We see your concerns,
Susan. Believe me, we do. And
we know your home is a *fine* one
for a young mutant. But *Krakoa* is
an *opportunity* for him to learn
about his people. About
his *future*.

With our
gates he would
only be steps
away.

I love you guys. You've
been *preparing* me
for this my entire
life. I just--

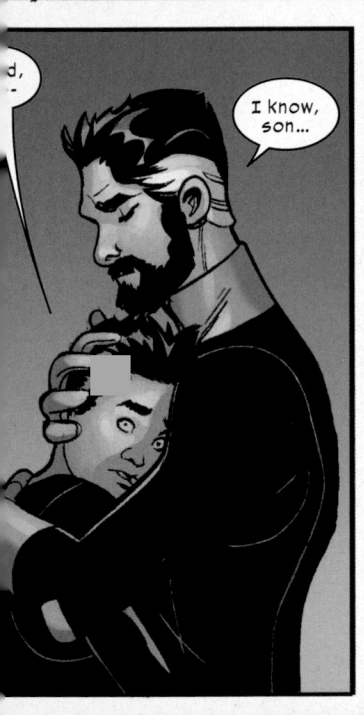

I know,
son...

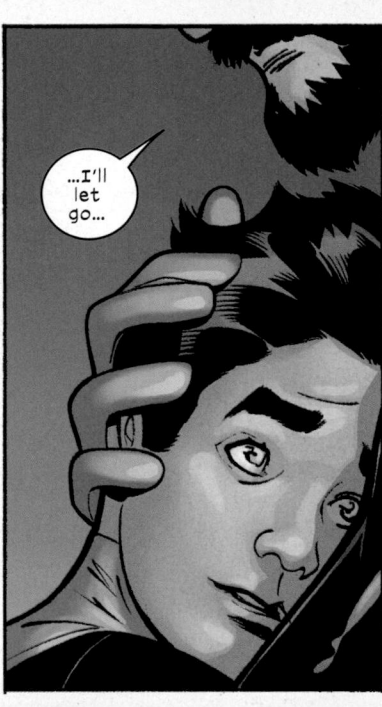

...I'll
let
go...

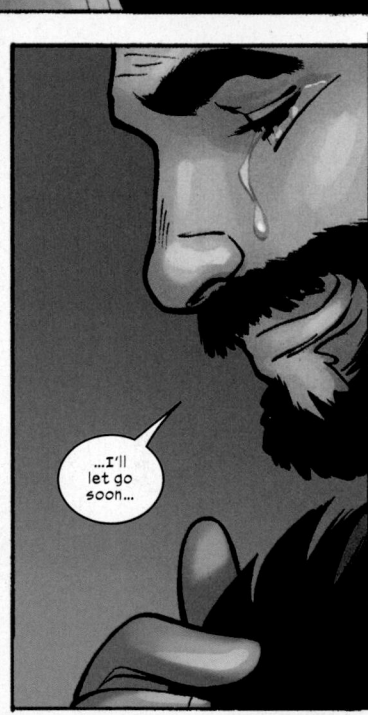

...I'll
let go
soon...

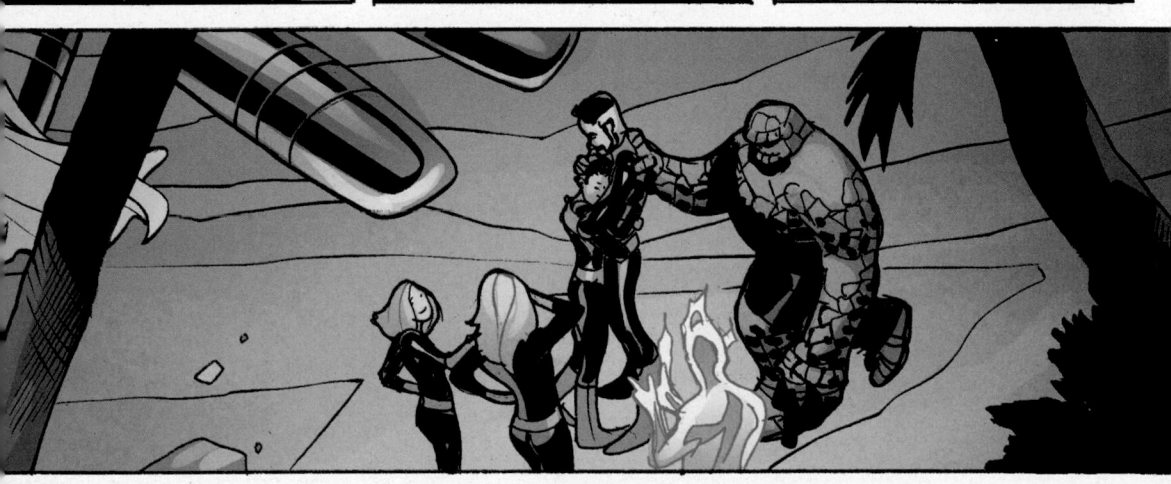

REED RICHARDS

Entry 662041 KRAKOAN GATES

While I can't pinpoint a total, Krakoan gates have emerged in most of the major cities on Earth. They allow instantaneous travel between gates and appear to be extremely resilient. They're remarkable on every level, and I can't help but wonder how these gates could change the world if Krako would allow the other 99.9% of th world's population--humans--to us them. The drastic reduction in carbo emissions alone would entirely ha global warming.

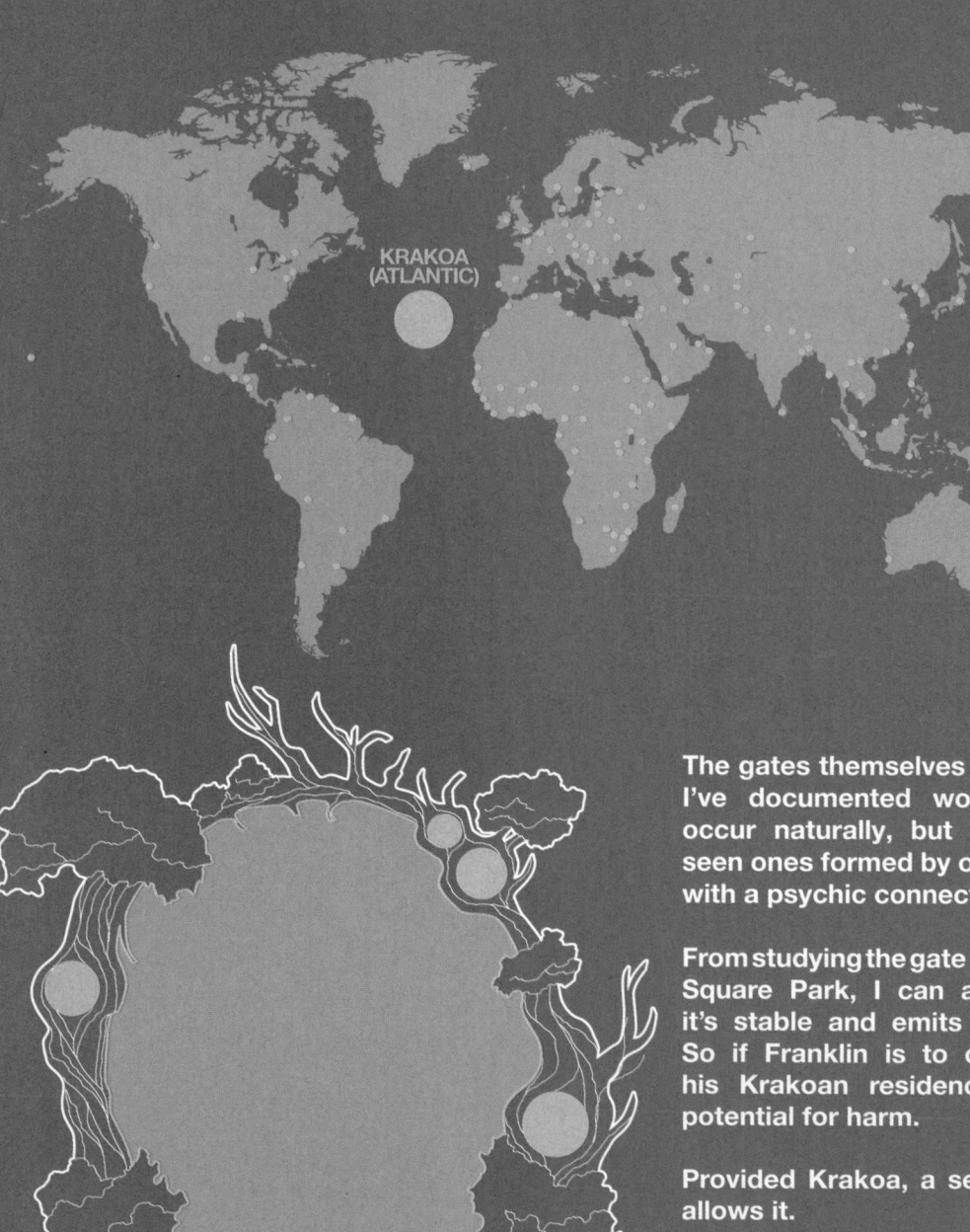

KRAKOA
(ATLANTIC)

KRAK
(PACIF

The gates themselves fascinate I've documented wormholes occur naturally, but rarely ha seen ones formed by organic ma with a psychic connection.

From studying the gate in Washing Square Park, I can ascertain it's stable and emits no radiat So if Franklin is to continue his Krakoan residency, I see potential for harm.

Provided Krakoa, a sentient isl allows it.

KRAKOAN GATE
diagram 20260-C

I *still* can't determine the cause of your overall *power loss...*

SZWAAHHH

ee
ks
er.

koa.

...but for *some* reason, when you *expend* energy on *Krakoa...*

...it doesn't *deplete* as quickly.

It's super weird, Dr. McCoy, but thanks for--

Wait! What *time* is it?

11:00.

Ah! I'm going to be *late* for *dinner!*

It's
00 in the
orning.

Not back *home* it isn't!

Would you mind...

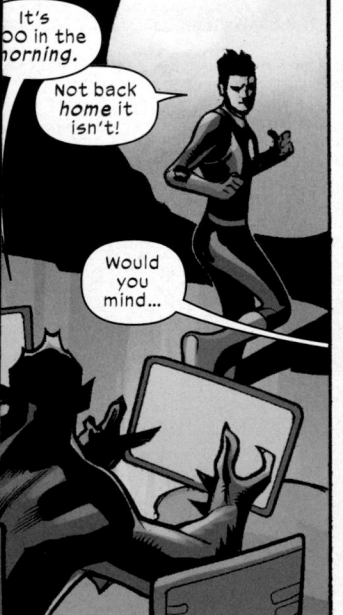

...if we *joined* you?

Erik and I have business in *New York...*

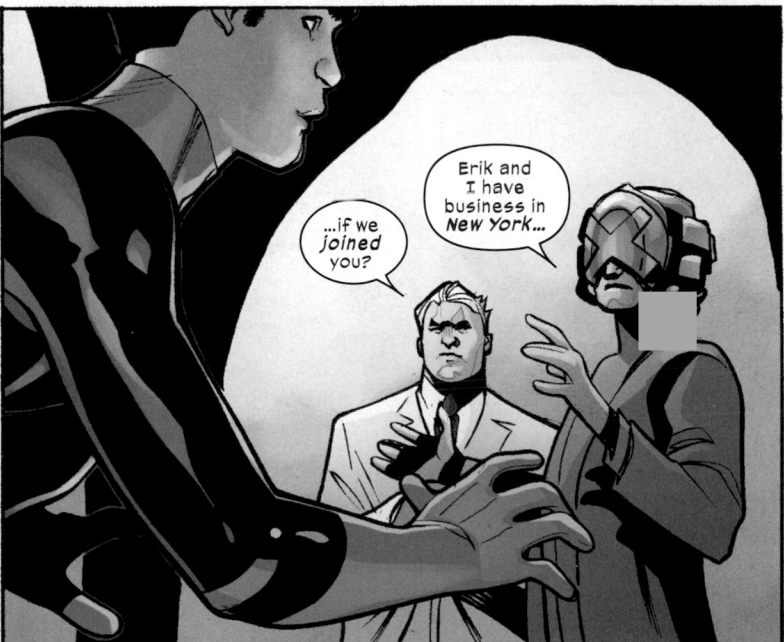

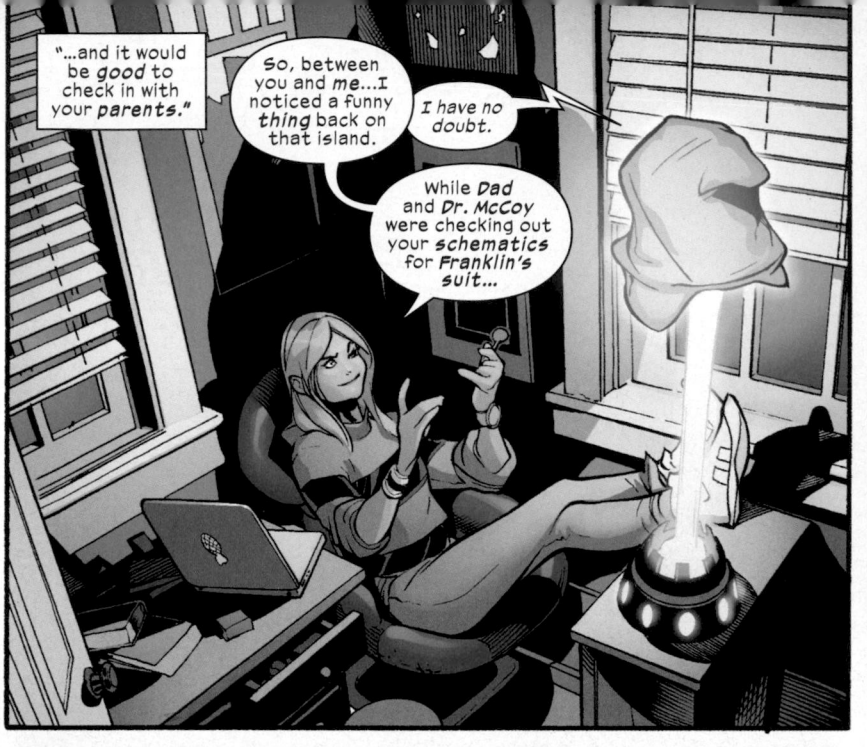

"...and it would be *good* to check in with your *parents*."

So, between you and me...I noticed a funny *thing* back on that island.

I have no doubt.

While *Dad* and *Dr. McCoy* were checking out your *schematics* for *Franklin's* suit...

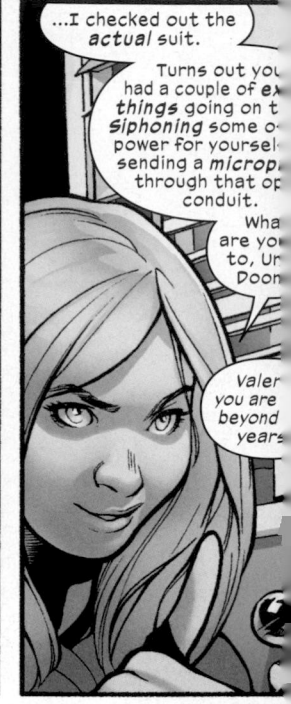

...I checked out the *actual* suit.

Turns out you had a couple of *ex* things going on t siphoning some o power for yoursel sending a *microp* through that o conduit.

Wha are yo to, Ur Doon

Valer you are beyond years

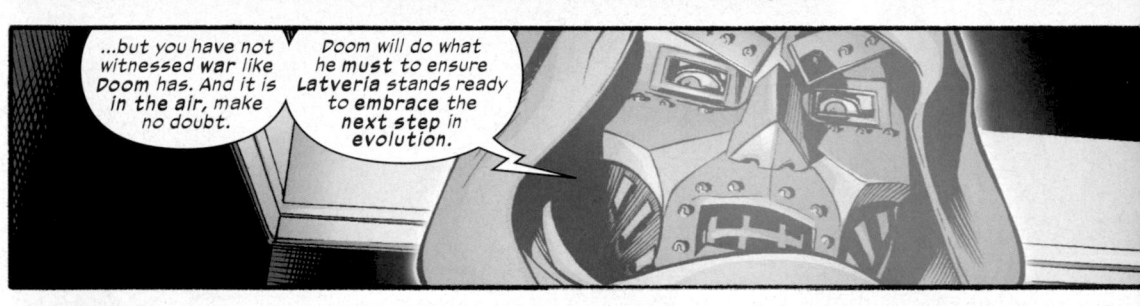

...but you have not witnessed *war* like *Doom* has. And it is *in the air*, make no doubt.

Doom will do what he *must* to ensure Latveria stands ready to *embrace* the *next step* in *evolution*.

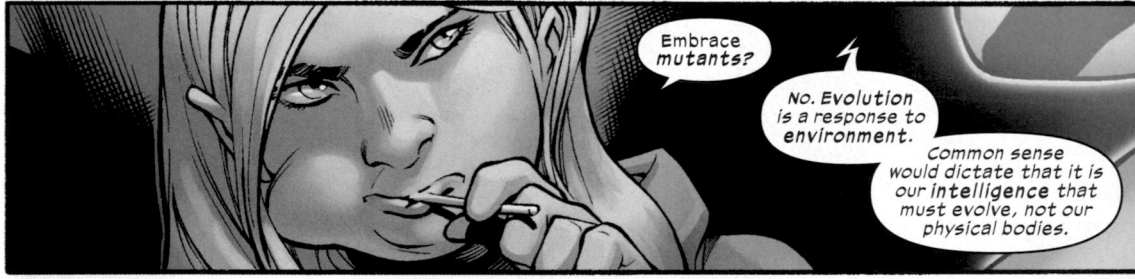

Embrace *mutants?*

No. Evolution is a response to *environment.*

Common sense would dictate that it is our *intelligence* that must evolve, not our *physical bodies.*

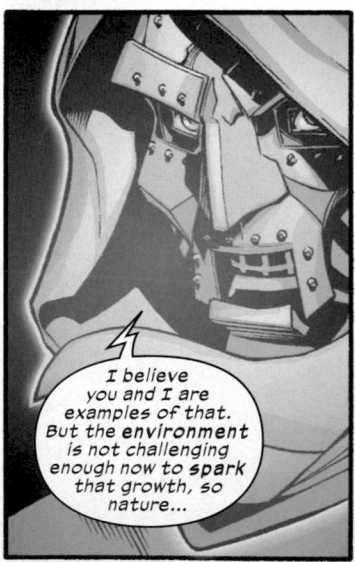

I believe you and I are examples of that. But the *environment* is not challenging enough now to *spark* that growth, so nature...

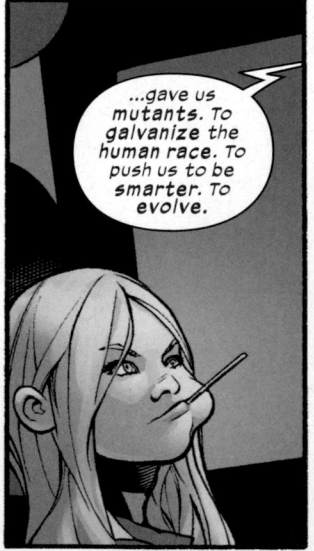

...gave us *mutants.* To galvanize the human race. To push us to be *smarter.* To *evolve.*

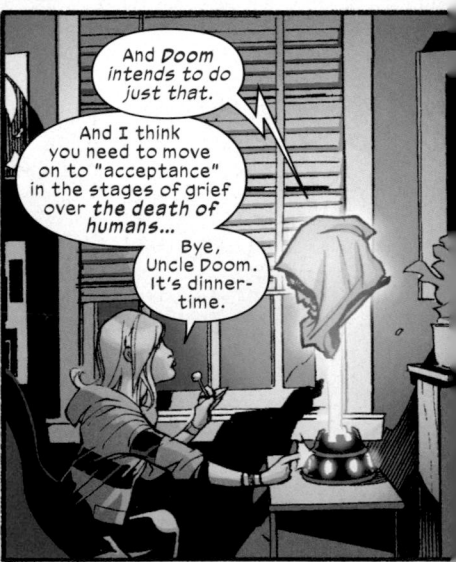

And *Doom* intends to do just that.

And I think you need to move on to "acceptance" in the stages of grief over *the death of humans...*

Bye, Uncle Doom. It's dinner-time.

Well, look what the *cat* dragged in...

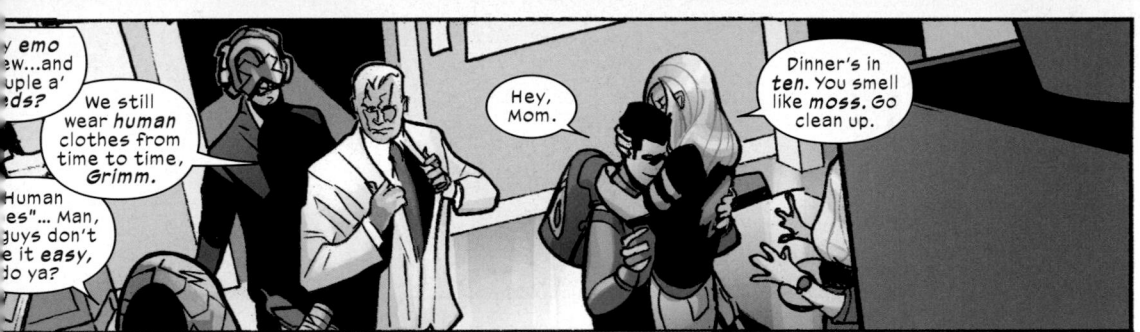

...y emo
ew...and
uple a'
ds?

We still wear *human* clothes from time to time, *Grimm*.

Human
es"... Man,
guys don't
e it *easy*,
do ya?

Hey, Mom.

Dinner's in *ten*. You smell like *moss*. Go clean up.

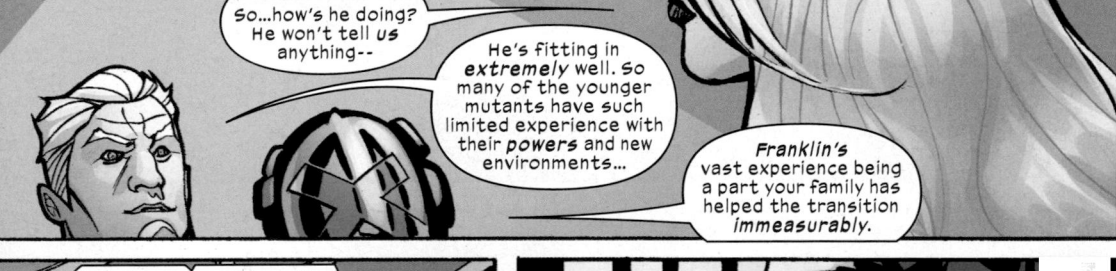

So...how's he doing? He won't tell *us* anything--

He's fitting in *extremely* well. So many of the younger mutants have such limited experience with their *powers* and new environments...

Franklin's vast experience being a part your family has helped the transition *immeasurably*.

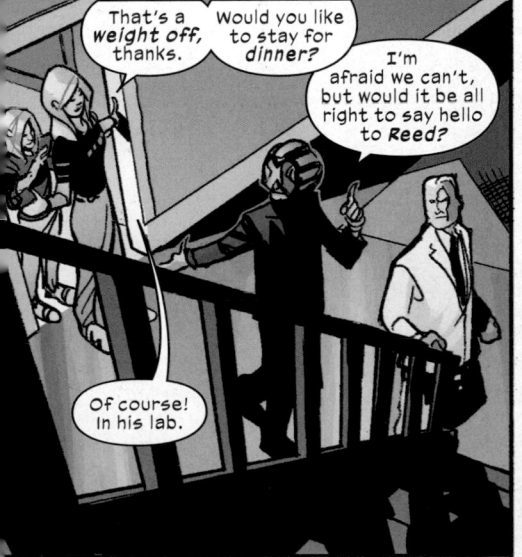

That's a *weight off*, thanks.

Would you like to stay for *dinner*?

I'm afraid we can't, but would it be all right to say hello to *Reed*?

Of course! In his lab.

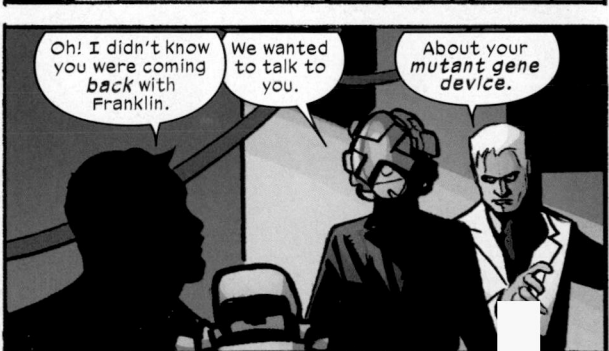

Johnny, I told you, I'd be down when I'm--

Oh! I didn't know you were coming *back* with Franklin.

We wanted to talk to you.

About your *mutant gene device*.

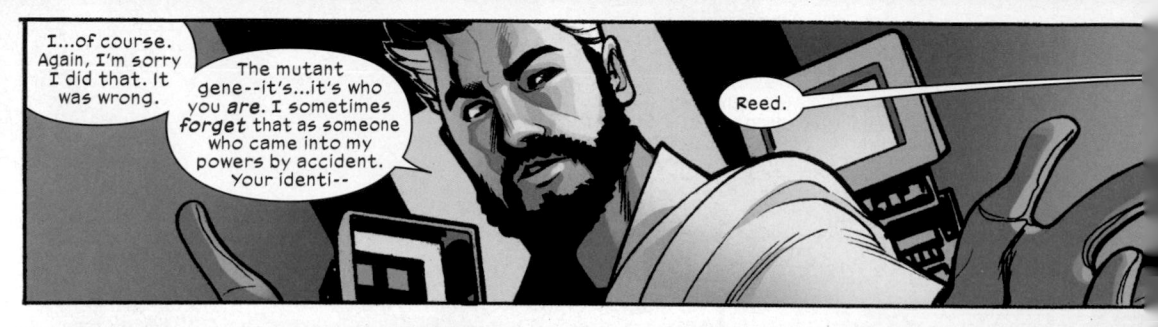

I...of course. Again, I'm sorry I did that. It was wrong.

The mutant gene--it's...it's who you *are*. I sometimes *forget* that as someone who came into my powers by accident. Your identi--

Reed.

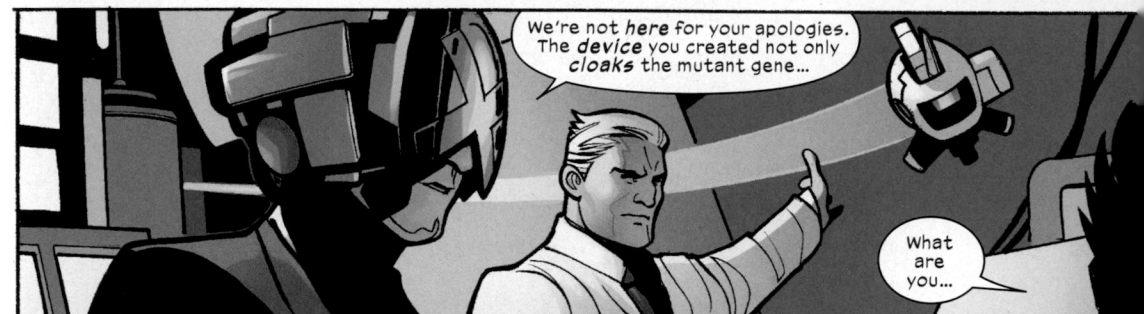

We're not *here* for your apologies. The *device* you created not only *cloaks* the mutant gene...

What are you...

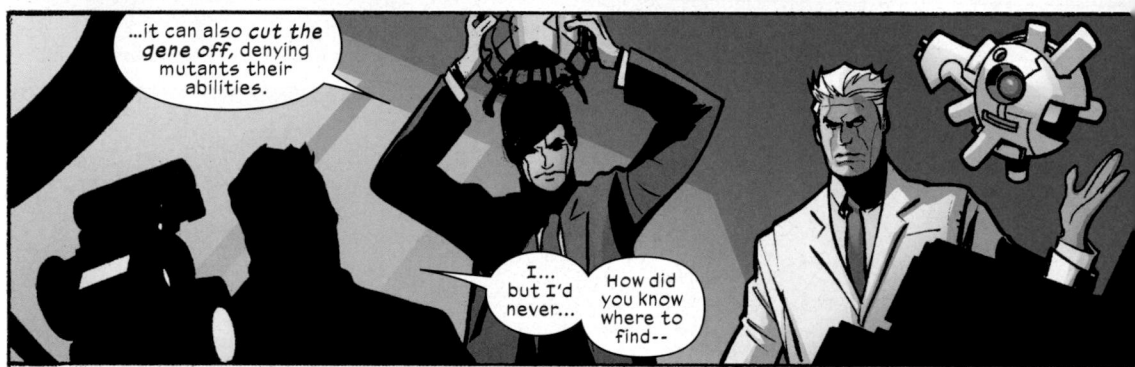

...it can also *cut the gene off,* denying mutants their abilities.

I... but I'd never...

How did you know where to find--

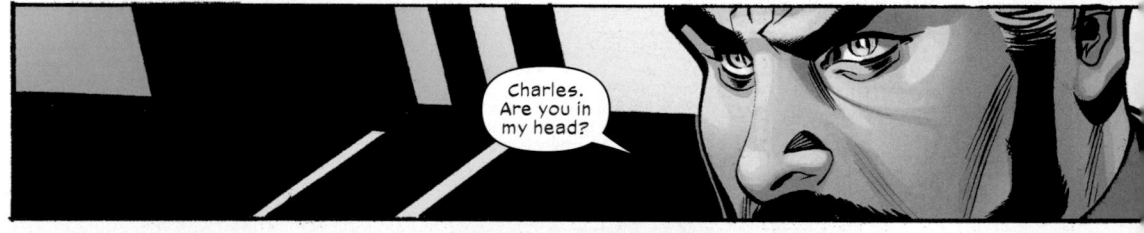

Charles. Are you in my head?

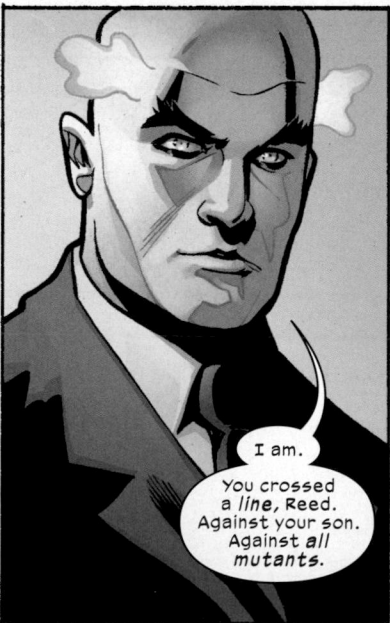

I am.

You crossed a *line,* Reed. Against your son. Against *all* mutants.

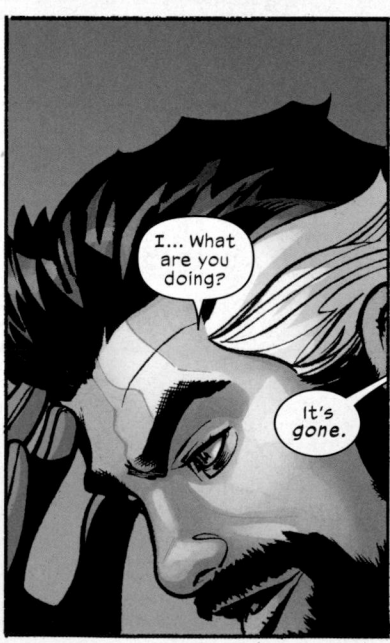

I... What are you doing?

It's *gone.*

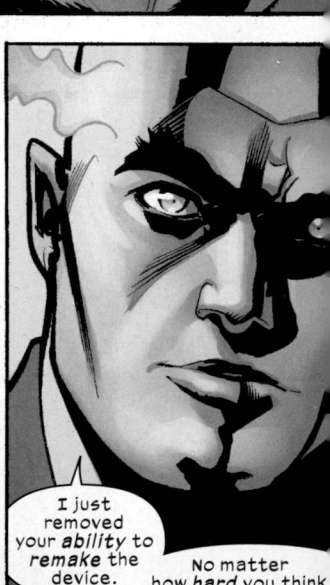

I just removed your *ability* to *remake* the device.

No matter how *hard* you think about it, tossing an turning in bed, trying to the jigsaw puzzle toget

.it will always
nissing pieces.
is mercy, Reed.
cy for a man who
't understand the
nsequences of
nis actions.
The old me,
when you and I
in the Illuminati,
d take one more
ep after this...
I would erase your memory of me doing this to you.
But that was then.
This is now.
I want you to remember.
This is not a game to us. This is our right to survive.
You don't get to do whatever you want anymore, Richards. Your wild, unchecked actions are now being checked.
KZSH!
lcome
he new
orld.

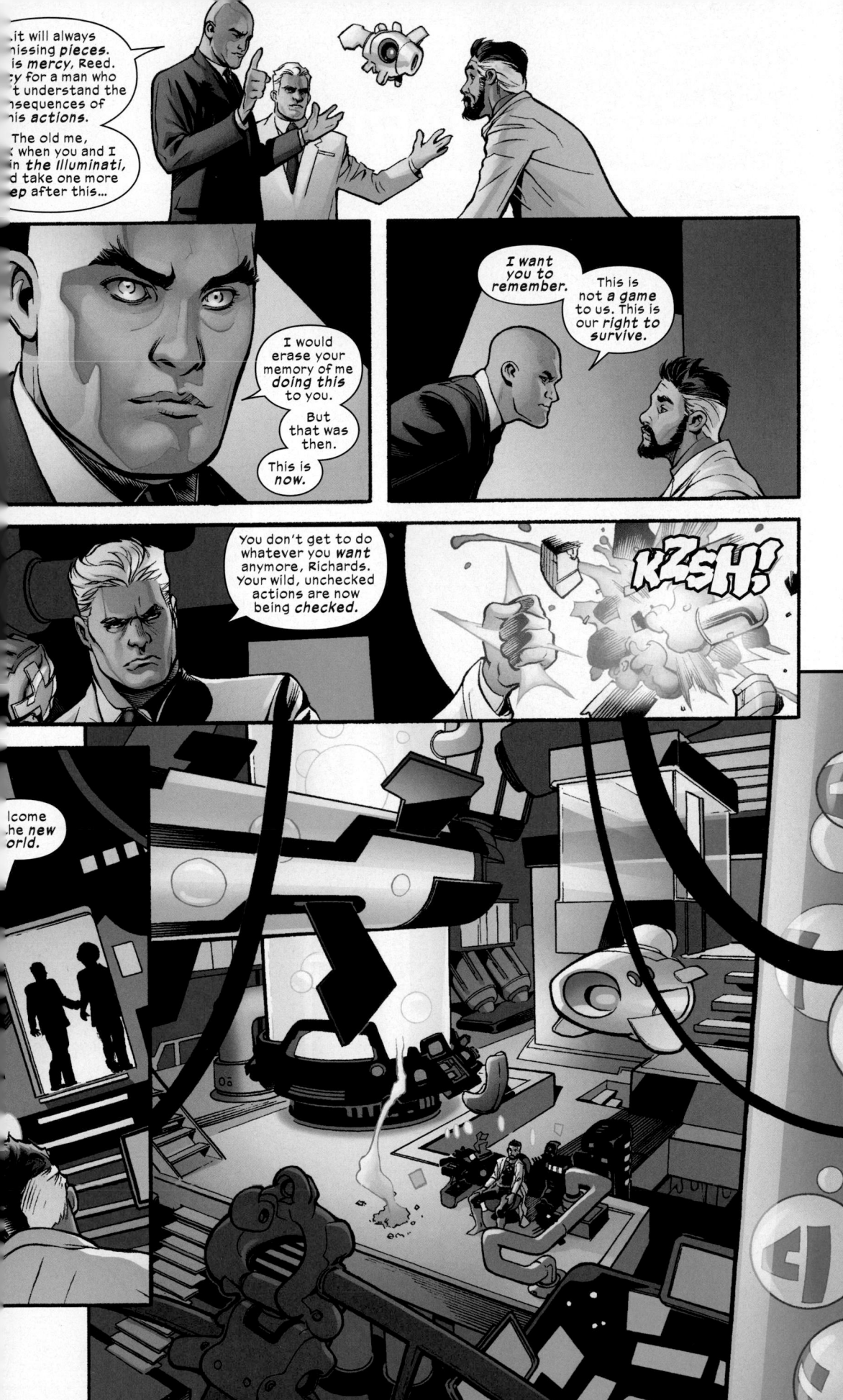

REED RICHARDS

Entry 661007 THE CODE-X

With the recent Krakoan gate appearing in New York City, coupled with Franklin's curiosity about the mutant island, I feel it's only a matter of time before he attempts to use one to gain access to Krakoa. And while I understand his interest, I don't want him to be a part of that new society until I can discern if it's safe or not. Cha Xavier's global positioning and tactics worrisome to say the least.

Because the gates seemingly just accep mutants, I've created the Code-X.

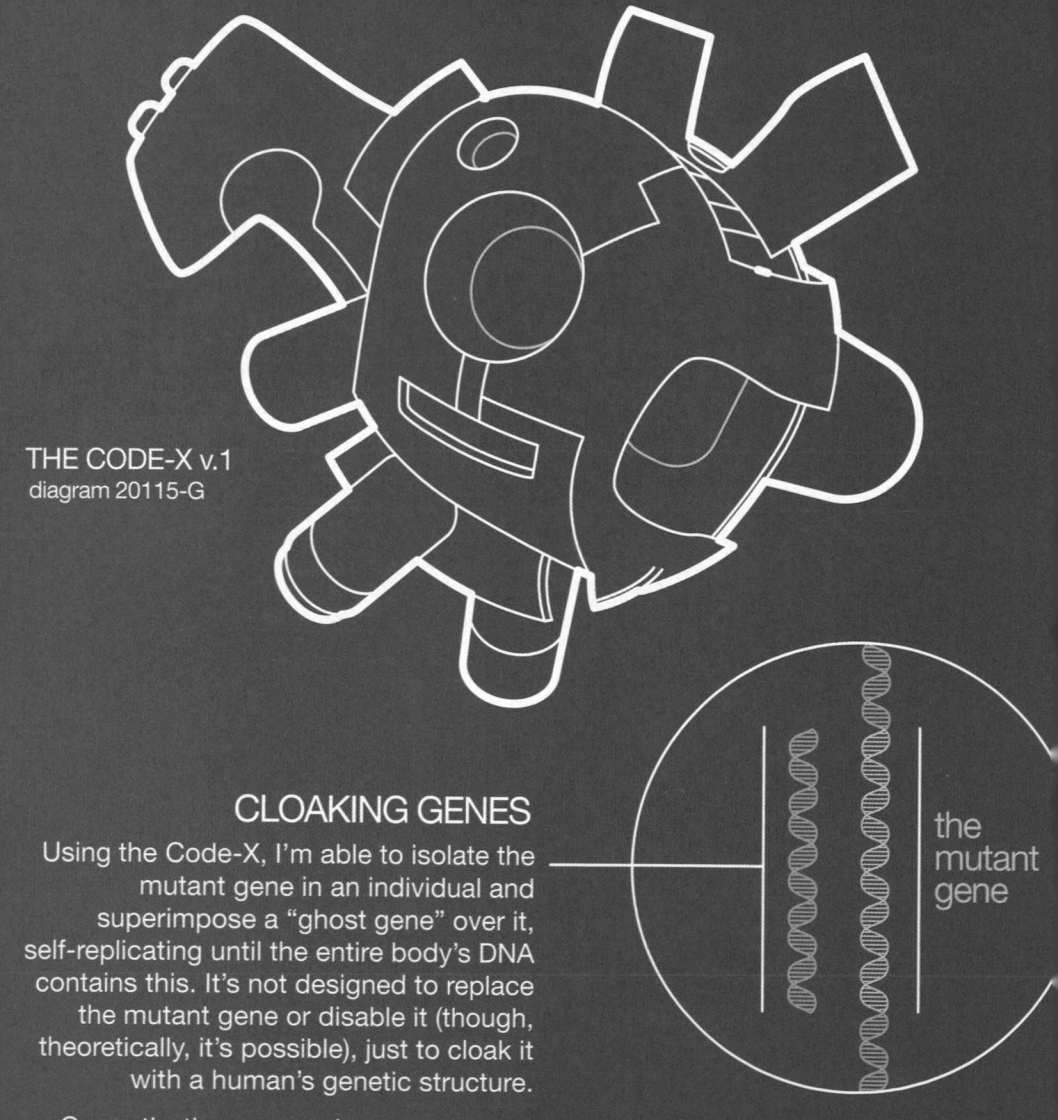

THE CODE-X v.1
diagram 20115-G

CLOAKING GENES

Using the Code-X, I'm able to isolate the mutant gene in an individual and superimpose a "ghost gene" over it, self-replicating until the entire body's DNA contains this. It's not designed to replace the mutant gene or disable it (though, theoretically, it's possible), just to cloak it with a human's genetic structure.

Currently, the process lasts roughly ten days until the "ghost gene" fades away.

the mutant gene

REED RICHARDS

Entry 661007 THE

With the recent Krakoan gate appearing n New York uriosity about the mutant island, I feel 's only a matter of time before he ttempts to use one to gain access to his nterest, I don't want him to be a part of nat new society until I can discern if it's safe or nc 's global some to say the least.

Because just accept mutants, I've created the Code-X.

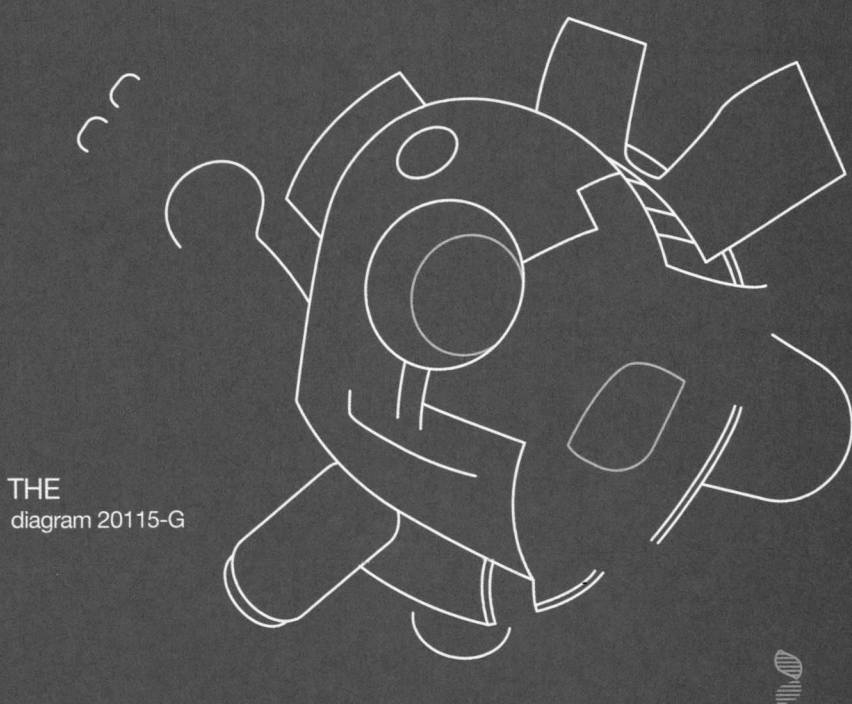

THE
diagram 20115-G

CLOAKING

able to isolate the mutant gene in an individual and superimpose it, self-replicating until the entire body's DNA It's the gene or disable it (though, theoretically, it's possible), just to cloak it with a genetic structure.

Currently the process lasts roughly ten days "ghost gene" fades away.

the

gene

REED RICHARDS

Entry 661007

01 FLOWERS VARIANT MEGHAN HETRICK

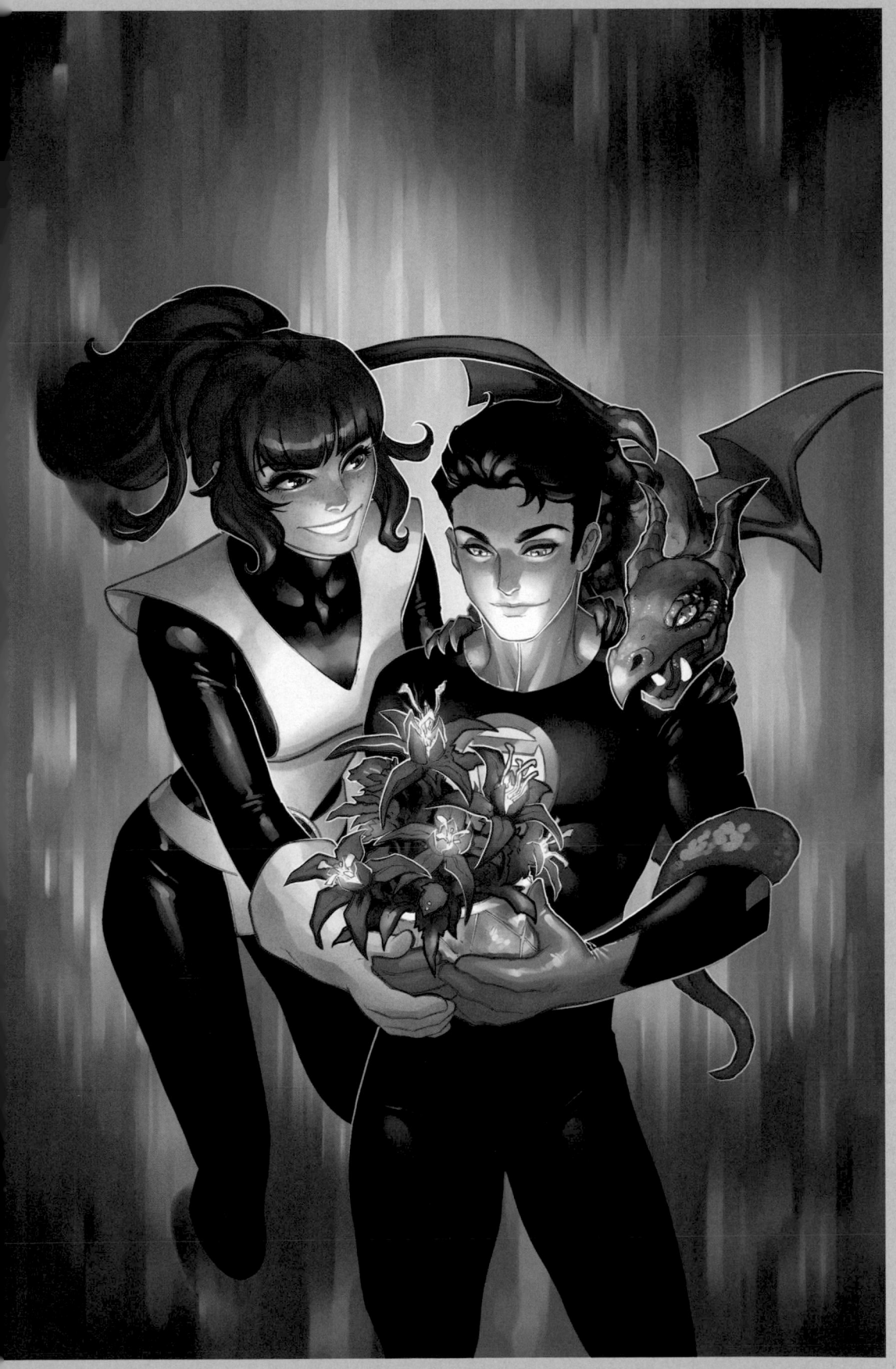

02 FLOWERS VARIANT MEGHAN HETRICK

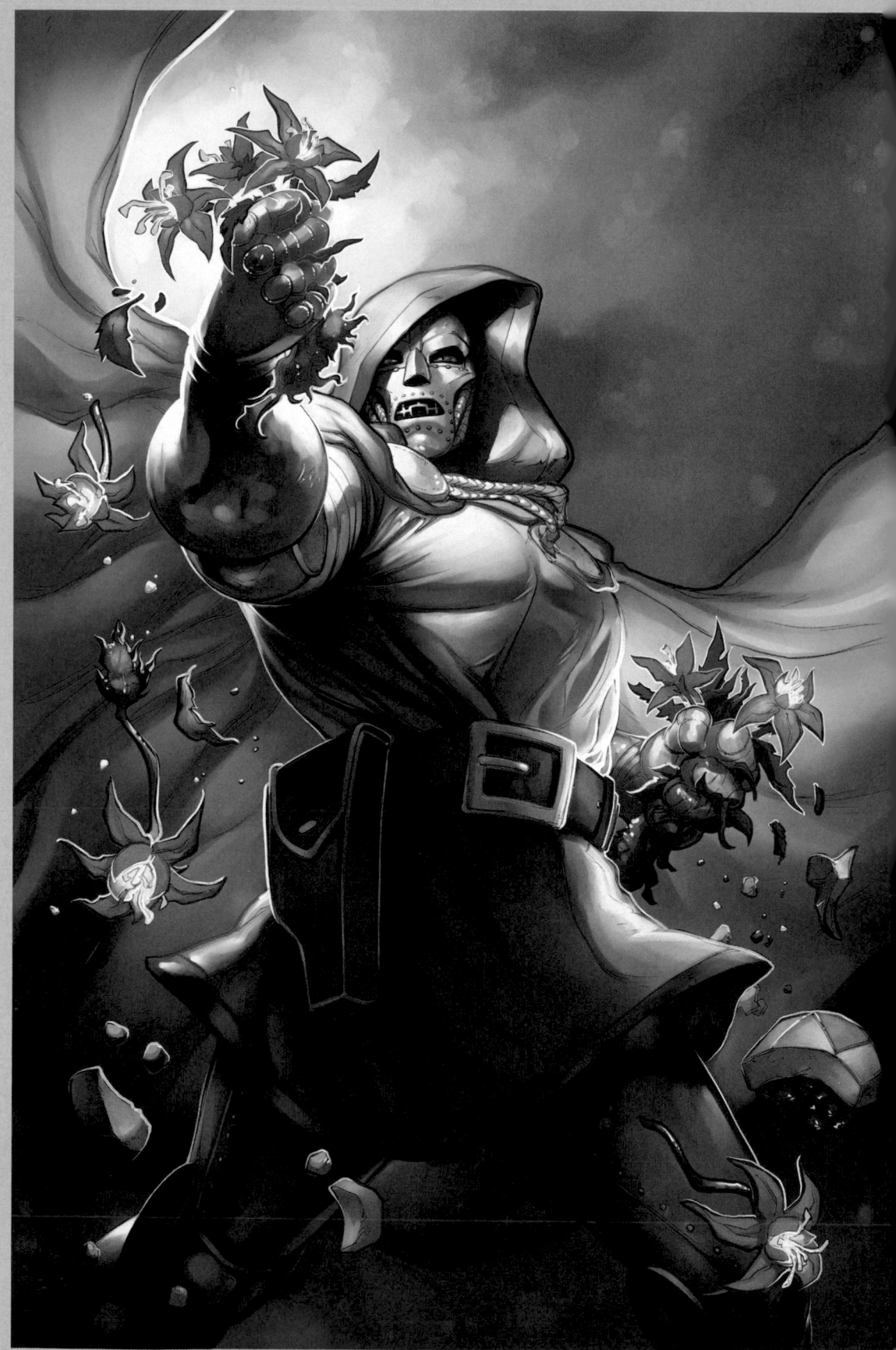

03 FLOWERS VARIANT MEGHAN HETRICK

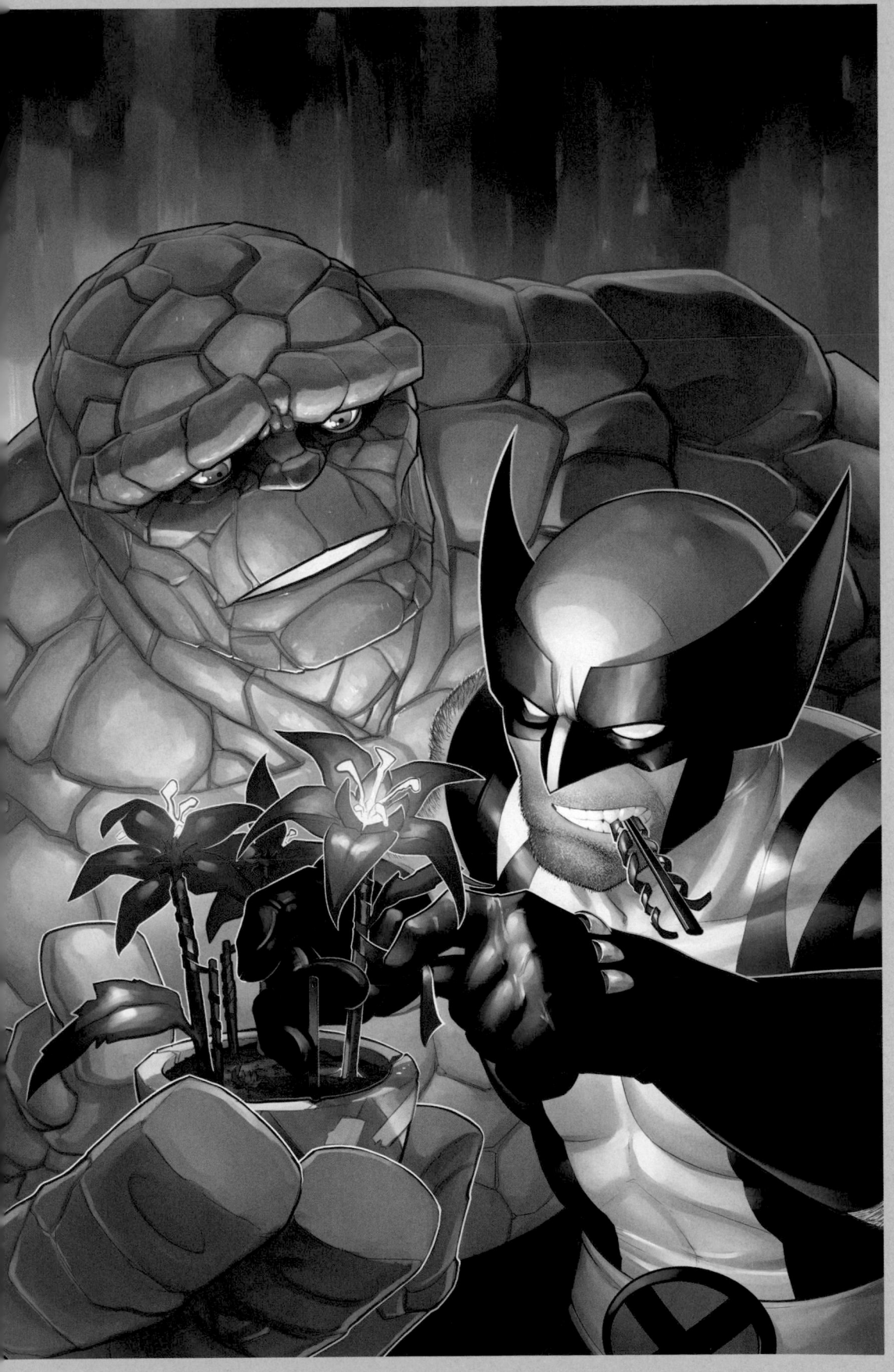

04 FLOWERS VARIANT MEGHAN HETRICK

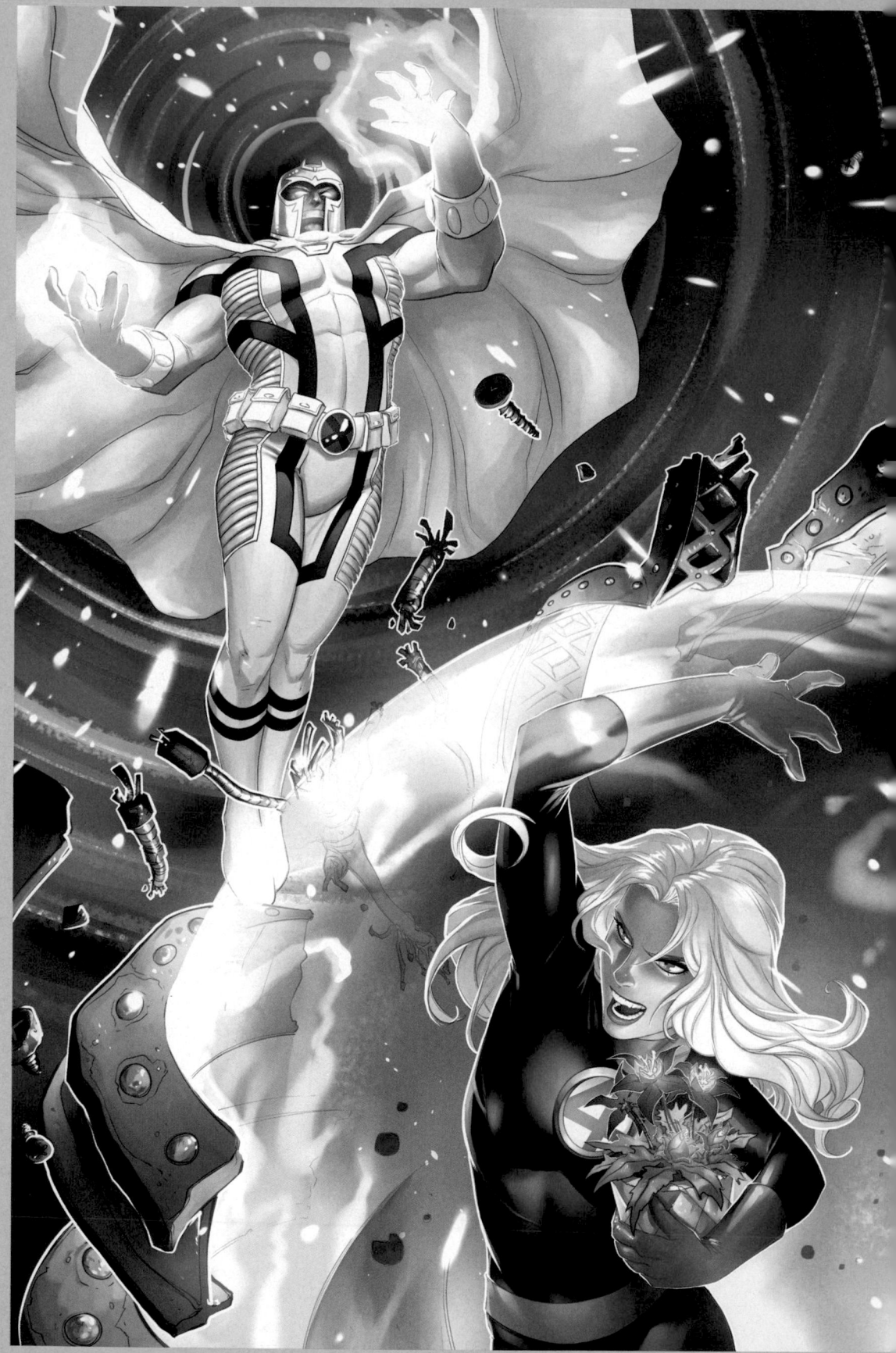

01-04 CONNECTING VARIANTS MARK BROOKS

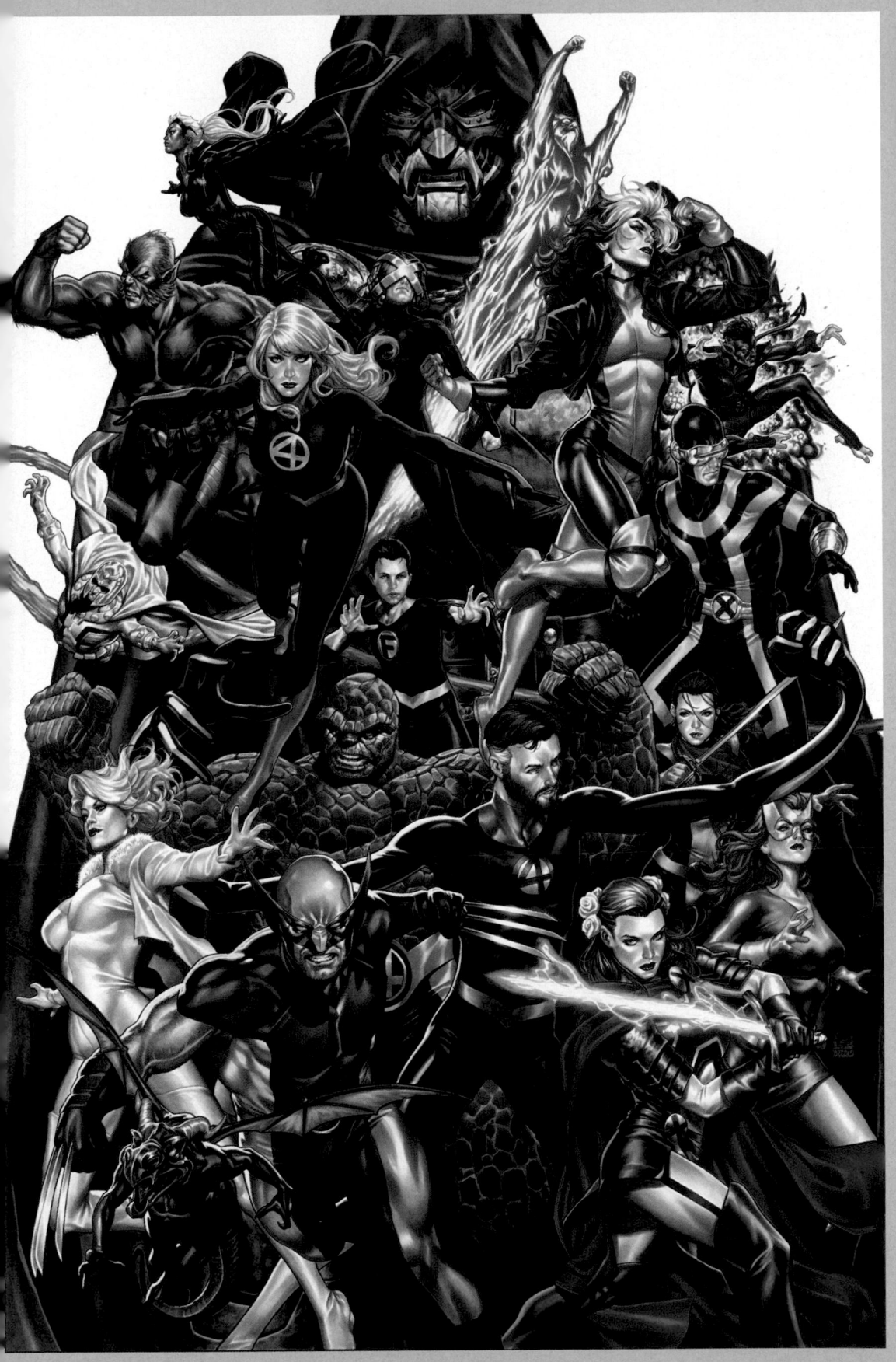

ROMITA

01 HIDDEN GEM VARIANT JOHN ROMITA SR. + MORRY HOLLOWELL

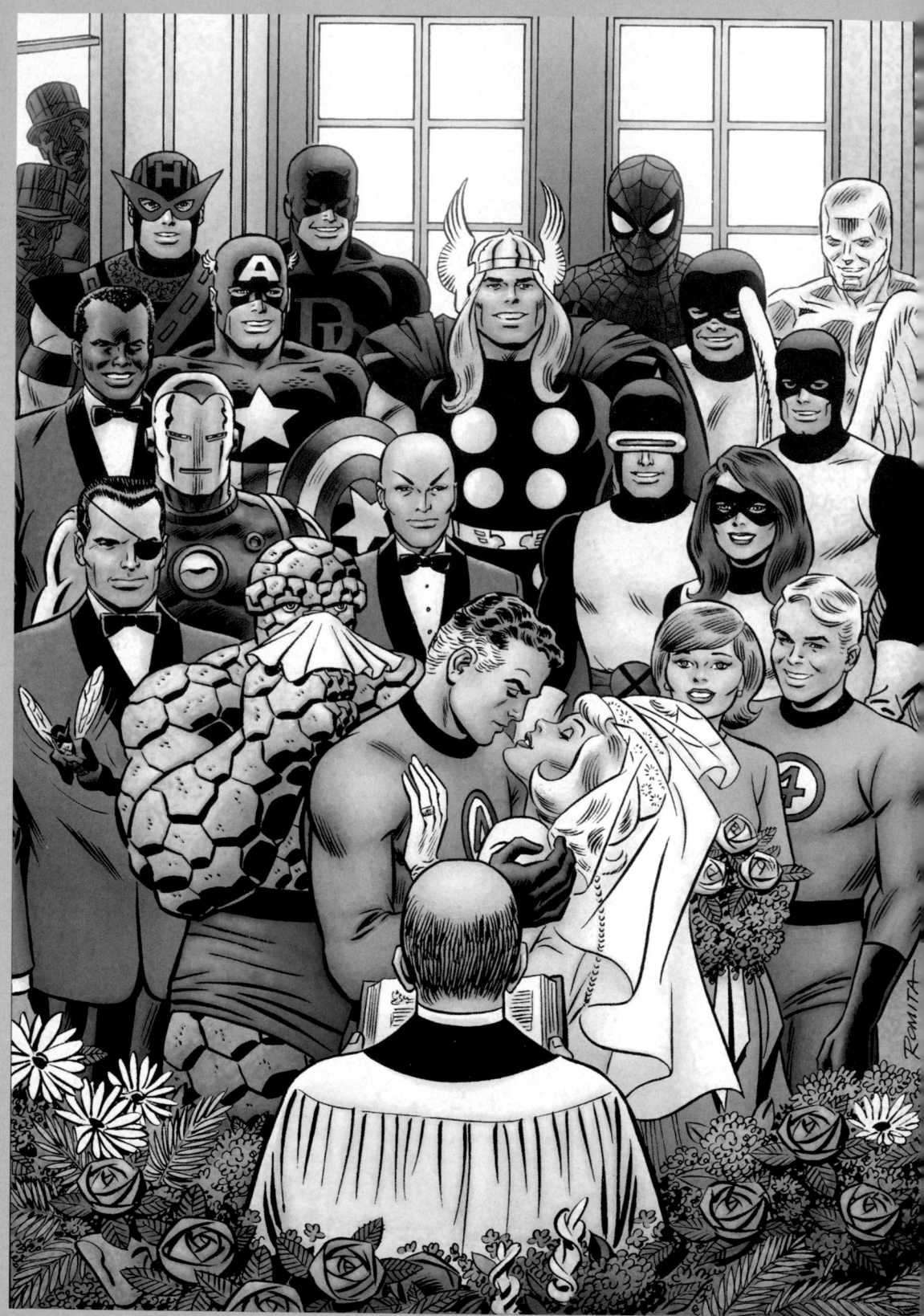

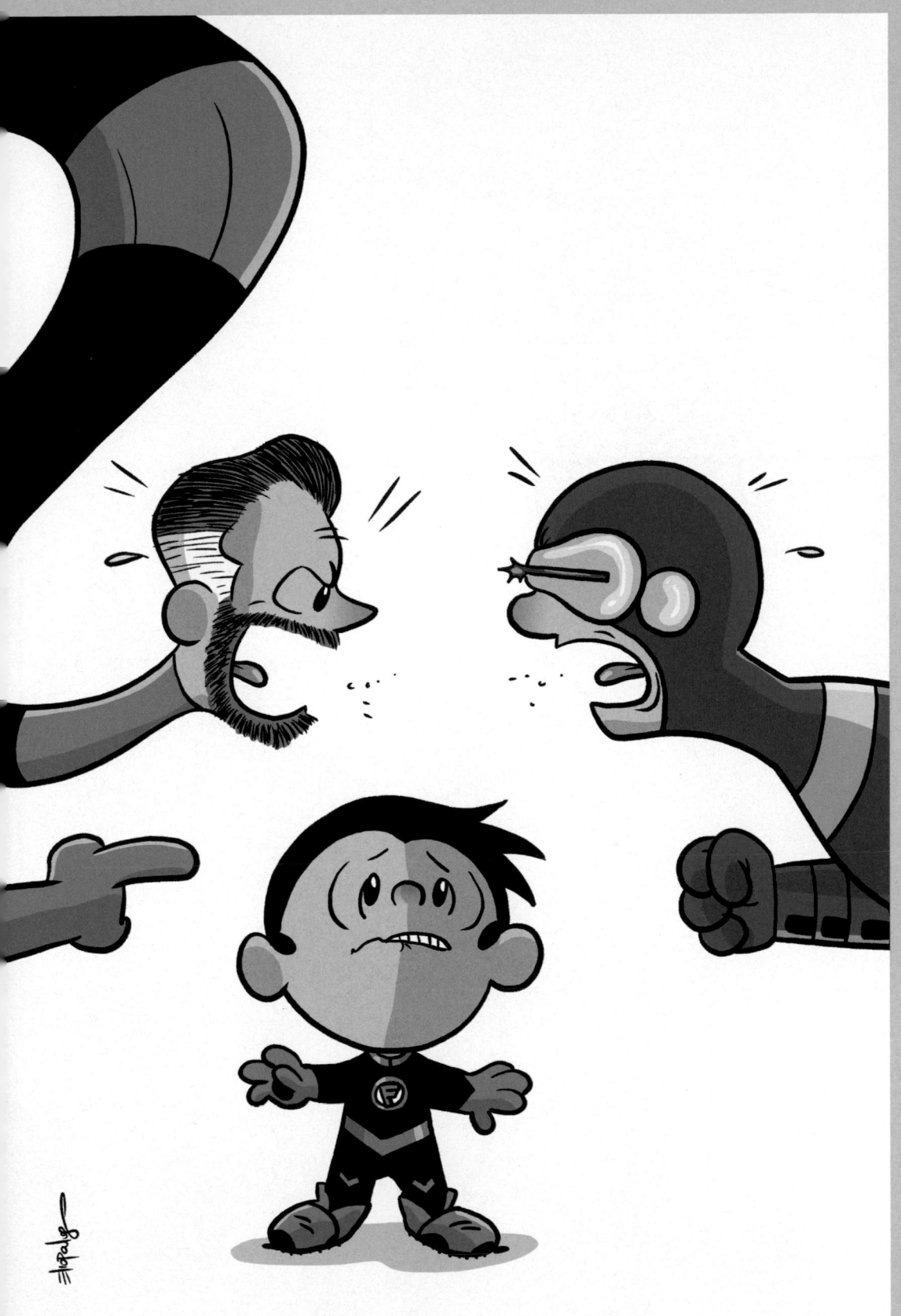

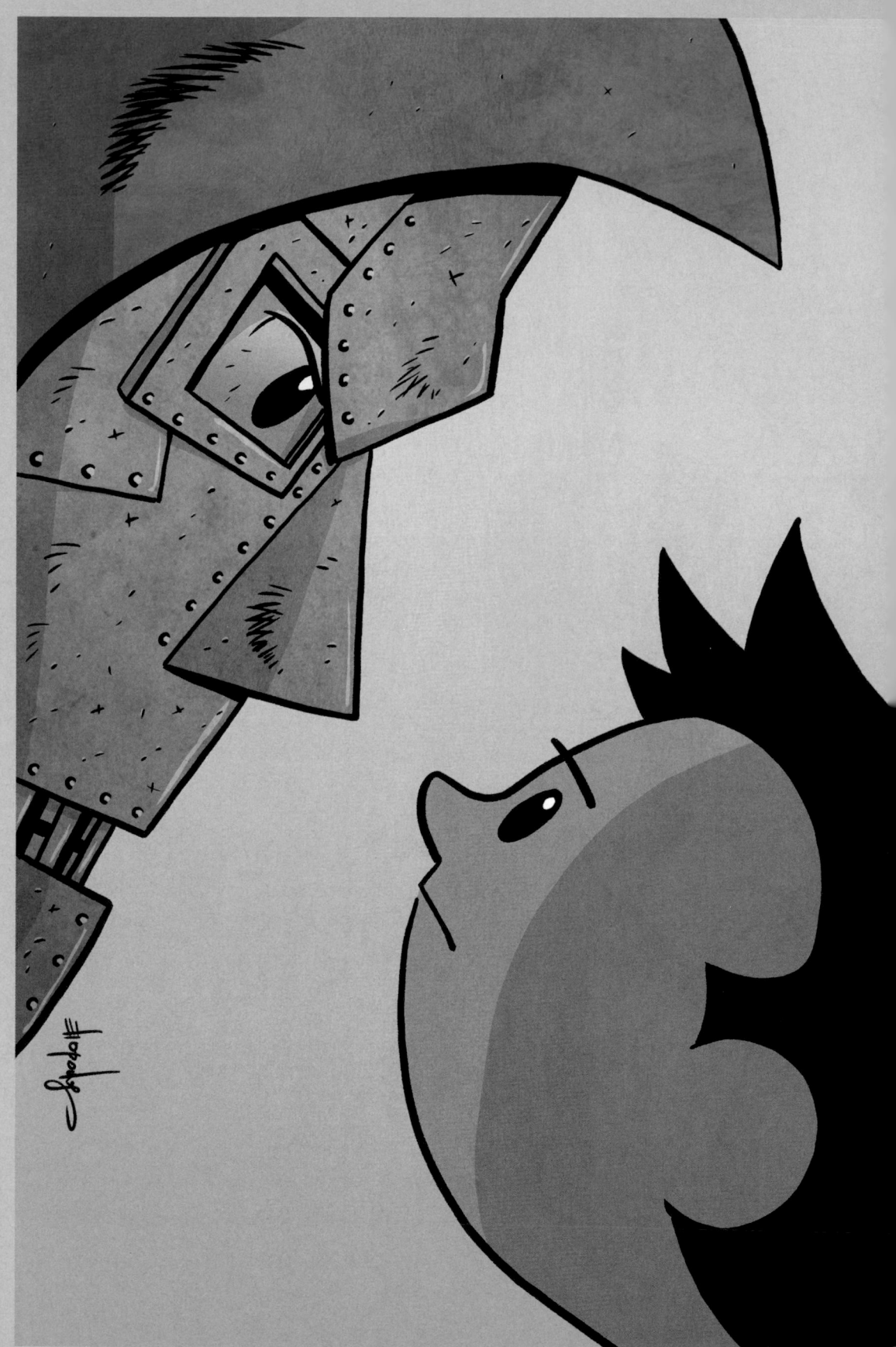

CHRIS ELIOPOULOS

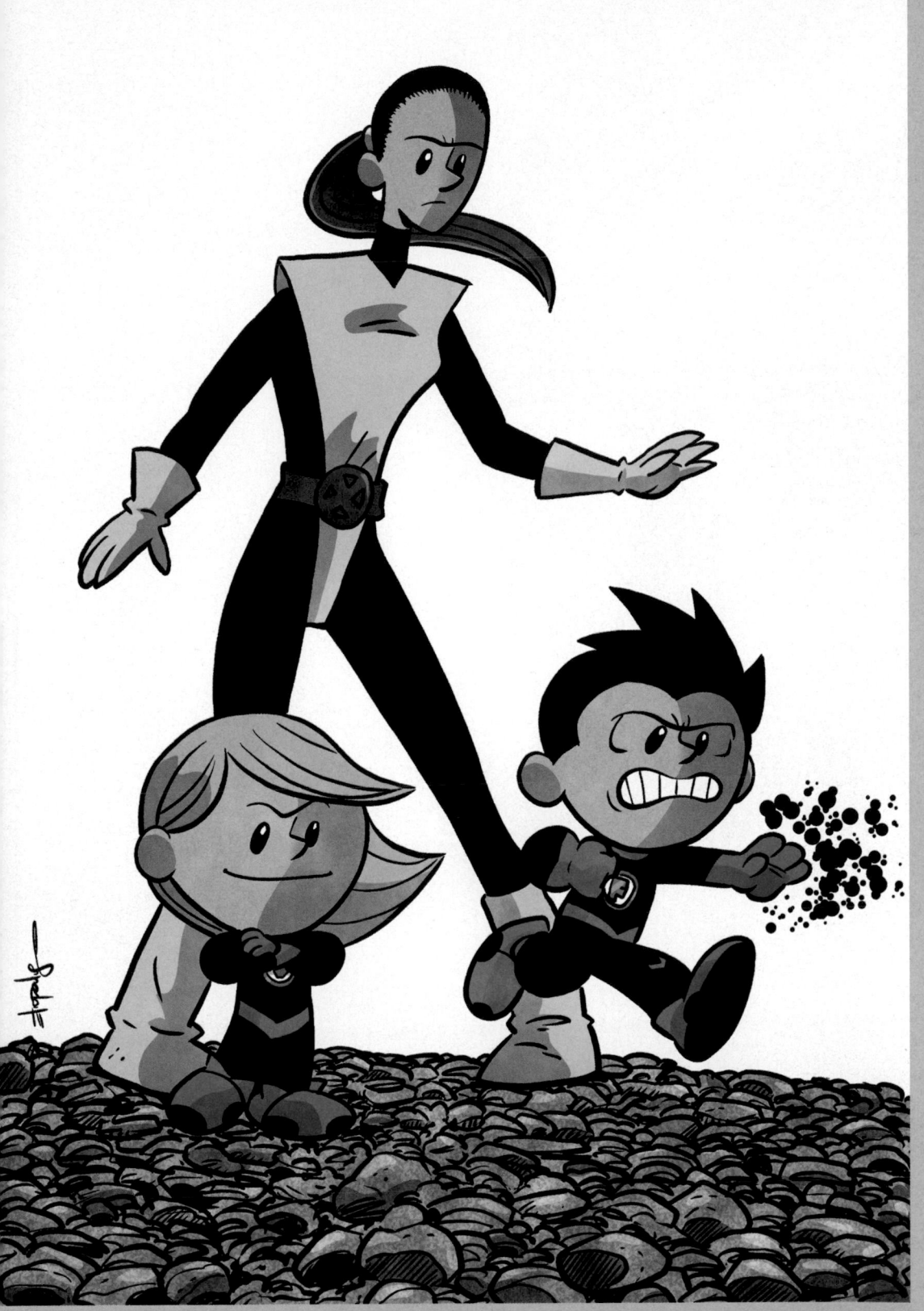

04 VARIANT CHRIS ELIOPOULOS

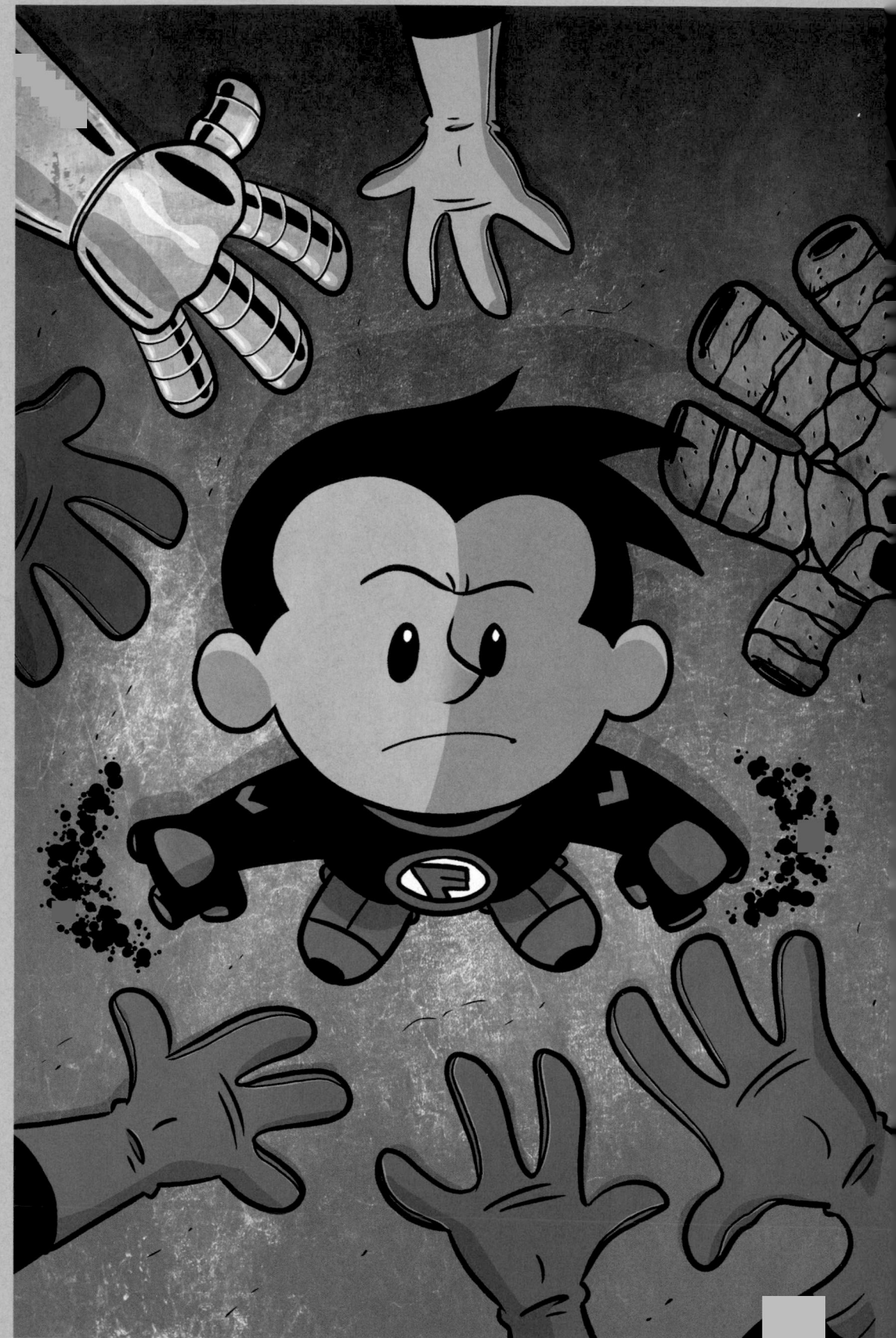

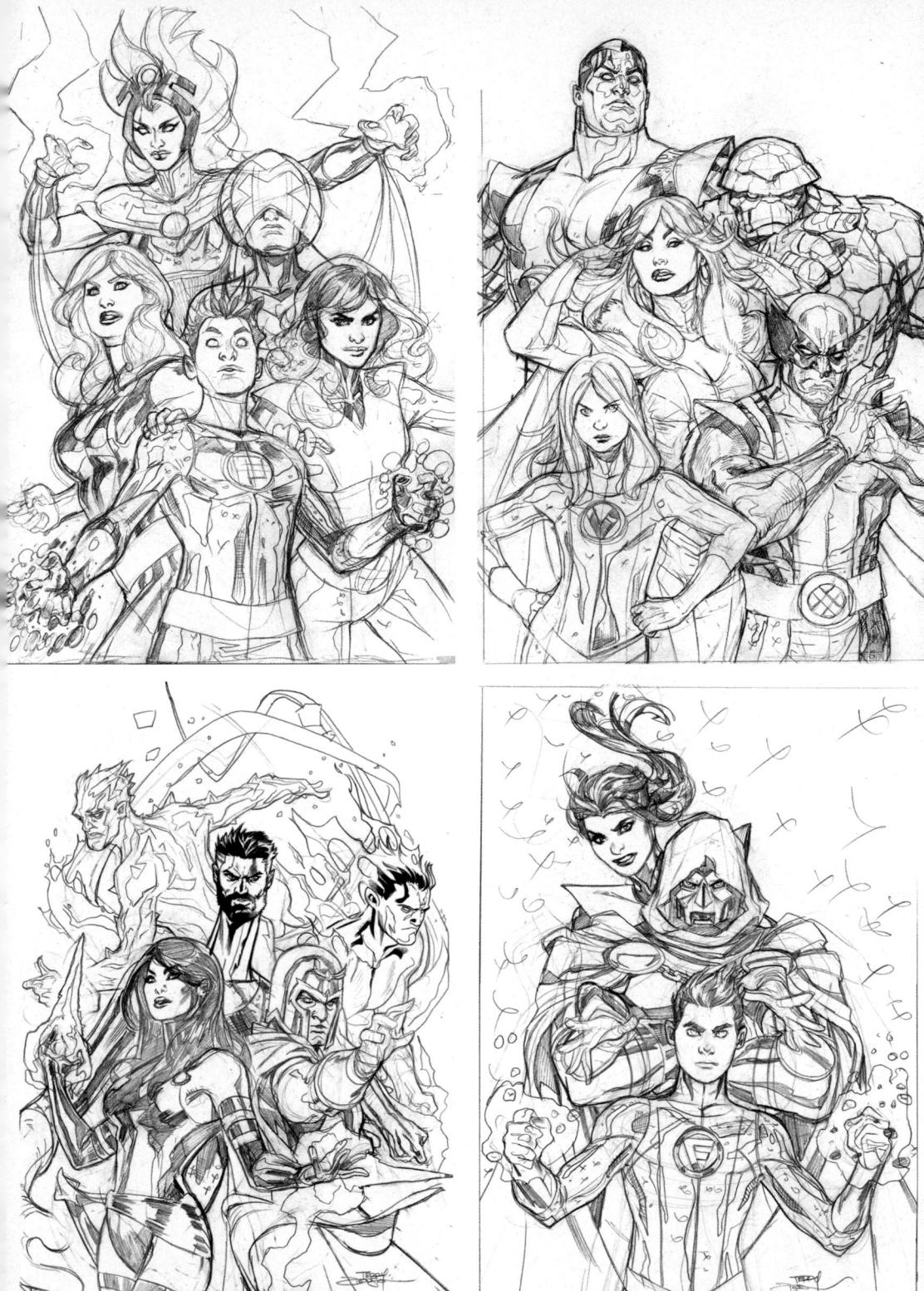

X MEN+
FANTASTIC
FOUR
ZDARSKY+
DODSON+
MARTIN
1

X MEN+
FANTASTIC
FOUR
ZDARSKY+
DODSON+
MARTIN
1

X MEN+
FANTASTIC
FOUR
ZDARSKY+
DODSON+
MARTIN
1

01-04 FLOWERS VARIANTS PENCILS MEGHAN HETRICK

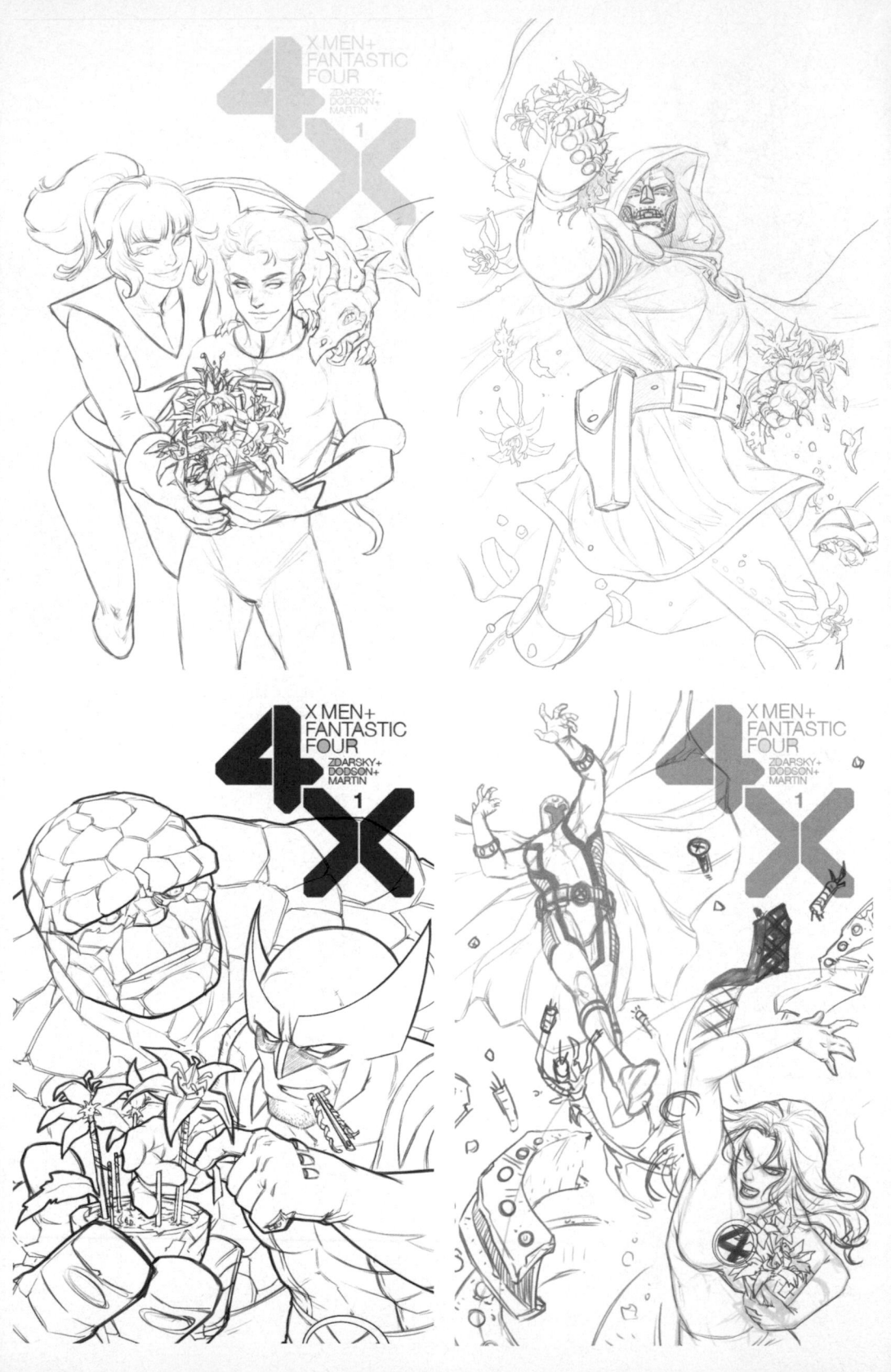

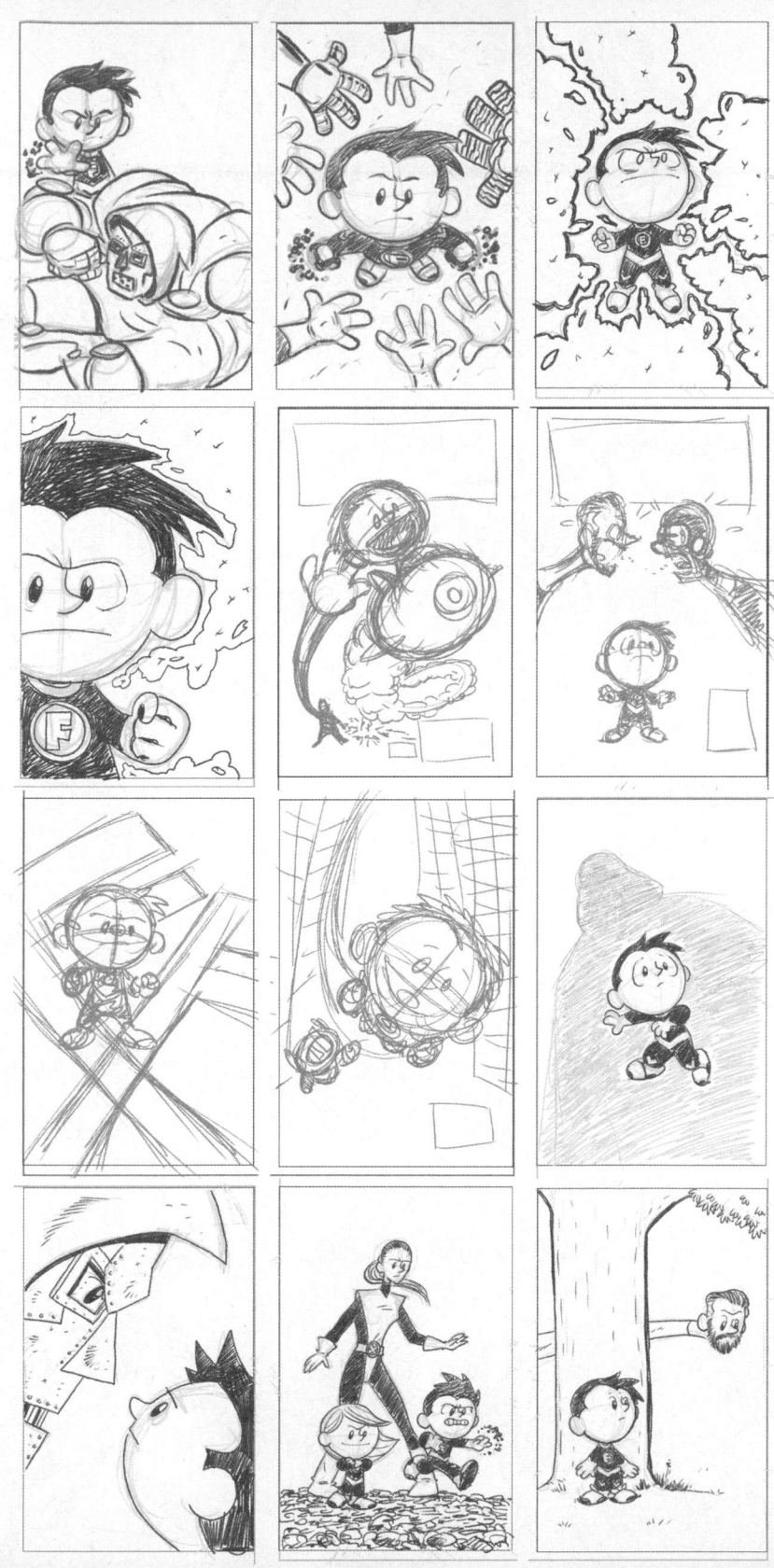

01-04 CONNECTING VARIANTS PENCILS MARK BROOKS

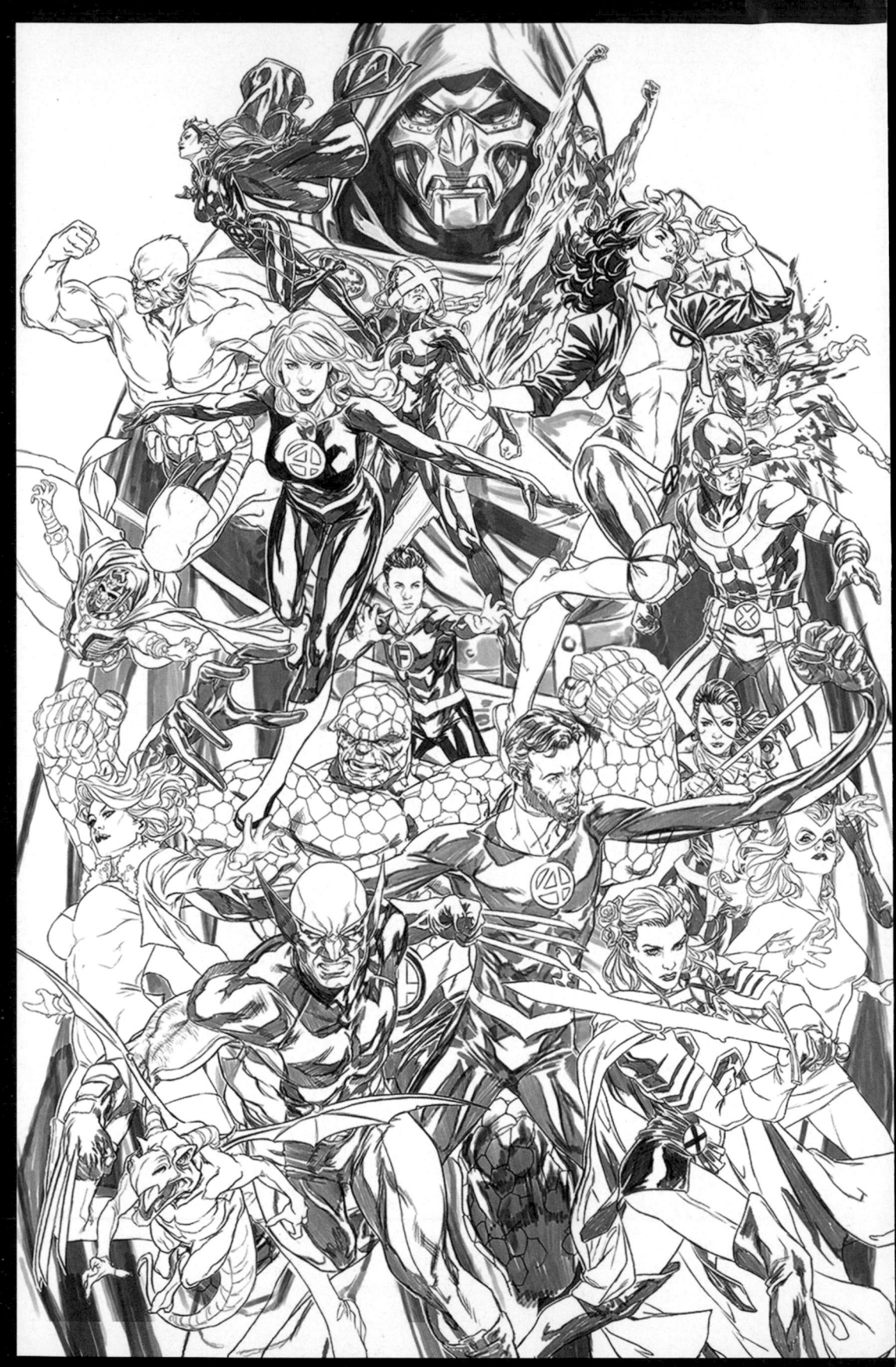